Ubuntu System Administration Guide

Ubuntu Desktop, Server, security, and DevOps automation

Mattias Hemmingsson

bpb

www.bpbonline.com

First Edition 2025

Copyright © BPB Publications, India

ISBN: 978-93-65895-124

LIMITS OF LIABILITY AND DISCLAIMER OF WARRANTY

To View Complete
BPB Publications Catalogue
Scan the QR Code:

www.bpbonline.com

Dedicated to

This book is dedicated to you, the reader who has opened it and is taking the first steps on your Linux journey.

I am honored to be a part of that adventure with you.

My family and friends, thank you for your unwavering support and encouragement throughout this incredible challenge.

About the Author

Mattias Hemmingsson is a seasoned IT professional with over two decades of experience in designing, building, and securing modern IT infrastructure. With deep roots in cloud computing, DevOps, and system architecture, he has successfully led the development and operations of high-availability systems for mission-critical environments, especially within the financial sector, where stability and performance are non-negotiable.

Mattias specializes in a wide range of technologies, including Kubernetes, Docker, Jenkins, GitLab CI, and cloud platforms such as AWS and Google Cloud. His skill set spans server orchestration, infrastructure as code, and containerized application delivery. A true advocate for developer productivity, he has implemented CI/CD pipelines, automated monitoring systems, and scalable platform services that have helped teams deploy faster with greater reliability.

Security is a cornerstone of Mattias's expertise. He has worked extensively in IT security and compliance, securing high-performance payment gateways and writing security policies to meet industry and regulatory standards. He actively manages vulnerability assessments, runs enterprise-grade security scanners, and participates in incident response operations. His security knowledge bridges the technical and procedural, ranging from configuring firewall rules to training development teams in secure coding practices.

As a full-stack developer, Mattias works with both Python and JavaScript, building frontend and backend systems using popular frameworks like Next.js and Vue. He brings a unique blend of hands-on coding ability and infrastructure mastery, making him equally at home writing applications or deploying them in scalable, production-ready environments.

Mattias also plays an active role in the tech community. He co-hosts the DevSecOps Talks podcast and YouTube channel, where he shares insights on the intersection of development, operations, and security. He teaches classes on DevSecOps practices and serves as the local organizer for one of Stockholm's tech meetups, helping others stay informed and connected in the ever-evolving world of IT.

Through his blog, Life and Shell, Mattias documents his professional journey, sharing practical tips and deep dives into real-world solutions for fellow developers, sysadmins, and security professionals. His work reflects a passion not just for running services, but for securing them, ensuring they are both compliant and resilient.

Whether building infrastructure, writing code, or leading training sessions, Mattias brings a comprehensive understanding of modern systems from their initial setup to their long-term security and scalability.

About the Reviewers

❖ **Nathan Molete** is a skilled Linux DevOps engineer with a strong background in cloud computing, automation, and infrastructure management. With extensive experience in Linux systems administration, networking, and application deployment, he specializes in ensuring the reliability, scalability, and security of enterprise IT environments.

Nathan is proficient in automation tools like Ansible and Terraform, enabling efficient configuration management and **infrastructure as code** (**IaC**) practices. He has expertise in containerization technologies, including Docker and Podman, as well as orchestration platforms like Kubernetes and Minikube. His hands-on experience with CI/CD pipelines, using Jenkins and Git, allows him to streamline software delivery and improve operational efficiency.

Working in both production and test environments, he is responsible for maintaining optimal system performance, troubleshooting complex issues, and implementing best practices for high availability and security. His knowledge spans across web servers such as Apache and NGINX, database management with MySQL and PostgreSQL, and cloud platforms like Azure.

Passionate about open-source technologies, Nathan continuously seeks to enhance systems and workflows through automation and innovation. With a detail-oriented and problem-solving mindset, he plays a crucial role in optimizing IT infrastructure, ensuring seamless operations, and driving digital transformation within organizations.

❖ **Cyrus** is a software developer, educator, and content creator with expertise in React, Next.js, and modern web technologies. He has developed educational platforms, built scalable web applications, and created a LinkedIn Learning course, Testing in React with Vitest, completed by over 1,000 learners. Passionate about empowering others, Cyrus shares insights on testing performance optimization and cutting-edge tools, helping developers build smarter, more efficient applications.

Acknowledgement

I want to express my sincere gratitude to all those who contributed to the completion of this book.

First and foremost, I extend my heartfelt appreciation to my family and friends for their unwavering support, patience, and encouragement throughout this journey. Your belief in me has been a constant source of strength.

I am especially thankful to my colleagues and friends from Fareoffice, Enterprise Car Rental, and Booli. Your valuable input, insights, and constructive feedback have been instrumental in shaping the direction and content of this book.

A special note of thanks goes to my close friends and neighbors for your patience in listening, your thoughtful feedback, and your enduring support. Your honest perspectives helped refine and elevate the quality of the work.

I am also deeply grateful to BPB Publications for their expert guidance and dedication in bringing this book to life. Your professionalism and support made the publishing process a smooth and rewarding experience.

I would like to sincerely appreciate the reviewers, technical experts, and editors who contributed their time and expertise to reviewing this manuscript. Your insightful comments and suggestions have significantly enhanced its clarity, depth, and accuracy.

Lastly, to the readers, thank you for your interest and support. Knowing that this book may inform, inspire, or assist you is the most rewarding outcome of all.

To everyone who played a part in making this book a reality, thank you.

Preface

Linux is swiftly establishing itself as the foundation of today's digital infrastructure, playing a central role in everything from personal desktops and enterprise-grade web servers to cutting-edge cloud platforms, smart home devices, and embedded IoT systems. Its presence extends into nearly every corner of computing. Whether you are browsing a website, deploying an app in the cloud, or working on a development project, chances are that Linux is working behind the scenes.

For aspiring developers, IT professionals, and system administrators, learning Linux is not just an option, it is a strategic advantage. Seasoned professionals often recommend starting with Linux before venturing into other tools such as Docker, Kubernetes, or even advanced cloud-native frameworks. Why is that? Because Linux provides deep insight into how operating systems function. It teaches you how processes run and interact, how file systems are organized, how networks are structured and secured, and how permissions and users are managed. These are the core concepts that underpin all modern computing tools.

By mastering Linux, you develop a strong mental model of how systems operate—one that allows you to troubleshoot more effectively, script more efficiently, and deploy with greater precision. It builds the kind of confidence that lets you approach complex technologies like container orchestration, virtualization, and continuous integration pipelines with a solid understanding of what is really happening behind the scenes.

This book is centered on Ubuntu, one of the most accessible and widely adopted Linux distributionsributions in the world. Ubuntu is known for its balance of power, simplicity, and versatility. It delivers the full capabilities of Linux in a package that is approachable for newcomers yet robust enough for professionals managing enterprise environments. With its regular updates, strong community support, and broad compatibility with both open-source and commercial software, Ubuntu serves as an ideal entry point into the Linux ecosystem.

Whether you are looking to replace your current operating system and use Ubuntu as your daily desktop driver, or you are interested in deploying servers, managing virtual machines, hosting applications, or building your own cloud infrastructure, this book will walk you through everything you need to get started. Ubuntu provides a secure, stable, and customizable platform that can grow with your needs, supporting everything from basic productivity tasks to advanced server-side operations, software development, and DevOps workflows.

In short, learning Ubuntu and Linux opens doors. It gives you the freedom to explore, experiment, and take control of your computing environment. It lays the groundwork for further exploration into the vast world of open-source technologies.

This book is your roadmap to getting there, with practical guides, hands-on exercises, and real-world use cases that will help you build both confidence and capability as a Linux user.

Chapter 1: Getting Familiar with Ubuntu Ecosystem - This chapter introduces the Linux and Ubuntu ecosystem, starting with the history of Linux and its evolution into one of the most widely used operating systems. It explores the Linux stack, popular distributions, and Ubuntu's development, release cycle, and various editions. The chapter highlights the growing importance of Linux in servers, IoT, and cloud computing. Readers are also introduced to key Ubuntu-based systems like Mint and Pop!_OS, and other Linux distributionsros like Red Hat and Alpine. To prepare for upcoming hands-on exercises, the chapter concludes by guiding readers to create GitHub and Blogger accounts for saving code and documenting progress.

Chapter 2: Install, Upgrade, and Configure Ubuntu Desktop - This chapter guides readers through installing and configuring Ubuntu Desktop. It begins with downloading the Ubuntu ISO, creating a bootable USB using tools like Etcher, and performing installation via USB or dual-boot with Windows. It covers pre-installed Linux options, basic troubleshooting, and verifying hardware compatibility. The chapter also introduces software installation using the Ubuntu Software Center, Snap Store, and terminal commands. Readers learn how to update and upgrade Ubuntu, manage apps, and back up configurations using the .config folder and Git. By the end, users will have a fully functional Ubuntu system ready for further customization.

Chapter 3: Environments and Window Managers - This chapter explores customizing Ubuntu with the i3 tiling window manager, offering efficient window navigation through keyboard shortcuts. It covers installing and configuring i3, setting screen resolutions, adding custom startup scripts, and improving usability with tools like sound controllers, screenshot utilities, and lock screens. The chapter also introduces essential productivity tools, including email clients, password managers, file encryption with PGP, and communication apps like Slack and Teams. For developers, it explains setting up Git, creating SSH keys, and using code editors like VS Code and PyCharm. By the end, readers have a fully personalized and productive Ubuntu environment.

Chapter 4: Setting up Firewall, VPN, and Wi-Fi Networks - This chapter covers essential networking tools in Ubuntu, focusing on connectivity and security. It explains how to configure DHCP and static IP addresses, connect to VLANs and wireless networks, and mask your device's MAC address for privacy. It introduces VPN setup using OpenVPN and WireGuard, and demonstrates encrypting DNS traffic with DNSS for added protection. Readers also learn to configure custom firewall rules using iptables and safeguard their systems with ClamAV antivirus. By the end, users can confidently connect to, secure, and manage networks on Ubuntu Desktop in both personal and professional environments.

Chapter 5: Preparing Virtualization Environment - This chapter introduces virtualization in Ubuntu using KVM, enabling users to run multiple isolated operating systems on a single host. It covers installing KVM, setting up network bridges, and creating **virtual machines (VMs)**. Readers learn to manage VM settings, take snapshots, and enable device passthrough like GPUs. The chapter also explores alternative tools such as VirtualBox, VMware, and Vagrant for VM creation and sharing. Guidance is provided on converting VM image formats for compatibility across platforms. By the end, users can effectively create, configure, and manage VMs and virtual environments for both testing and development purposes.

Chapter 6: Up and Running with Kubernetes and Docker - This chapter introduces Docker and Kubernetes as essential tools for containerized development. It covers Docker installation, running a Minecraft server container, and managing multi-service applications like WordPress and Metabase using Docker Compose. Readers learn to connect multiple containers, persist data, and streamline development with local volumes. The chapter then transitions to Kubernetes using Minikube, demonstrating how to deploy WordPress and MySQL with Kubernetes manifests. Key concepts include namespaces, services, deployments, and load balancers. By the end, readers can run, scale, and manage containers locally using Docker and Kubernetes for efficient, isolated application development and testing.

Chapter 7: Install Ubuntu Server on Metal, Cloud, and Network - This chapter explores various methods to install and manage Ubuntu Server across physical machines, virtual environments, and cloud platforms. It covers using SSH keys for secure access, installing via USB or VM, and deploying on cloud providers like Google Cloud and Hetzner. Readers also learn about scalable server provisioning using **machine as a service (MAAS)**, including PXE booting and automated installations. Concepts like cattle vs. pets emphasize treating servers as disposable for easier management. By chapter's end, users can confidently set up single or multiple Ubuntu Servers suited to local or enterprise-grade infrastructure..

Chapter 8: Keeping Check on Your Ubuntu Server - This chapter explores tools and techniques for monitoring and securing Ubuntu Servers. It begins with basic Linux commands like top, netstat, and du for local performance insights. For GUI monitoring, Cockpit is introduced, while Grafana, Prometheus, and Node Exporter enable the visualization of scalable server metrics. Filebeat, Elasticsearch, and Kibana are used for centralized log collection and analysis. Security tools such as Fail2Ban and OSSEC help detect intrusion attempts and automate responses. Readers learn to create dashboards, configure alerts, and integrate logs and metrics into unified views—building a robust foundation for proactive server management and security.

Chapter 9: Setup Advanced Network, Firewall and VPN Servers - This chapter guides configuring Ubuntu Server as a network firewall and router. It covers setting up network interfaces, VLANs, and routing using Netplan, and securing traffic with iptables. You learn to install and configure dnsmasq as both a DHCP and DNS server, enabling client IP management and domain resolution. The chapter also details creating secure VPN tunnels using OpenVPN and WireGuard, including certificate generation and client-server configurations. By the end, you'll have a fully functional Ubuntu-based router capable of secure communication and traffic control for both local and remote networks.

Chapter 10: Running Virtualization Server Environment - This chapter explores setting up an Ubuntu Server as a virtualization host using KVM. It guides installing and managing VMs via CLI, desktop GUI (Virtual Machine Manager), and a web interface (Cockpit). The chapter also introduces containerization using Podman, a Docker alternative, to deploy a monitoring stack with Grafana, Prometheus, Loki, and Promtail. Detailed setup for container-based metrics and log collection from multiple servers is provided, using podman-compose. The chapter concludes by contrasting virtualization and containers, emphasizing containers for lightweight, scalable service deployment and preparing readers for Kubernetes in the next chapter.

Chapter 11: Setup Webserver, Deploy and Run Webapps - This chapter explores setting up web servers and deploying web applications on Ubuntu. It begins with installing Apache and NGINX, configuring domains, and serving web content. Two databases are introduced: MariaDB (SQL) and MongoDB (NoSQL), including setup, usage, and backup processes. Practical deployments include WordPress and Observium, demonstrating PHP app hosting and virtual host configurations. Rocket.Chat is deployed via Docker, connected to MongoDB. The chapter also covers performance tuning for web servers and emphasizes using proper database users for security. By the end, readers can host, optimize, and manage web apps and databases on Ubuntu Servers.

Chapter 12: Kubernetes Run and Setup - This chapter guides readers through setting up a Kubernetes cluster on Ubuntu Servers using kubeadm. It covers preparing master and worker nodes, disabling swap, and installing core components. The chapter introduces Helm for managing Kubernetes packages and demonstrates deploying essential services like OpenEBS for storage, Prometheus and Grafana for monitoring, and Traefik with MetalLB for ingress and load balancing. A full WordPress deployment, including MySQL, is configured and accessed using both NodePort and ingress routes. The chapter concludes with basic kubectl commands for troubleshooting and managing the cluster, forming a strong foundation for further automation.

Chapter 13: Task Automations, CI/CD Pipeline, and Service Deployment - This chapter focuses on automating infrastructure tasks using Bash, Ansible, and Terraform to ensure repeatable, reliable server and service setups. It starts with creating reusable Bash scripts, then advances to Ansible for managing tasks across multiple servers via Docker containers. The chapter introduces building and pushing Docker images, running host-level tasks from containers, and deploying applications to Kubernetes using Terraform. These automation techniques form a complete CI/CD pipeline foundation. By the end, readers gain the tools to configure, deploy, and manage services efficiently, marking a transition to professional DevOps practices within Linux and Ubuntu environments.

Code Bundle and Coloured Images

Please follow the link to download the
Code Bundle and the *Coloured Images* of the book:

https://rebrand.ly/ou09t8w

The code bundle for the book is also hosted on GitHub at
https://github.com/bpbpublications/Ubuntu-System-Administration-Guide.
In case there's an update to the code, it will be updated on the existing GitHub repository.

We have code bundles from our rich catalogue of books and videos available at
https://github.com/bpbpublications. Check them out!

Errata

We take immense pride in our work at BPB Publications and follow best practices to ensure the accuracy of our content to provide with an indulging reading experience to our subscribers. Our readers are our mirrors, and we use their inputs to reflect and improve upon human errors, if any, that may have occurred during the publishing processes involved. To let us maintain the quality and help us reach out to any readers who might be having difficulties due to any unforeseen errors, please write to us at :

errata@bpbonline.com

Your support, suggestions and feedbacks are highly appreciated by the BPB Publications' Family.

Did you know that BPB offers eBook versions of every book published, with PDF and ePub files available? You can upgrade to the eBook version at www.bpbonline. com and as a print book customer, you are entitled to a discount on the eBook copy. Get in touch with us at :

business@bpbonline.com for more details.

At **www.bpbonline.com**, you can also read a collection of free technical articles, sign up for a range of free newsletters, and receive exclusive discounts and offers on BPB books and eBooks.

Piracy

If you come across any illegal copies of our works in any form on the internet, we would be grateful if you would provide us with the location address or website name. Please contact us at **business@bpbonline.com** with a link to the material.

If you are interested in becoming an author

If there is a topic that you have expertise in, and you are interested in either writing or contributing to a book, please visit **www.bpbonline.com**. We have worked with thousands of developers and tech professionals, just like you, to help them share their insights with the global tech community. You can make a general application, apply for a specific hot topic that we are recruiting an author for, or submit your own idea.

Reviews

Please leave a review. Once you have read and used this book, why not leave a review on the site that you purchased it from? Potential readers can then see and use your unbiased opinion to make purchase decisions. We at BPB can understand what you think about our products, and our authors can see your feedback on their book. Thank you!

For more information about BPB, please visit **www.bpbonline.com**.

Join our book's Discord space

Join the book's Discord Workspace for Latest updates, Offers, Tech happenings around the world, New Release and Sessions with the Authors:

https://discord.bpbonline.com

Table of Contents

CHAPTER 1

Getting Familiar with Ubuntu Ecosystem

Introduction

In this chapter, we will be introduced to Linux and Ubuntu. We will start by discussing the creation of Linux. Then, we will go into Ubuntu and look at how it began, understand Ubuntu releases, and cover some of the different versions of Ubuntu. Finally, we will cover other Linux distributions and how they are different from Ubuntu. Additionally, we will discuss what parts make up the Linux stack.

We encourage you to create a blog page and an account by the end of the chapter so that you are ready for the subsequent chapters in the book.

Structure

In this chapter, we will cover the following topics:

- Linux history
- Linux stack
- Usage and stats of Linux
- Ubuntu history
- Ubuntu releases
- Ubuntu versions

- Other Linux distributions
- Create GitHub and blogger account

Objectives

By the end of the chapter, we will understand how Linux started and how the different parts of the Linux stack are put together. We will also understand the difference between different Linux versions and how Ubuntu is versioned and released.

Linux history

Linux was created by *Linus Torvalds*, a computer science student at the *University of Helsinki*, in 1991 at the age of 21. What started as a small hobby is today one of the most used operating systems.

At first, *Linus* named the invention Freax, but one of the administrators at FUNET, where the project was uploaded, did not like that name and renamed it to Linux.

Tux, the penguin mascot as depicted in *Figure 1.1*, was chosen by *Linus* after a small penguin bit him during a visit to the *National Zoo and Aquarium* in *Canberra*.

Figure 1.1: Tux

Today, you can find the Linux kernel development on GitHub. **https://github.com/torvalds/linux** and follow the development there, and today, there are over 13k contributors to the Linux kernel. Refer to the following link: **https://en.wikipedia.org/wiki/Ubuntu**

Linux stack

The Linux kernel is the base of all Linux operations systems. It is the one that boots and adds all the drivers. If the car brand is named Ubuntu, the engine is the Linux kernel. On top of the Linux kernel, we can choose/build different operating systems, such as Ubuntu and Red Hat.

Now, to use your Linux system as a desktop computer, you would also need some type of windows manager. In this book, we will look more at the windows manager i3 and the default windows manager in Ubuntu GNOME.

Usage and stats of Linux

The usage of Linux and Ubuntu is growing fast. Today, Linux is the primary OS used by our supercomputers. It powers NASA servers and is the most used OS for IoT devices.

In the cloud, it is the dominant OS, with 90% of all OS running Linux. Linux is also the OS powering the Kubernetes cluster, which is becoming the default platform for hosting applications. Some other stats from Linux are as follows:

- Web servers also completely rely on Linux. According to Linux server statistics, of the top 1 million web servers, 96.3% employ Linux environments.

- The Linux kernel development report reveals that 90% of the workload deployed on the cloud is based on the Linux system.

- 65 SpaceX missions were completed using Linux-powered technology, according to the latest Linux statistics.

- According to the latest Linux distributions statistics, Ubuntu is the most popular Linux distributions (32.8%), followed by Debian (14.4%) and CentOS (10.8%).

Ubuntu history

One of the most used Linux operating systems is Debian, and Ubuntu is based on Debian. Ubuntu was built by the British company *Canonical* and is set to be a friendly and easy-to-use Linux system. The first release was Ubuntu 4.10, which was released in October 2004. Today, a lot has happened, and Ubuntu has now released version 22.04.

There is a base version of Ubuntu. Ubuntu Desktop are the desktop for laptops, office, and home computers with a GUI. Ubuntu Server runs on servers on both cloud and metal, and Ubuntu Core is used to run on IoT devices.

https://en.wikipedia.org/wiki/Ubuntu

Ubuntu releases

Ubuntu is released twice yearly, one version on 04 April and one on 10 October. The release makes up the name with the year. Ubuntu 22.10 will be released in October 2022. So, how long is then a release supported? Well, that depends. Ubuntu makes **long-term support** (**LTS**) releases, and the LTS releases are supported for ten years. If you plan to set up a server that will run longer or a desktop to work on, consider using the LTS releases. However, if you want the latest kernels and tools, you can look at the newest release. In this book, we will recommend installing the LTS releases. Ubuntu also provides tools to upgrade from the LTS release to the next one.

More on the Ubuntu releases is found here, **https://ubuntu.com/about/release-cycle**.

Ubuntu version

Ubuntu and the Linux kernel are open-source, which has led many developers to make their own version of Ubuntu. People who wanted to use another graphical desktop environment on a particular version of Ubuntu for schools or music studios.

Some of the different versions of Ubuntu are as follows:

Mint

Linux Mint is based on Ubuntu and the XFC Windows desktop. Mint Linux is pre-filled with many of the standard tools to get you started and working quickly after installation.

Linux Mint is an operating system for desktop and laptop computers. It is designed to work out of the box and comes fully equipped with the apps most people need.

You can find more information on Mint Linux and download links at **https://linuxmint.com/**.

Pop

System76 is a company building Linux computers, and its operating system is based on Ubuntu.

Pop!_OS is designed for fast navigation, easy workspace organization, and fluid, convenient workflow. Your operating system should encourage discovery, not obstruct it.

You can find more info on Pop Linux and download links at **https://pop.system76.com/**.

LXLE

Lxle is a light version of Ubuntu. We used computers that were low in resources but still needed to be able to be used in a secure and updated way.

The developers of LXE describe it as light on resources and heavy on functions. LXLE is based on Ubuntu, and it is super-fast to boot up.

You can find more info on LXLE and download links at **https://lxle.net/**.

Other Linux distributions

Ubuntu is based on the Linux distributionsro called **Debian**, but there are more Linux OSs than Ubuntu. Raspberry Pi OS is another famous OS based on Debian. However, there are many more. Kali Linux is a Linux OS specially built for hackers. It includes all the tools you would need as a hacker and runs easily from a USB stick.

But our Linux distributions does not stop with the Debian family. There are more families of Linux.

Red Hat has Red Hat Enterprise Linux, a stable Linux distributionsro that many companies use. It includes open-source software and Red Hat's own software. Fedora Linux will be the next Red Hat Linux. In Fedora, we see the latest software and kernel versions. If you start using Docker, you will get to know **Alpine Linux**. Alpine is a minimal Linux perfect for building small Docker images, **https://www.alpinelinux.org/**.

Regarding Kubernetes, new Linux distributionsributions release unique builds for running containers. The most famous are Flatcar and CoreOS, where Flatcar is a fork of CoreOS. AWS has also released its own Linux build for containers called **Bottlerocket**.

One new project is Talos Linux, a special Linux distributionsro only made to run Kubernetes. One special part of Talos Linux is that it does not have any external access, and all configs are used using API calls.

To read more and get installation instructions on the special Linux distributionsro, visit the following links in the chapter's reference section.

Let us look at the difference between Linux versions:

It is all about how you use your computer and server. On your laptop, run Ubuntu LTS, and run Ubuntu LTS on my home server. Then, you can reuse the tools and script, for example, to set up backup and access.

However, flatcar Linux is run in the Kubernetes cluster, which is good for running containers and Kubernetes.

We may have some servers that run Red Hat, and the difference is, for example, the package manager. In Ubuntu, as you will learn in this book, the package tool is called **apt**.

The command installs **apache** on a Ubuntu/Debian Linux:

```
1. apt-get install apache
```

However, on a Red Hat server, your package manager is named **yum**. So, to install the Apache web server, you would run.

```
1. yum install httpd
```

They both will install the Apache web server, but the way you type the command for installing Apache is different. The same command in Alphine Linux would be as follows:

```
1. apk add apache
```

There are some differences in this way, but as you will learn to use **apt** in this book, it is simple to move to a Red Hat-based Linux, and the base of how you install the package is the same. You only need to find the right command.

Create GitHub and blogger account

In this book, we will use code and configuration files when we set up our desktop and install services like a web service on our Ubuntu Server. We will build Docker apps to run

WordPress and other apps and save all our work, both the code and what we have done, by setting up a GitHub account and a Blogger account.

Git

During this book, you will be working with code and configurations, and keeping your code and settings is good practice to save them in a Git Repo.

You will, for example, save all your `.config` files in a Git Repo so that all your Ubuntu settings will be saved.

One of the most used platforms for storing code using git is **https://github.com**. Before we start writing code, we will set this up.

Blog

We hope that this book will teach us new things. To remember everything and have it as a reference, it is a good idea to set up a small blog to write down the different tasks. One example of a free blog hosting is **https://www.blogger.com**.

Book Git Repo

This book also has a GitHub repo. All code and examples are stored in that repo. Feel free to clone or fork the repo to your GitHub repos so that you can test and run the example code.

https://github.com/bpbpublications/Ubuntu-Linux-in-30-days

Conclusion

A student at the *University of Helsinki* started using Linux as a free OS. It is free to use, and the kernel is available at GitHub.com. From the Linux kernel, a new and different Linux OS has arrived. Ubuntu is the famous one we will use in this book. However, there are also unique Linux OS for running clusters ore security audits. So, depending on your task, you can find a Linux OS best suited for your needs.

In the next chapter, we will install Ubuntu by learning how to install it and getting started using it on our desktops.

References

- https://getfedora.org/en/coreos?stream=stable
- https://flatcar-linux.org/
- https://www.talos.dev/
- https://aws.amazon.com/bottlerocket/

CHAPTER 2
Install, Upgrade, and Configure Ubuntu Desktop

Introduction

In this chapter, we will follow the steps to install Ubuntu. We will start by downloading the Ubuntu image, burning or copying the image to a USB flash drive, booting a computer from the USB drive, and following the steps to install Ubuntu. When a computer is running Ubuntu, we will look at the Ubuntu package manager and install our first Ubuntu packages.

Structure

In this chapter, we will discuss the following topics:

- Installing Ubuntu
- Pre-installing Ubuntu
- Dual-boot Windows/Ubuntu
- Boot Ubuntu and install
- Ubuntu running
- Install software
- Software store
- Updating Ubuntu

- Upgrading Ubuntu LTS
- .config folder

Objectives

By the end of this chapter, we will be able to download iso Linux files from the internet and create bootable USB. Boot up live Linux distributionsributions and run basic commands to find issues before installing Ubuntu.

We will also be able to install Ubuntu Linux and install packages from the Ubuntu Software Center.

Installing Ubuntu

Today, you can install Ubuntu on almost all laptops, computers, and servers. You can even install Ubuntu on Apple laptops.

When installing Ubuntu today, we used a USB drive on which we installed Ubuntu. You can use this USB drive to boot up your computer first to test out Ubuntu and verify that the network drivers are working.

We always keep a USB drive with Ubuntu to help us boot up and troubleshoot issues with our servers and computers. Once booted from the USB drive, Ubuntu also provides the option to install the operating system onto the hard drive, allowing it to boot without the USB drive.

If you are using an older computer, the same approach can also be done with CD discs.

Later in this book, you will also understand how to install servers over the network to install servers automatically.

Pre-installing Ubuntu

Today, there are several companies that provide computer pre-installation with Ubuntu. *Dell* has a full line of computers already preinstalled:

https://www.dell.com/en-us/lp/linux-systems

Another brand is *Lenovo*, which also has its own line of Linux computers:

https://www.lenovo.com/us/en/d/linux-laptops-desktops/?orgRef=https%253A%252F%252Fsearch.brave.com%252F

Starlab has also create there Starbook preinstalled Ubuntu laptop. It is a fully open-source computer from BIOS, Firmware, and Ubuntu running as OS.

https://se.starlabs.systems/

There are also many new, smaller companies that provide Linux computers, like Framework, which is a modular laptop where you can replace parts yourself. It comes preinstalled with Windows, but the community around Linux is large. **https://community. frame.work/t/ubuntu-21-04-on-the-framework-laptop/2722**

When we talk about preinstalled Linux computers, we also need to add system76 **https:// system76.com/**. They have been building powerful Linux computers for a long time.

Dual-boot Windows or Ubuntu

It is possible to dual-boot Ubuntu and Windows from the hard drive. To do that, we need to follow the given steps:

1. First, we need to install Windows on the computer.

2. Then, install Ubuntu beside Windows.

3. Now, in grub, the boot tools for Ubuntu detect the Windows options, and when you boot your computer, there is an option to boot into Windows.

4. If you added Windows after Ubuntu, you could simply update grub, and it will detect and set up the Windows boot options.

Boot Ubuntu and install

To get started, we will need the following:

- We need a computer to download and set up our Ubuntu USB drive.

- A USB drive with more than 4GB of storage.

First, we need to download the Ubuntu version we will be using. You can follow the given steps:

1. Go over to the Ubuntu download page and download the Ubuntu Desktop,

   https://ubuntu.com/download/desktop

2. Download the ISO file to your computer.

3. When we have the ISO file on our computer, we must write it to the USB drive. There are many different tools that we can use. If you already have a Ubuntu Desktop, then Ubuntu has a program called **Create Startup Disk**.

Making boot USB with Etcher

To make a bootable USB drive, we need to flash the Ubuntu iso to a USB key. To do that, we use a tool called **Etcher**.

https://www.balena.io/etcher/

Etcher works on Linux, Windows, and MAC. It is a great tool for writing Linux images for Ubuntu, Raspberry, and any other Linux distributions. *Figure 2.1* illustrates the startup screen on Etcher as follows:

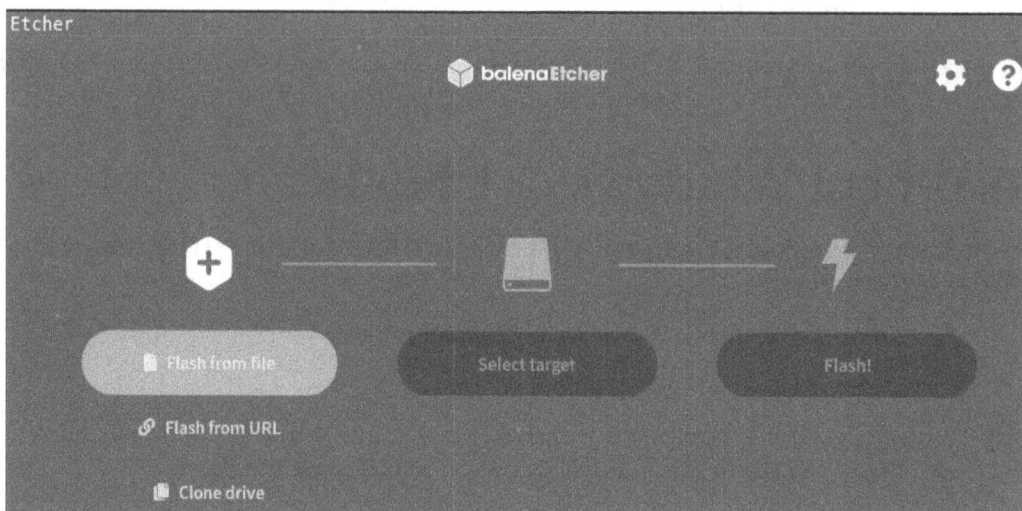

Figure 2.1: Etcher tool for making USB drives

Start by selecting the Ubuntu image we have downloaded and the destination USB drive, as shown in *Figure 2.2*:

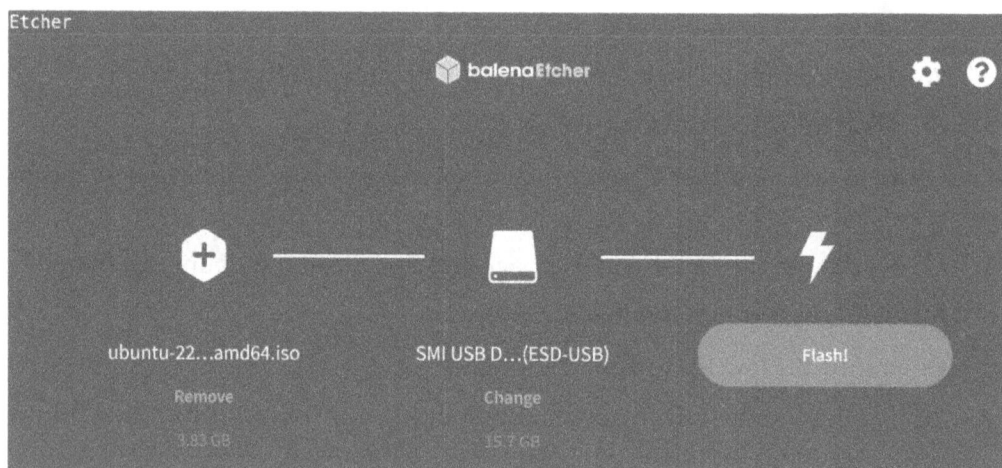

Figure 2.2: Etcher with selected ISO and USB drive

After we have selected the iso, we need to choose the drive where we want the iso to be flashed. Etcher is brilliant and should only show the USB drives here.

Now press **Flash**, and the image will flash to the USB drive as shown in *Figure 2.3* and *Figure 2.4*:

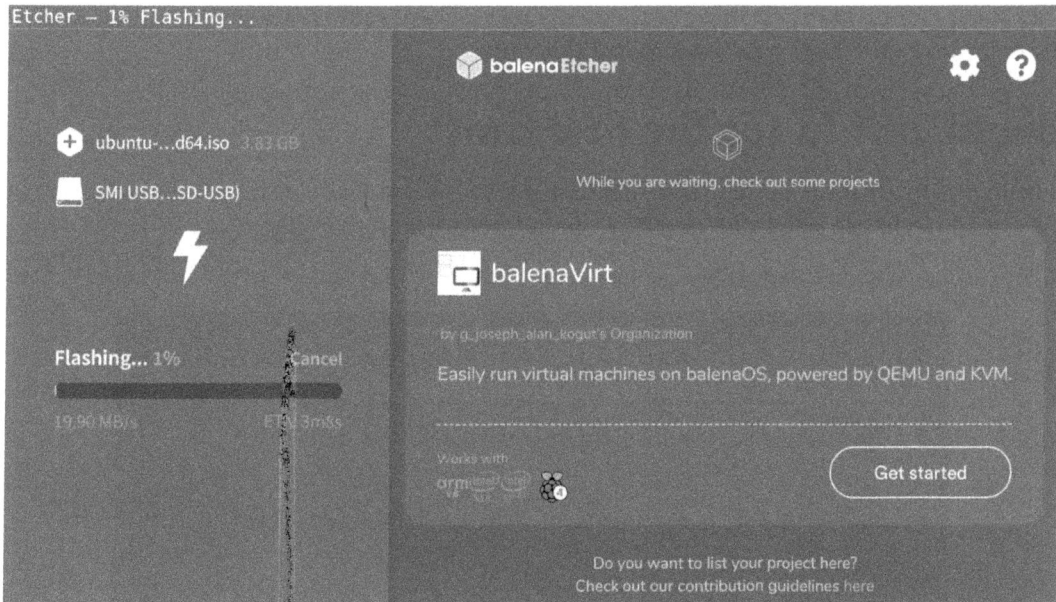

Figure 2.3: Etcher flashing the image to the USB drive

When Etcher is **Flashing** the image to the USB drive, it needs admin access to write the boot data into the USB drive; if it fails, ensure you are running as the admin.

Once Etcher has completed flashing the USB, it will show a ready message, as shown in *Figure 2.4*:

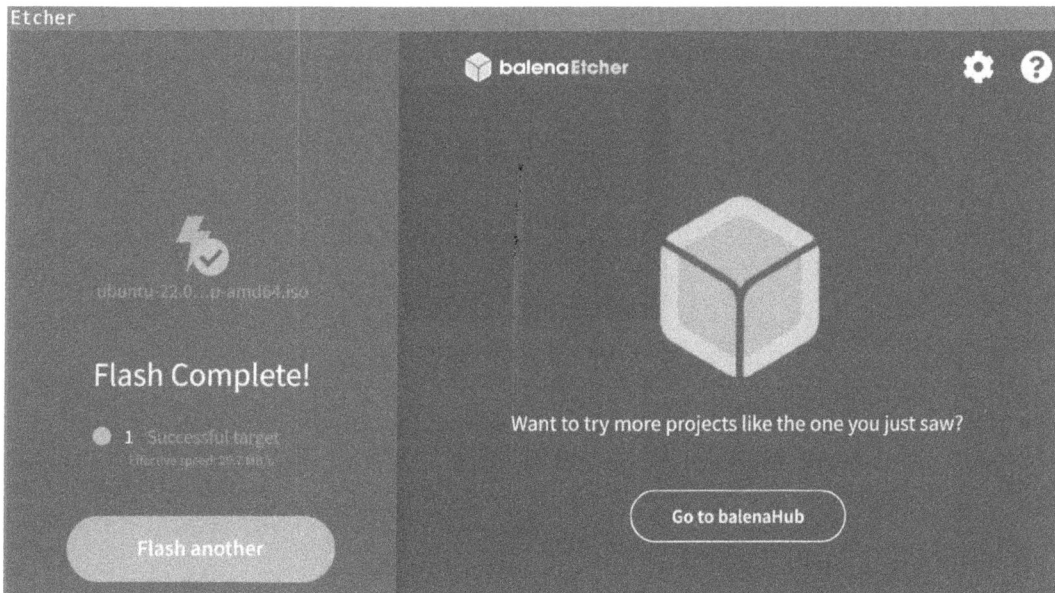

Figure 2.4: Etcher has flashed a USB drive complete

Let Etcher complete the flashing of the USB Drive. Then, remove the drive and attach it to the computer on which you want to install Ubuntu.

Boot Ubuntu for the first time

It is time to boot Ubuntu. Insert the USB drive into the computer and boot it up. Now, you may need to choose what device you want to boot from in the BIOS.

Figure 2.5 shows the Ubuntu boot menu:

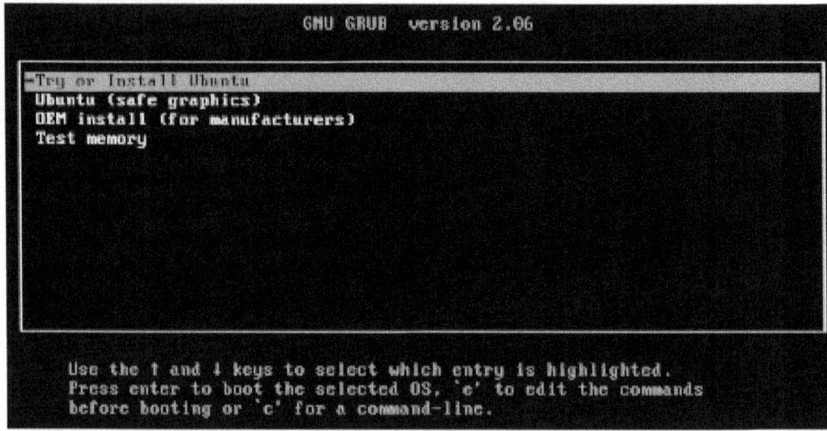

Figure 2.5: Ubuntu USB drive start menu as default will start Ubuntu

When the computer boots up for the first time, you get the option **Start or install Ubuntu** Press *Enter* to boot Ubuntu. Now Ubuntu is booting from USB drive, so keep in mind the performance will be slow as shown in *Figure 2.6:*

Figure 2.6: Ubuntu is starting up

The preceding figure is the Ubuntu load screen when Ubuntu is starting up. When Ubuntu has loaded, you are presented with the choice to try or install Ubuntu as shown in *Figure 2.7:*

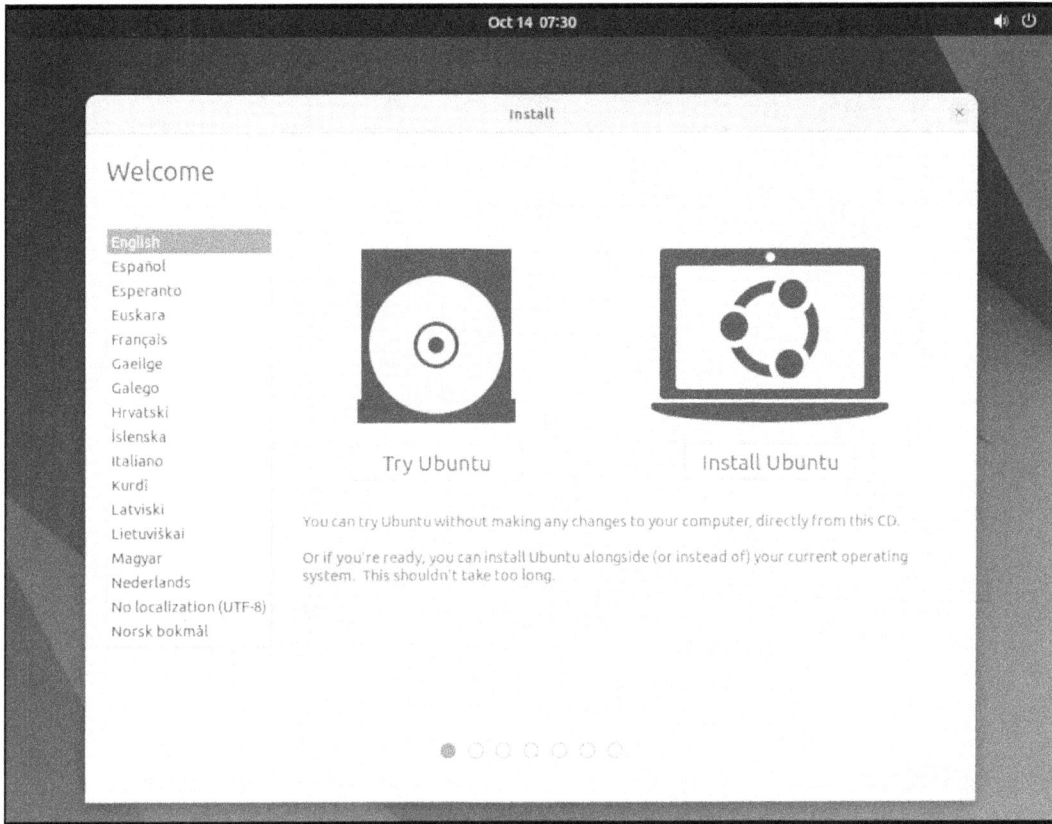

Figure 2.7: Choose an action after Ubuntu has started

Here, you can choose to install and proceed with the installation, or press **Try** and perform some pre-checks. Feel free to press **Install** and skip the pre-checks.

Pre-checks before installations

Now that we have a running Ubuntu booted from a USB drive, let's do some pre-checks to ensure that things are working.

Figure 2.8 shows the settings menu to use to connect to a network:

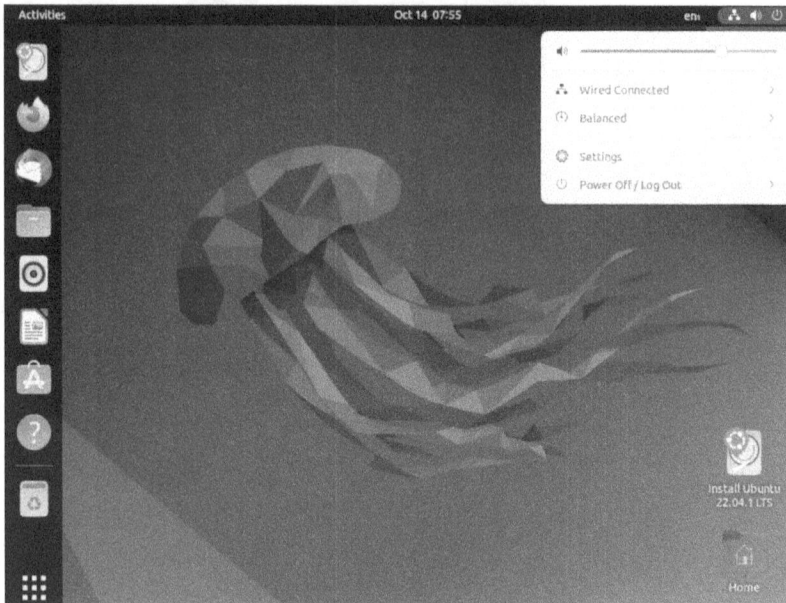

Figure 2.8: *Ubuntu Desktop with the menu to the left and to the top right, the settings panel has dropped down*

When we connect Ubuntu to a network, we can open Firefox to test our internet connection; *Figure 2.9* shows Ubuntu where we have opened the **Firefox Web Browser**:

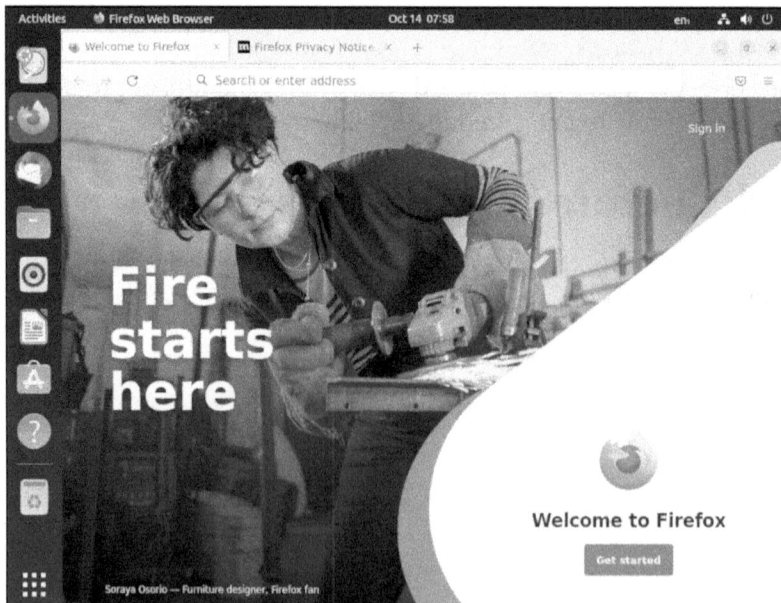

Figure 2.9: *Firefox started on Ubuntu*

The first check is to verify we have a working network connection. Connect to your ethernet or Wi-Fi access point and start Firefox to test the network.

Verify computer device

When Ubuntu is installed, it loads all the drivers for the different devices on the computer, from network cards to video cameras. However, sometimes Ubuntu can have problems setting up a device, and the following command can help you troubleshoot and find a resolution.

After the command's output is obtained and the device ID is searched on the Internet, Ubuntu guides users through using the device in Ubuntu.

Commands

You can run the following command to list all USB devices connected to your Ubuntu:

`lsusb` -vvv

Figure 2.10 shows how the command looks when its run on the installed Ubuntu:

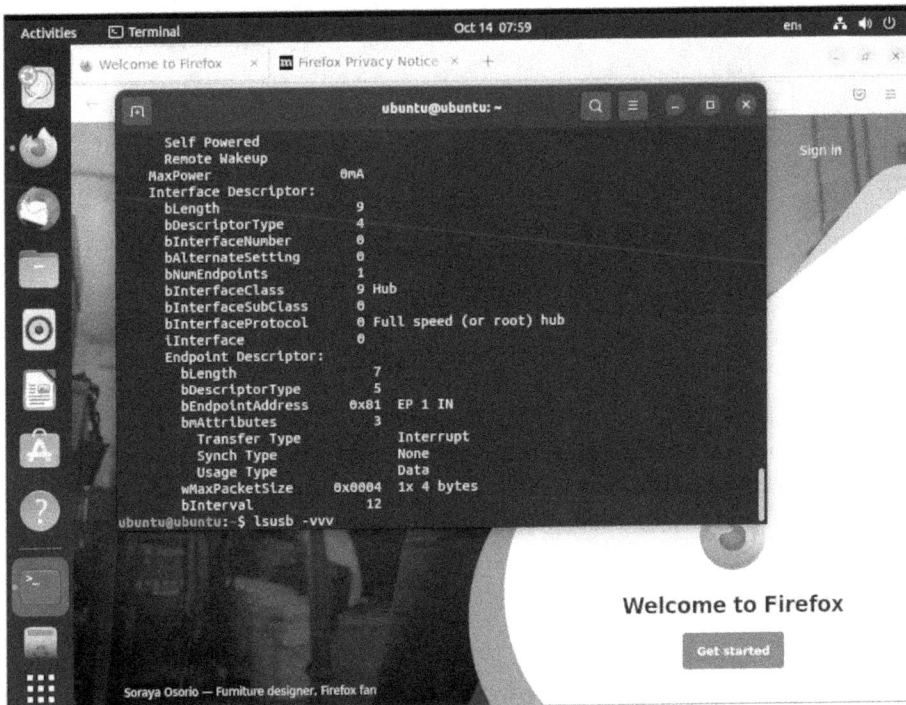

Figure 2.10: *The output of lsusb -vvv*

Figure 2.10 shows the output of the command `lsusb -vvv`. The command will print all the detected USB devices connected to the computer.

The following command will list all PCI devices connected to your Ubuntu:

lspci -vvv

As shown in *Figure 2.11:*

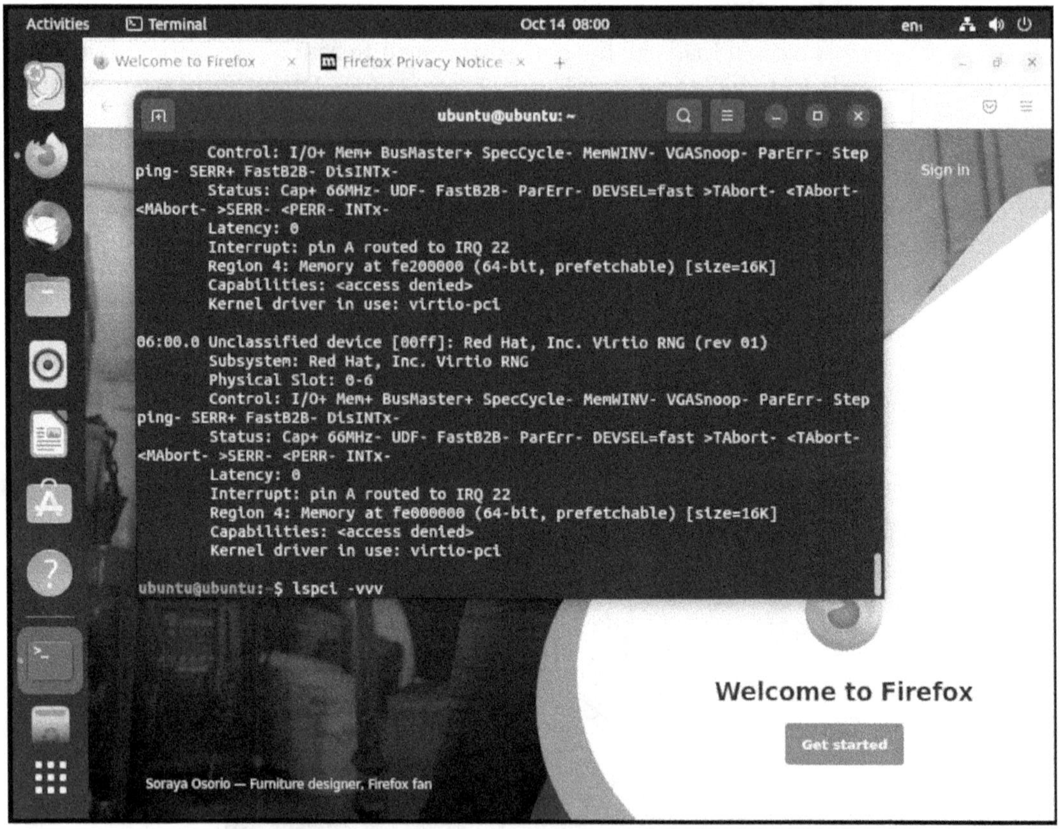

Figure 2.11: *The output of lspci -vv*

Figure 2.11 shows the output of the command **lspci -vvv**, which shows all the internal devices like network cards and more. If there are errors with the soundcard or network card, then this command will show what is detected. Verify that your devices are showing up, for example, a soundcard, microphone, and camera.

Installing Ubuntu

Now we are good to go and let us install Ubuntu on our computer. Start the guide on the desktop and follow the guide all the way. Ultimately, your computer will be rebooted, and you will disconnect the USB drive. The first option when installing Ubuntu is to select your language, as shown in *Figure 2.12:*

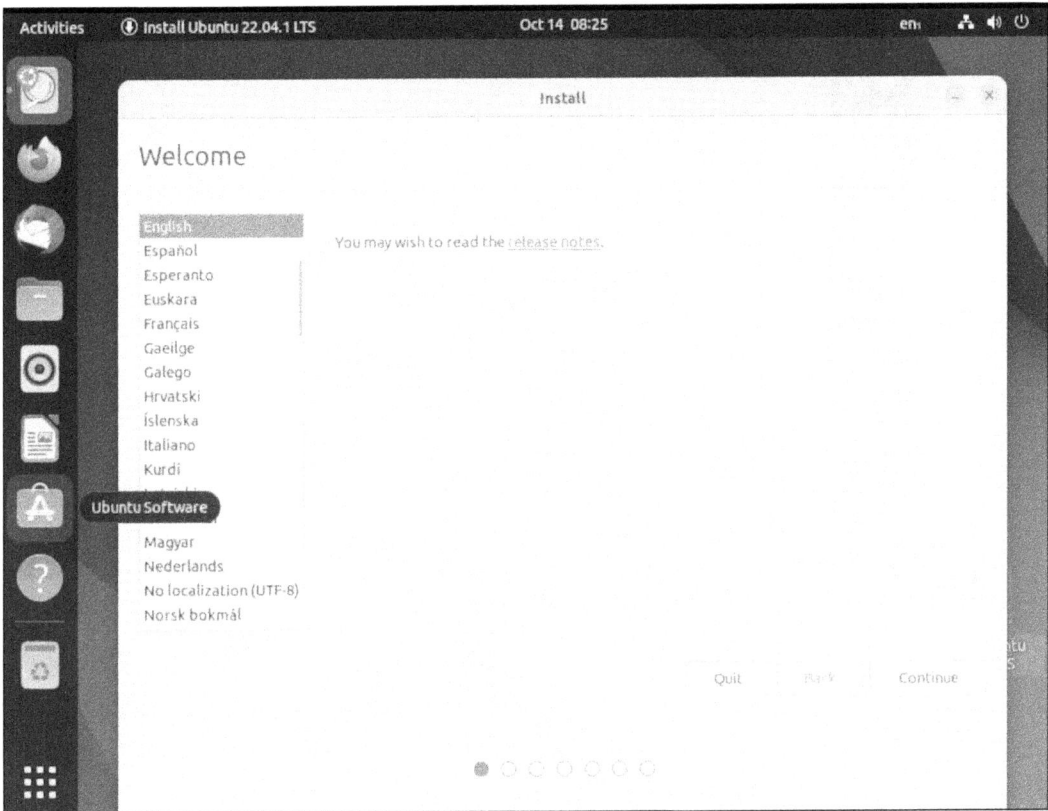

Figure 2.12: Selecting language for Ubuntu

First, choose the language for Ubuntu. All the menus and text that Ubuntu will communicate with you will use this language.

We recommend using English as a language, and if you can, use English. If you have issues, then search for them using the English names to make it easier to find the correct answers.

When your language is selected, it is time to choose your keyboard layout, as shown in *Figure 2.13*:

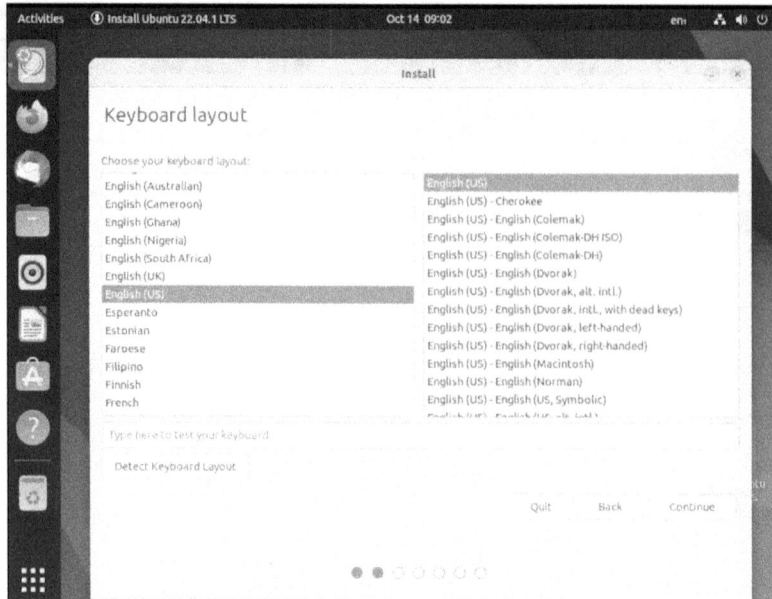

Figure 2.13: Selecting keyboard layout

Next, you set the keyboard you are using. Here, English is used as the language for Ubuntu, but with a Swedish keyboard layout. Choose your preferred keyboard layout.

Now we have set up the basics for the installation, and it is time to choose what kind of installation we want. *Figure 2.13* shows our installation options as follows:

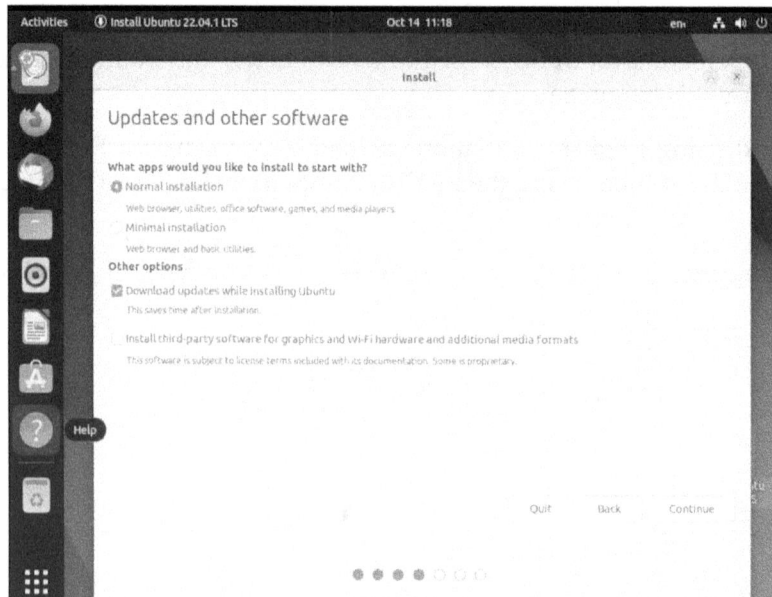

Figure 2.14: Update configuration and software installation

Update and other software

Now, we choose how we want to install Ubuntu. The default option, **Normal**, will install the base apps, including LibreOffice packages and other utility software. If you choose **Minimal**, Ubuntu only installs with base utils. It is easy to upgrade and install all apps. However, it is harder to downgrade to a minimal installation after using the normal installation.

If you have any GPU installed, choose the installed third-party software.

If you are unsure, we suggest enabling it.

After you install it, you can also enable third-party software from the desktop.

Installation type

This action is the one that will make changes that cannot be undone. Select the drive on which you want to install Ubuntu.

Later in this book, we will look more into how you can set up different disk partitions.

Figure 2.14 shows where we can add our changes to the hard drive. For the first time, we recommend using the first option to erase the hard drive and install Ubuntu as follows:

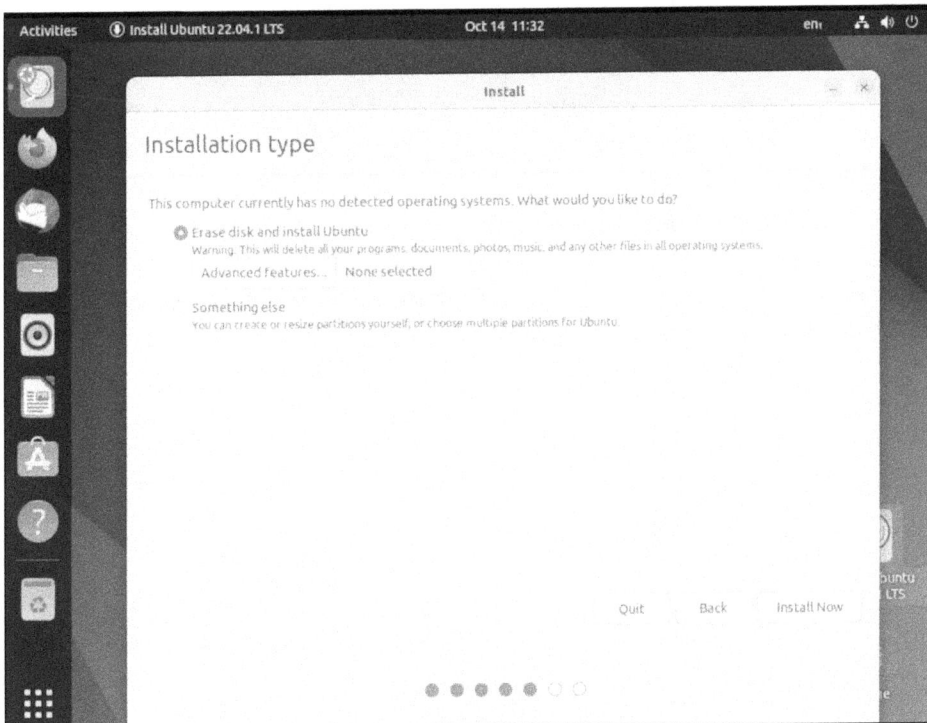

Figure 2.15: Installation type

Before Ubuntu makes the changes, a list box appears to verify the changes to the disk. As shown in *Figure 2.15*. To continue and make the changes to the disk, press **Continue**, and the installation will proceed. After this, your computer will be modified as follows:

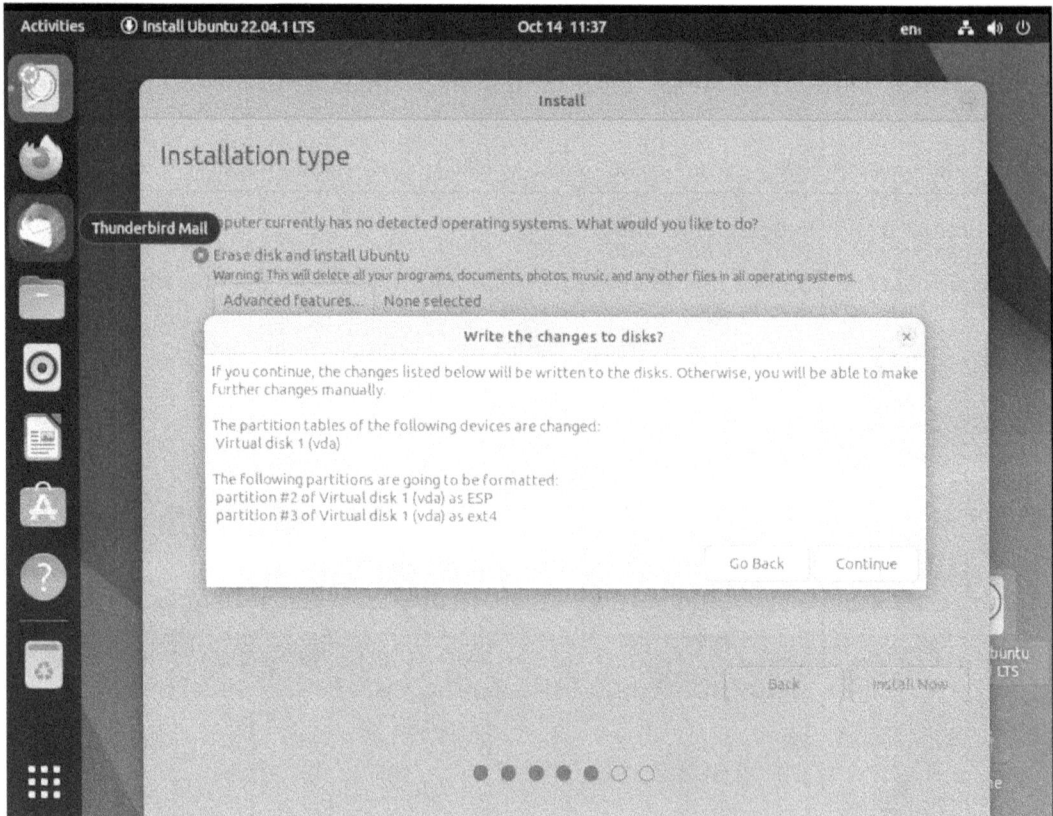

Figure 2.16: Confirmation to make changes to the disk before installation begins

The installation has begun in the background, and we are to set up our user info first. We are asked to set the correct time zone, shown in *Figure 2.17*:

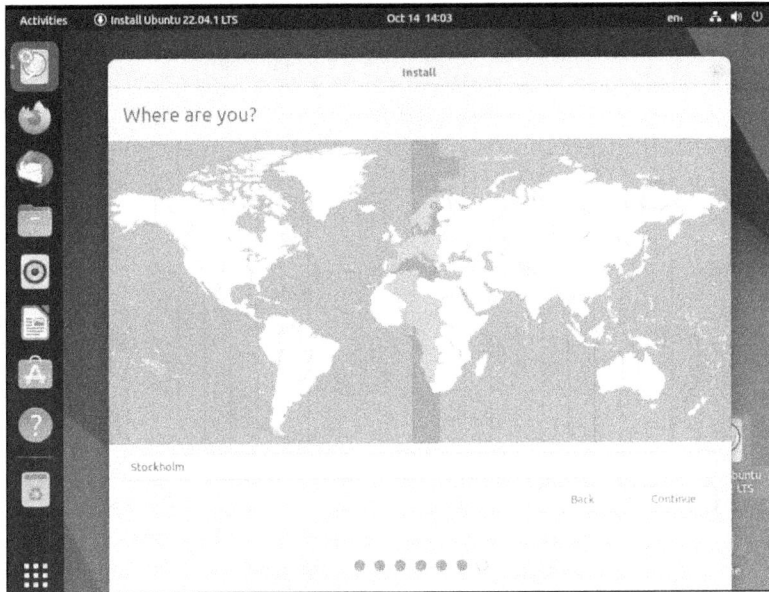

Figure 2.17: Select the time zone

The last information to add to the installation is your details, including your username and password. Please remember your username and password, as you will need them later to log in to Ubuntu.

Figure 2.18 shows the last page of the installation where you add your details:

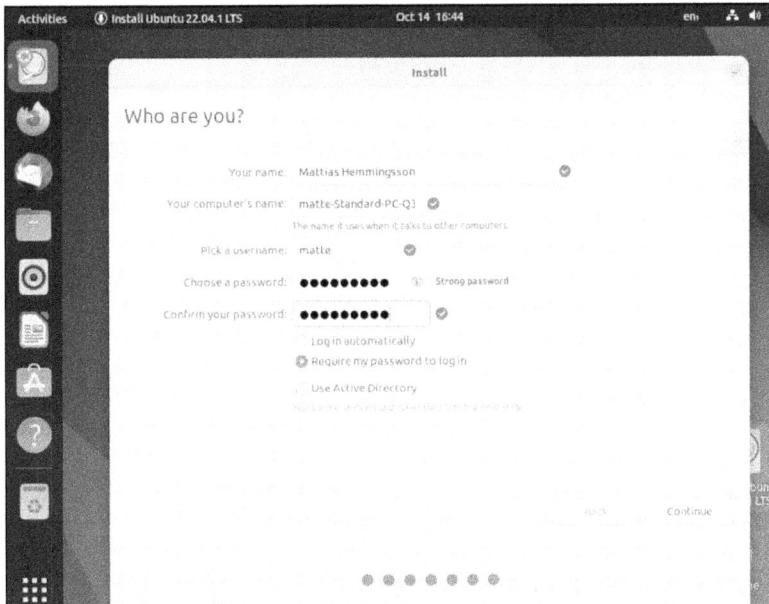

Figure 2.18: Setup your account and password, and name your computer

Now it is time to relax and let Ubuntu install. The installation time will be different depending on your computer's hardware. *Figure 2.19* shows Ubuntu installing:

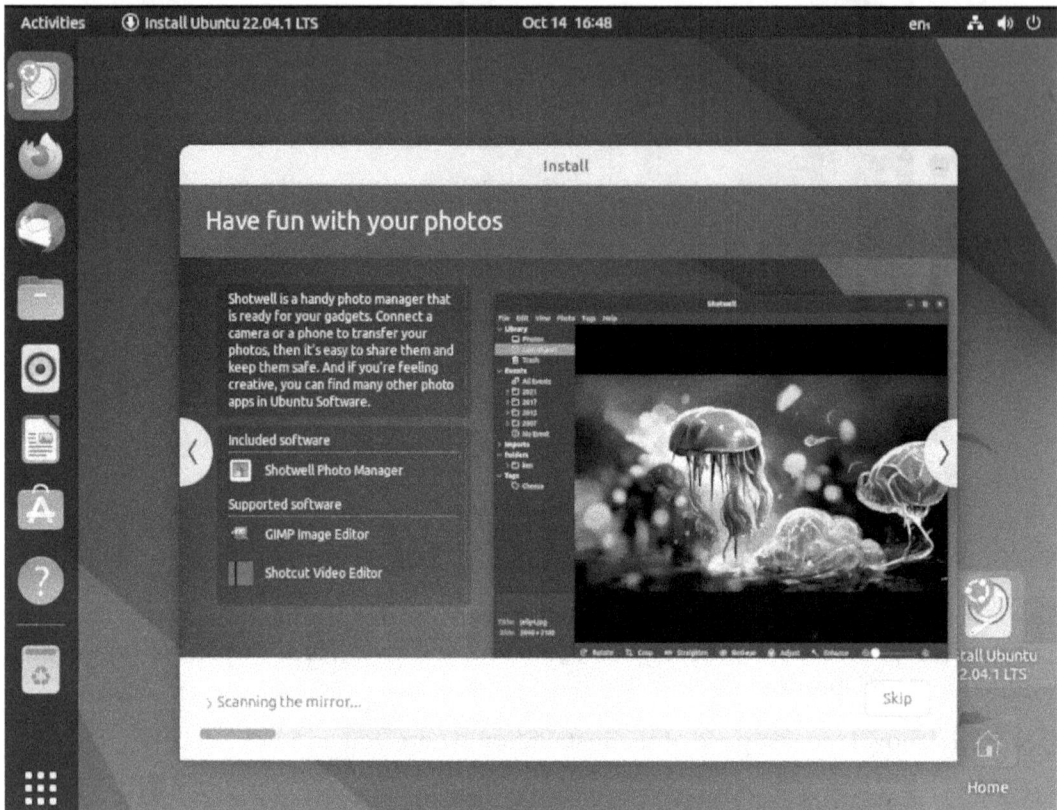

Figure 2.19: Installation is running

When Ubuntu has installed all the packages, it needs to be restarted, as shown in *Figure 2.20*. By pressing **Restart Now,** your computer will reboot, and the next time your computer boots, Ubuntu will be running.

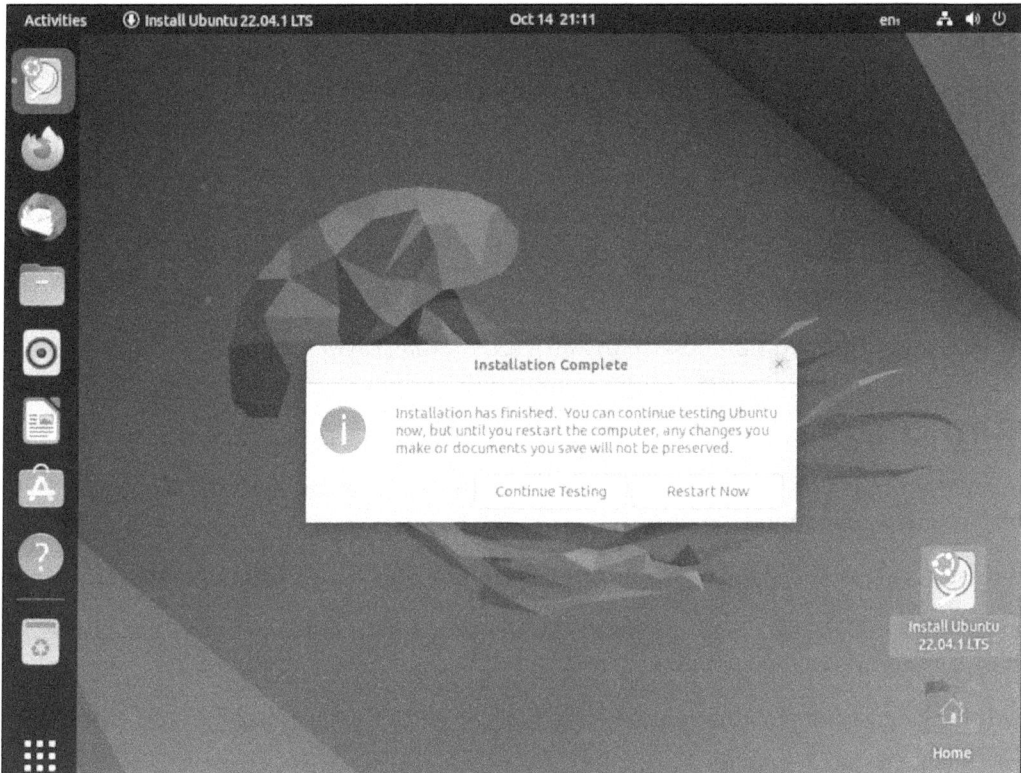

Figure 2.20: *Ubuntu installation complete*

Ubuntu running

Now you will have a running Ubuntu. The first task is to verify that everything is working. If your Ubuntu is working as it should, then jump into how to install apps.

Let us start with your first commands in Ubuntu.

Installing software

Installing software on Ubuntu is simple. You need the following steps for installing:

1. Install software from any of the two software stores.
2. Download the package from the web page and install it.
3. Connect your Ubuntu to the software's own repo and get direct access to updates.
4. Download an app image that runs without installation.

In this chapter, we will examine installing software from the store. Later in the book, we will discuss installing software using other methods.

Software store

The first store is the default Ubuntu Software Center, which is similar to an app store on a smartphone. It gives you access to all the standard tools and apps in Ubuntu and will also update apps for you.

You can access the store by starting the Ubuntu Software program. Search for the video player VLC and install it. You can also install software using the terminal.

```
sudo apt-get install vlc
```

The aforementioned command will install VLC media player.

Snap Store

The Snap Store is now built into Ubuntu software, and you can find all the apps from one interface: **https://snapcraft.io/store.**

Let us start by installing the Brave browser from the Snap Store, **https://snapcraft.io/brave**

You can also install Snap software from the Ubuntu Software Center ore by running Snap install commands in the terminal.

The following will install brave using the Snap Store in the terminal:

```
sudo snap install brave
```

Updating Ubuntu

It is recommended that you install most of your apps from the *Ubuntu software* store. This will install the correct packages, and all the surrounding packages needed for the app to run. Most importantly, it will keep track of and update your app for you.

In Ubuntu, open the *Software and Updates program*. The program will show you from which sources you are installing software. You can also install and enable software properties here.

Open the program called *Software Updater*. The program will update all the packages for you and keep your Ubuntu system up to date. If the tool finds a new update, it will send you a notification so that you can update your Ubuntu system.

You can also run the following command in the terminal:

```
1. sudo apt-get update
```

This will update the repos and find new packages that need to be installed:

```
1. sudo apt-get upgrade
```

This will upgrade all packages that have new versions.

Upgrading Ubuntu LTS

Ubuntu comes with its own update tool, which allows you to upgrade from the LTS version to the next version. This will allow you to keep your Ubuntu Server or desktop running for a long time while still updating it with the latest software.

In the terminal, run the command:

```
1.  #Here we have the -h flag to show the help section to the release
    upgrade command.
    sudo do-release-upgrade -h
```

It will find any new version and upgrade your Ubuntu LTS for you. You can also upgrade to a minor version by updating the configuration. The tool cannot upgrade the LTS before the first minor is released. So, if the LTS is released on 22.04, you can run the tool to upgrade when 22.04.01 is released.

.config folder

When we install apps onto our Ubuntu Desktop, all the application configuration is stored in the folder **.config**. Initially, it makes it a hidden folder, and it will not show up when you browse the folder. We will use this folder to save the script we use and the settings for different apps in the book. To keep this all, we will hold it all if anything happens to our Ubuntu installation. We will save it regularly to a Git Repo.

Conclusion

By the end of this chapter, we will have a running Ubuntu Desktop and have installed your first apps in Ubuntu, both from the powerful terminal and using the software store. We are now ready to go deeper into Ubuntu and Linux.

In the next chapter, we will make our desktop ready to work from. This includes adding tools for chat, email, and writing code.

Join our book's Discord space

Join the book's Discord Workspace for Latest updates, Offers, Tech happenings around the world, New Release and Sessions with the Authors:

https://discord.bpbonline.com

CHAPTER 3

Environments and Window Managers

Introduction

Ubuntu has all the comprehensive tools and software essential for our work. The widely used office tools now have packages compatible with Windows or operate in web browsers. This means that Ubuntu is a great operating system choice for professional work. You can also choose different types of windows managers with Linux.

In this chapter, we will look at a particular window manager called i3.

Structure

In this chapter, we will discuss the following topics:

- Install i3 window manager
- Commands to use in i3
- Working on Ubuntu
- Developing with Ubuntu

Objectives

In this chapter, we will discuss how to install the most popular tools in Ubuntu. You will also understand how to set up and use password manager to protect your passwords and encrypt files. We also understand how to connect your Ubuntu to a network using a VPN and personalize your system configuration. Additionally, we will also understand how to install and configure i3 windows manager and use a tilled windows manager.

Install i3 window manager

In Ubuntu, you can change the windows manager. We are using the window manager i3; now, you will learn to install and use it. You can always go back to the default windows manager by logging out and choosing the default windows manager. The i3 window manager is a tile manager, so everything you open will tile up. You can use short commands to control your desktop. It is also easy to command and control where apps will start.

Installing i3 windows manager is optional, showing different windows managers that can be used in Ubuntu. Open the terminal in your Ubuntu and type in the following command:

```
1. sudo apt install i3
```

This command will install the i3 windows manager and the essential tools to run and display the windows manager. When the installation is done, it is time to log in to your manager. To log in to the i3 windows manager, we must first log out from the current session. Then, choose the i3 windows manager and log in.

Refer to the following figure:

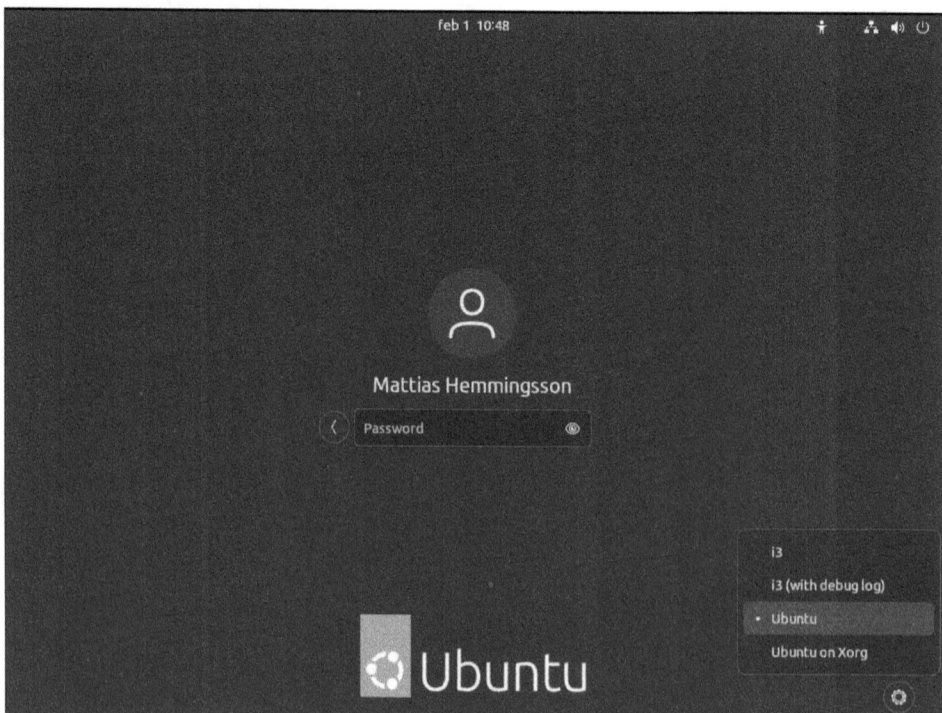

Figure 3.1: Ubuntu select desktop

If you want to log back into the default Windows GNOME, follow the same steps but choose the **Ubuntu** option. Do not worry when you log into the new i3 window. We may need to set up the screen before everything looks good.

Tiling

To open a web browser like Firefox or Brave, type *Win + D (Windows key + D)*, look at your screen, top left, type Firefox, and then press *Enter*. Now, Firefox will open beside the terminal, as shown in the following figure:

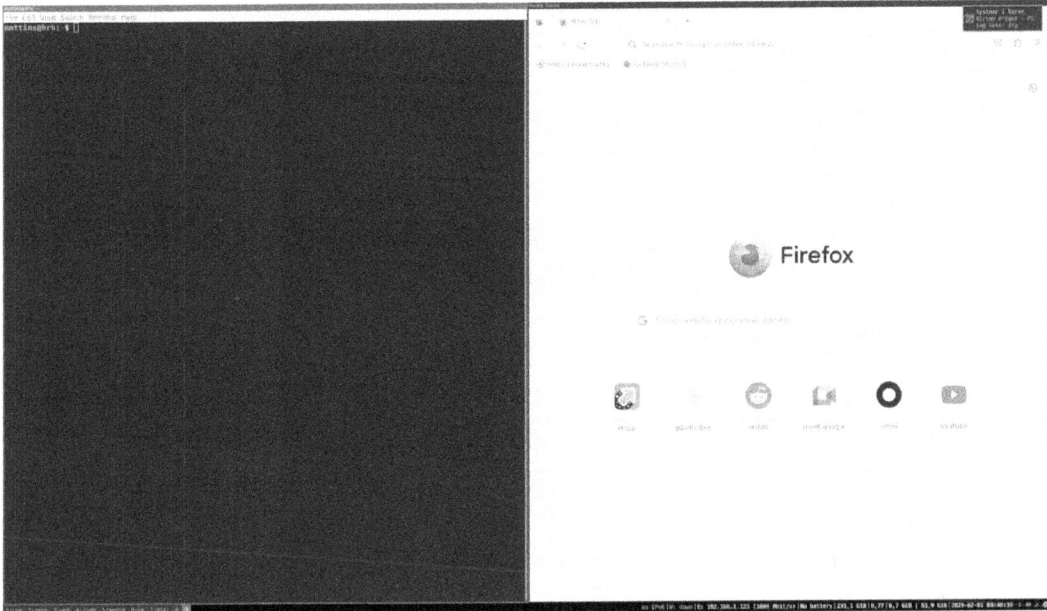

Figure 3.2: i3 tiling apps

As you see in the image, the windows are open beside each other, and there are no floating windows that you can drag around. i3 is a tiling windows manager; every app is open in full screen, or tiles to the program are already open.

1. Let us start by opening a terminal and see if we can set up the screen. Enter the combination *Win + Enter (Windows key + Enter)* at the same time. This command opens a new terminal instance.

2. If you need to set up your screen, follow the steps to configure it properly. This step is needed if you have multiple screens. In your terminal, now go to the folder **.config**:

   1. `cd .config`

3. Create the file **.XResources** notice the "." in the beginning:

   1. `nano .XResources`

4. Now, add the following:

    1. `Xft.dpi: 220`
    2. `Xcursor*size: 30`
    3. `Xcursor.size: 30`

5. Now, let us apply the values by typing the following command:

    1. `xrdb .XResources`

    Then, reload the Windows manager with the *Win + Shift + R (Windows key + Shift + R)* combination.

    The new settings will be applied, and the screen will change. The changes can be different. The setting above works for a Dell XPS with a 4k screen, and the values must be altered to fit other screen resolutions. Different screens will have different settings, and you can change the settings to your liking. Programs like Firefox need to be restarted to have the new settings applied.

6. Change your screen resolution or connect more screens to your computer. Then you need to tell **xrandr** in i3 to display the video on the new screen. Start with finding your screens:

    1. `#This command is used to set the size, orientation and/or reflection of the output of the screen`
    2. `xrandr`

7. This will print a long text of the connected screens and the different resolutions the screen can use:

    1. `xrandr --output <enter_screen_name> --auto`

8. Set the output of the screen **eDP-1** to auto:

    `xrandr --output <enter_screen_name> --mode 3840x2160 --right-of <enter_screen_name>`

9. This will add a second screen named from the **xrand** command **DP-1** and set the resolution to 3840x2160. Place the screen right of the laptop screen **eDP-1**.

    1. `xrandr --output eDP-1 --auto --output DP-1 --off`

10. Set the output to auto for the laptop screen **eDP-1** and then turn the image on the external **DP-1** off. They set the different settings and change between one and external screens. To change between different screens, a small bash script can be handy:

    a. Only laptop script:

        1. `mahe@comp:~/.config$ cat schreen_one.sh`
        2. `#!/bin/bash`
        3. `xrandr --output eDP-1 --auto --output DP-1 --off`

    b. Office script:

```
1. mahe@comp:~/.config$ cat schreen_office.sh
2. #!/bin/bash
3. xrandr --output DP-2 --mode 3840x2160 --right-of eDP-1
```

11. As you can see, the script is saved in me **.config** folder:

```
1. exec --no-startup-id xrdb ~/.config/.XResources
```

Add the above line to load your **-config/i3** config file to save and start your settings when you boot.

Extra commands

We also have the following command in the i3 configuration to take screenshots and open the sound controller:

```
1. bindsym $mod+XF86AudioMute exec pavucontrol # open sound control
```

We use this command to open the **pavucontrol** soundbar program:

```
1. bindsym Print exec gnome-screenshot
2. bindsym Control+Print exec gnome-screenshot -i
```

This is the command for taking screenshots.

Troubleshooting commands

If you add some commands and notice the short command is not working, always start with reloading the i3 config so the latest config is loaded. Then, test the command in a new terminal and use your account.

Commands in i3

i3 default comes with some basic commands for you. You have already used some but let us start on some basic ones. We are to open some programs in different windows and switch between them:

1. First, press *Win + D (Windows key + D)* and then type Firefox to launch the Firefox browser.

2. Now we are to change the windows:

   Win + 2 (Windows key + 2)

   This will open Windows 2. Looking at your bottom left, you see a two that is highlighted.

3. Start a new terminal here by pressing:

   Win + Enter (Windows key + Enter)

Now, you can toggle between the windows by pressing *Windows key + 1* or *Windows key + 2*.

i3 has many prebuild commands, as shown in the following tables:

- The basics are as follows:

Key combination	Purpose
Win+ Enter (Windowskey + Enter)	Open new terminal
Win + j (Windowskey + j)	Focus left
Win + k (Windowskey + k)	Focus down
Win + l (Windowskey + l)	Focus up
Win+ ; (Windowskey + ;)	Focus right
Win+ a (Windowskey + a)	Focus parent
Win + Space Bar (Windowskey + Space Bar)	Toggle focus mode

Table 3.1: Basics

- For moving windows:

Key combination	Purpose
Win + Shift –j (Windowskey + Shift + j)	Move window left
Win + Shift + k (Windowskey + Shift + k)	Move window down
Win + Shift + l (Windowskey + Shift + l)	Move window up
Win + Shift + : (Windowskey + Shift + ;)	Move window right

Table 3.2: Moving windows

- For modifying windows:

Key combination	Purpose
Win + f (Windowskey + f)	Toggle fullscreen
Win + v (Windowskey + v)	Split a window vertically
Win +h (Windowskey + h)	Split a window horizontally
Win + r(Windowskey + r)	Resize mode

Table 3.3: Modify windows

Look at the **Resizing containers/windows** section of the user guide.

- For changing the container layout:

Key combination	Purpose
Win + e (Windowskey + e)	Default
Win + s (Windowskey + s)	Stacking
Win + w (Windowskey + w)	Tabbed

Table 3.4: Changing the container layout

- Floating:

Key combination	Purpose
Win + ⇧ Shift + Space bar (Windowskey + Shift + Space Bar)	Toggle floating
Win + Left Click (Windowskey + Left click)	Drag floating

Table 3.5: Floating

- Using workspaces:

Key combination	Purpose
Win + 0-9 (Windowskey + 0-9)	Switch to another workspace
Win + ⇧ Shift + 0-9 (Windowskey + Shift + 0-9)	Move a window to another workspace

Table 3.6: Using workspaces

- Opening applications or closing windows:

Key combination	Purpose
Win + d (Windowskey + d)	Open application launcher (dmenu)
Win + ⇧ Shift + q (Windowskey + Shift + q)	Kill a window

Table 3.7: Opening applications/closing windows

- Restart or exit:

Key combination	Purpose
Win + ⇧ Shift + c (Windowskey + Shift + c)	Reload the configuration file
Win + ⇧ Shift + r (Windowskey + Shift + r)	Restart i3 in place
Win + ⇧ Shift + e (Windowskey + Shift + e)	Exit i3

Table 3.8: Restart/Exit

This is from the i3 website, and you can find it here:

https://i3wm.org/docs/refcard.html

Custom shortcuts

One advantage of i3 is that you can easily add your shortcuts. Then, you can run the command to open an application or script. We will now add some shortcuts to lock your screen and take screenshots. It is easy to add your command, open a terminal, and open the file **.config/i3/config**.

Open the file up with the text editor:

1. gedit .config/i3/config

The Windows key is set as the *Mod* key by default. But you can change this to any key you like. Some want to run this using the *ctr* key.

To change the **mod** key, modify the line:

1. set $mod Mod4

Change **Mod4** to the key you want to trigger commands with:

1. set $mod Control

Background image

Download an image to use as a background and place it in your **.config/background** folder. Install the package that sets the background for us:

2. sudo apt-get install feh

Let us add a background image in i3. Add the following line at the bottom of the file:

1. exec --no-startup-id feh --bg-fill ~/.config/background/image.jpg

Now, restart i3 with the **reload** command.

Lock screen

We will add a lock screen and a lock screen timer. So that your computer locks after 15 minutes. First, download an image you want to show when your screen is locked. Save the image in the folder **.config/i3/config/background**.

Install the package that we need:

1. sudo apt-get install xautolock i3lock.

Then add the following lines to your **.config/i3/config** file:

1. exec xautolock -time 15 -locker 'i3lock -i ~/.config/background/lock. png' &
2. bindsym $mod+1 exec i3lock -i ~/.config/background/lock.png

The first command starts with **exec** and tells i3 to run that command, and then it starts. So, **xautolock** runs in the background and will lock the screen after 15 minutes. It will then show the image **lock.png**. The second line that starts with **bindsym** sets when you press the **mod** button (Windows key as default) and l. It will run the command **i3lock** and lock the screen. Save the file and reload i3. Then press *mod+l* to test your screen lock.

Extra configs

Add the following to your config file:

```
1.  exec --no-startup-id nm-applet
2.  exec --no-startup-id blueman-applet.
```

This will start the applet in the bottom bar of i3 and show the network widget. So, you can right-click it and configure your network settings. It also adds the Bluetooth applet to connect to Bluetooth and configure any Bluetooth devices. If your computer lacks Bluetooth, you can remove that line.

To use the Bluetooth applet, install the packages:

```
1.  sudo apt-get install blueman
```

Extra Trix with i3

One of the excellent features of i3 is that you can auto-start the app when your computer starts up. So, the Brave browser always ends up on screen 1. Slack and Discord always start on screen 2. This way, you can easily set up your perfect working setup and save time. To do this, we need to edit our config file for i3:

```
1.  #Namming your screens
2.  set $ws1 "1:com"
3.  set $ws2 "2:term"
4.  set $ws3 "3:web"
5.  set $ws4 "4:code"
6.  set $ws5 "5:media"
7.  set $ws6 "6:vm"
8.  set $ws7 "7:misc"
```

Then, adding the following to your configuration will name the screens. You can alter the name to suit your screens:

```
1.  #My programs to start
2.  #w2
3.  #
4.  exec --no-startup-id i3-msg 'workspace 2:term; exec i3-sensible-
    terminal'
```

```
 5. exec --no-startup-id i3-msg 'workspace 2:term; exec i3-sensible-
    terminal '
 6. #w3
 7. exec i3-msg 'workspace 3:web; exec /snap/bin/brave'
 8.
 9. #w1
10. exec i3-msg 'workspace 1:com; exec /snap/bin/Slack'
11. exec i3-msg 'workspace 1:com; exec /snap/bin/discord'
12. #w3
13. exec i3-msg 'workspace 4:code; exec /snap/bin/code'
14.
15. #w4
16. #exec --no-startup-id i3-msg 'workspace 4:Wec; exec /usr/bin/code'
17. #assign [class="code"] 2:code
18. for_window  [class="Slack"] move to workspace 1:com
19. for_window  [class="discord"] move to workspace 1:com
20. for_window  [class="Brave-browser"] move to workspace 3:web
```

These commands start the different apps on the different screens (workspaces). In the end, assign them to the screen (workspace).

Then i3 starts up, and Slack also starts up. However, before Slack had fully started. The i3 startup has already moved to the next screen. Then, Slack is lunch in the wrong workspace. The **for_windows** command resolves this by moving Slack to the correct screen (workspace).

Work on Ubuntu

Today, Ubuntu has lots of features, you can access chat, email, and video tools from your Ubuntu with native apps.

Email

Thunderbird is an email client that can connect to most email providers. We will connect with a Gmail account and then sync email, contacts, and calendar events. Start by installing **thunderbird**. This only needs to be done if you choose the minimal installation during the installation of Ubuntu:

```
1. sudo apt-get install thunderbird
```

When Thunderbird is installed, we can launch the app. The first time Thunderbird runs, a startup guide is launched. The guide asks for your name and email. When you use Gmail or any of the big email providers, Thunderbird will autodetect the servers needed. It will also connect and sync all your contacts and calendar events.

Password manager

A password manager allows you to have one password you need to remember. Other functions will be saved in the password manager, and when you want to log into a site, you will ask your password manager for the credentials. This makes creating new best-practice passwords for every site and tool you use easy. Here, we will use the Bitwarden password manager. You will install it both as a plugin in your browser on your smartphone and as an app inside Ubuntu. Start by going to the site **https://bitwarden.com/** and registering an account. Now, start your browser and download and install the Bitwarden extension for your browser.

For Chrome and Brave, go to:

https://chrome.google.com/webstore/search/bitwarden

For Firefox:

https://addons.mozilla.org/en-US/firefox/addon/bitwarden-password-manager/

When the extension is installed, log in to your Bitwarden account. Pin the extension to your bar. Refer to the following figure:

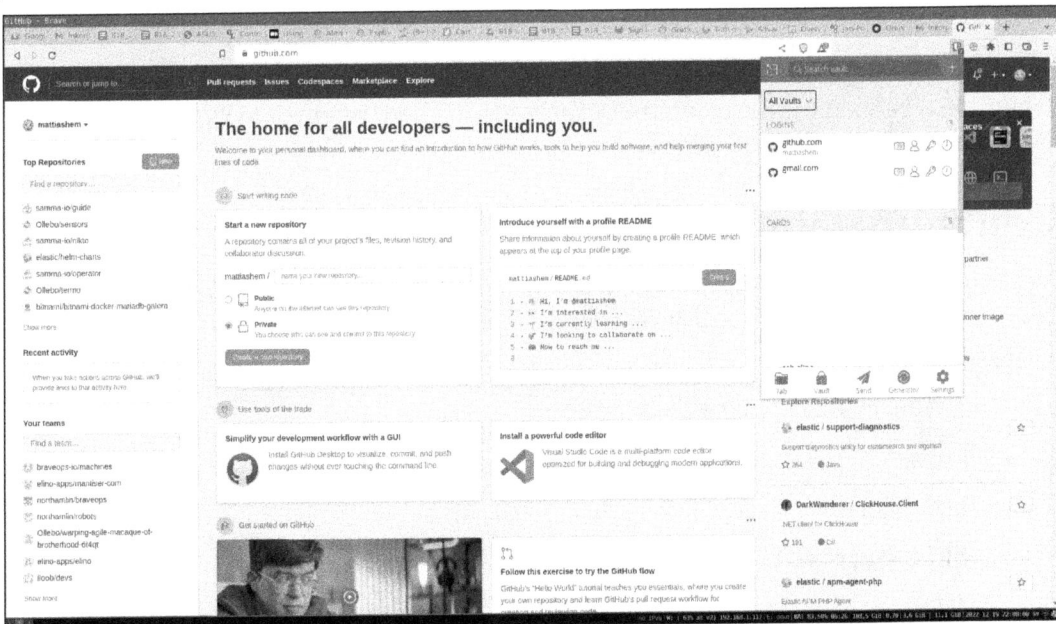

Figure 3.3: Firefox with Birtwarden plugin

Here is the Bitwarden plugin listing all my accounts with username and password for GitHub. Easy to use and use to login. When Bitwarden is installed, you can easily create new credentials for new sites and update the password for your current logins.

PGP encryption

PGP is a tool that encrypts and decrypts files. Using a public and private essential structure, you can encrypt using the public key and decrypt using the private key. When you are to receive an encrypted file, you send your public key to the sender. The sender then encrypts the files with your public key. Only you can decrypt and read the file with your private key. This is the best practice when sending information over the Internet in email or sensitive chat messages. You can also easily integrate PGP into Thunderbird and encrypt emails. Start the tool called **Seahorse**. It should be installed by default by Ubuntu. Create a new GnuPG key and type in your email and password.

Encrypt a file:

```
1. gpg --output file.txt.gpg --encrypt --recipient matte.hemmingsson@
   gmail.com file.txt
```

Here, the file is encrypted with the public key that belongs to the email:

matte.hemmingsson@gmail.com

To decrypt:

```
1. gpg --output file.txt --decrypt file.txt.gpg
```

Now, the files are in clear text again. To encrypt a file and send it. Import the public key of the person receiving the file using the Seahorse tool. Then, run the **encrypt** command and use the recipient's email and the file you want to encrypt.

Communication tools

Working today means we have more tools than email and docs. Today, we use chat tools to communicate with colleagues or friends. The most used are Teams from Windows, Slack, and Discord.

All of them are available in the Snap Store:

- **https://snapcraft.io/Slack**
- **https://snapcraft.io/teams**
- **https://snapcraft.io/discord**

Download them and start up the clients. You can go to the **Slack.com** homepage and create your channel. Both Slack and Teams are messaging applications, where you can send and chat between teams. They both can start voice and video calls and share the screen. Discord comes from pure voice-to-voice and is built for in-game talk between players. Today, it also supports text, video, and screen sharing. Both Slack and Discord are great tools for communication with colleagues and friends.

Watching video on Ubuntu

There are several tools to play videos. One of the best tools is the VLC media player. With VLC, you can play almost any media format and stream video directly from a source, such as an IP camera.

We have already installed VLC, but here are the commands again:

```
1. sudo apt-get install vlc
```

We will use VLC to stream a video from a camera. The command will start VLC and connect it to the stream. It then opens a window and shows the video with the image. The stream from the IP camera is here:

```
1. vlc rtsp://10.100.0.90:554/s2
```

The following figure shows the stream from an IP camera displayed with VLC:

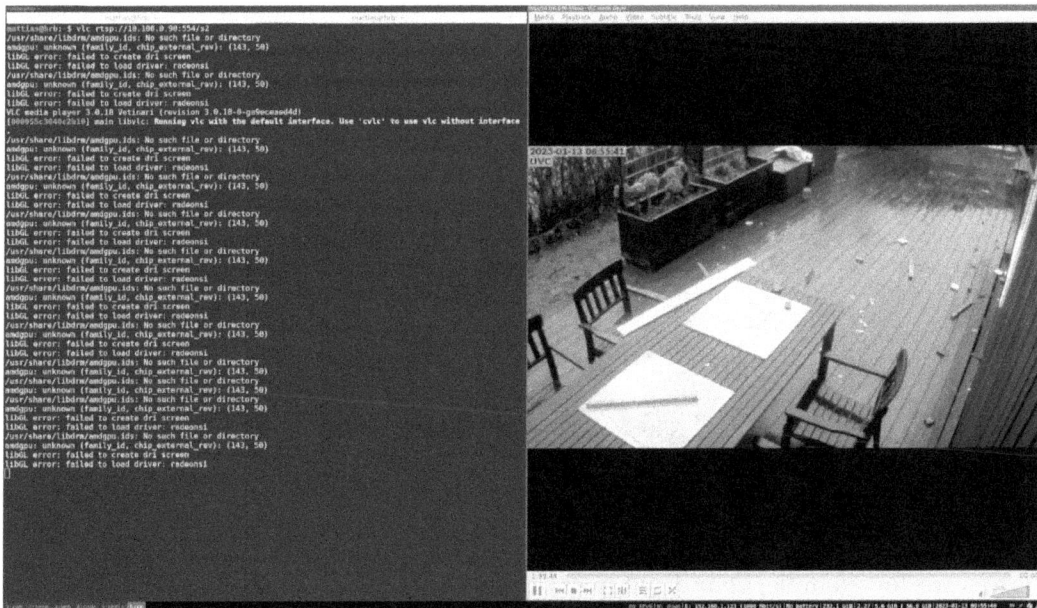

Figure 3.4: Showing VLC stream

Stream your desktop live

OBS Studio is a tool to stream live video from your desktop to the largest streaming platforms.

OBS Studio connects multiple inputs, like your screen and webcam, into one stream. Then, you can send that stream to any streaming service or save it as a video file.

You can download and read more about OBS from the following link:

https://obsproject.com/

To install OBS, run the following commands:

1. `sudo add-apt-repository ppa:obsproject/obs-studio`
2. `sudo apt update`
3. `sudo apt install ffmpeg obs-studio`

After installing and starting OBS, you are greeted with the start screen shown in the following figure:

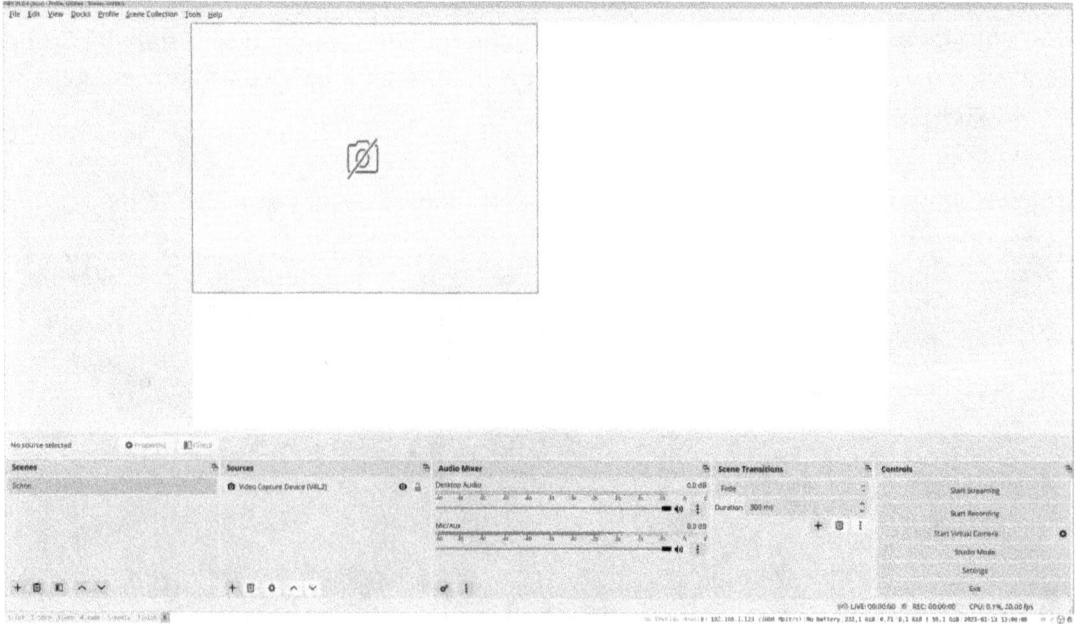

Figure 3.5: OBS Studio start window

Figure 3.7 shows the window at the start of OBS Studio. Here, you can select your scenes and sources.

Sources are, for example, your desktop or your webcam.

OBS Studio then combined the different sources into one scene and streamed that scene.

In *Figure 3.6*, we can see the stream from my desktop:

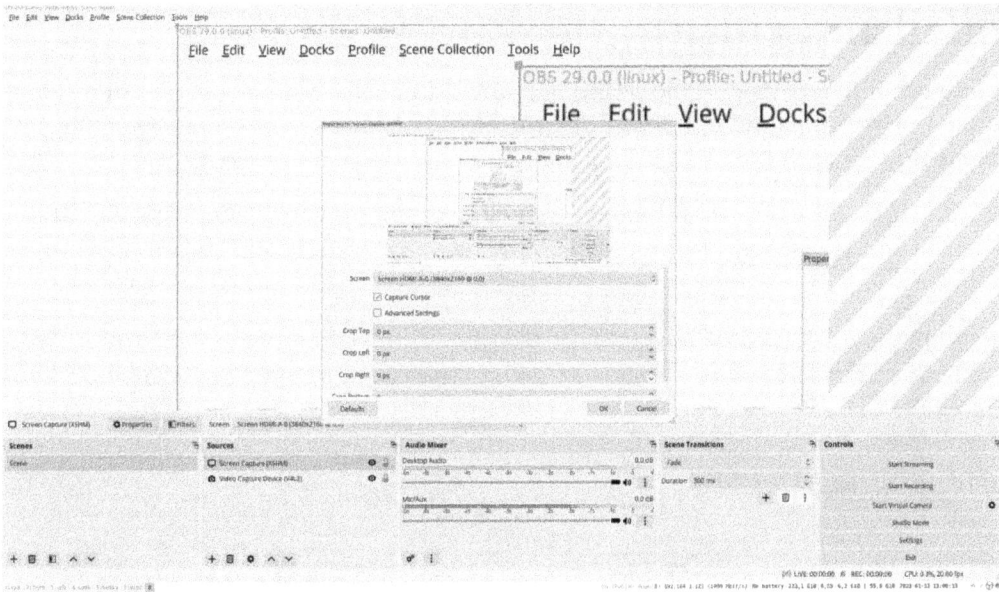

Figure 3.6: OBS Studio with screen capture source

You can move more sources to your desired layout when you add them. After adding your sources and arranging them, it is time to stream your video to a streaming service. OBS Studio has integrated support for several video streaming platforms. Select a video platform or a custom one in the settings menu and start streaming. The example shown in the following figure shows how to set a stream:

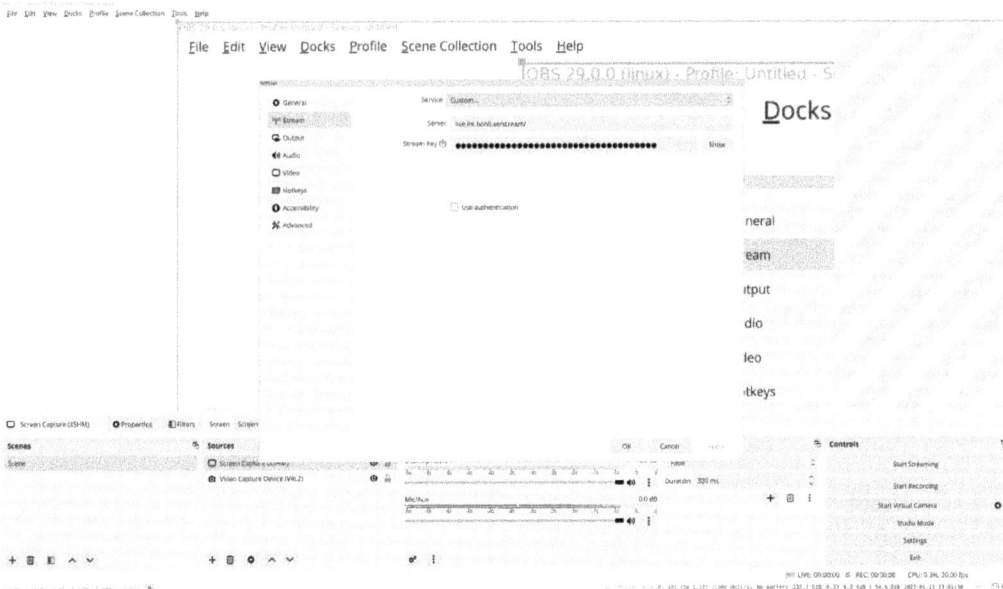

Figure 3.7: OBS Studio stream settings

Sound and video

Ubuntu can mix and control the sound in many different ways. Most of the time, it is easy and only plays the sound out on the default speaker. However, you may sometimes want better control over the sound, and for that, different tools can be used.

Pavucontrol is one of the tools that allows you to easily set your default speaker. It is also set so that music is played on your headphones and system sounds are on your main speaker.

The following figure shows how you can select auditor setting in pavucontroll:

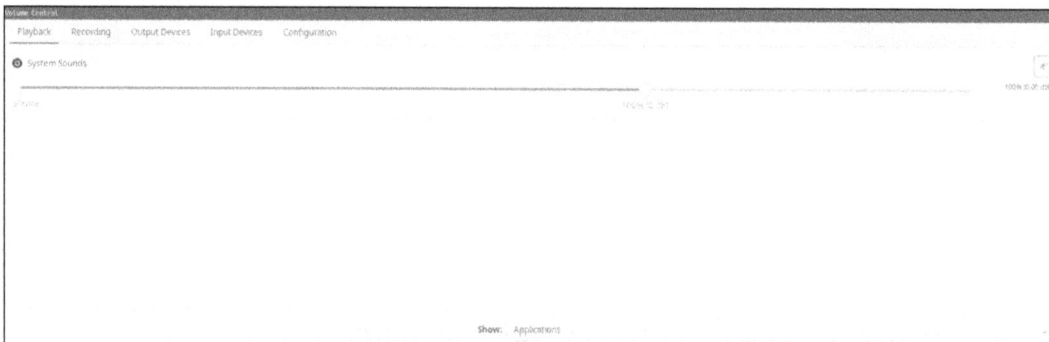

Figure 3.8: Pavucontrol sound config

Webcam

Video devices such as a webcam will be detached automatically. The default video cam player in Ubuntu is Cheese. If you use the minimal installation options, then you need to install **cheese** to use it:

```
1. sudo apt-get install cheese
```

Then you can start Cheese; it autodetects webcams and connects to them. Cheese also has some video effects that you can add to your stream.

Syncing files

Syncing files from your local computer to a cloud provider is harder than on other OS. Many large cloud providers with cloud storage do not have native sync clients for Ubuntu. However, there are other clients you can use, as follows:

- **Google Drive:** For syncing files between Google Drive and Ubuntu, the app OpenDrive can be a good option:

  https://flathub.org/apps/details/io.github.liberodark.OpenDrive

- **Dropbox:** It is a storage provider that provides a native app for syncing files. You can easily download and install the app from the following URL:

  https://www.dropbox.com/install-linux

- **Mega:** It is cloud storage with a native Linux app that you can use to sync files:

  https://mega.io/desktop

- **Resillio:** If you are syncing files with friends or to your server, then Resillio is a great tool. You can choose two folders on different computers and then sync them. You can also add more folders in different locations and nodes where you want the data synced:

  https://www.resilio.com/

Developing with Ubuntu

Ubuntu is a great platform to work from as a developer, DevOps, or Linux admin. All the tools you need work in Ubuntu, and some only work in Linux today.

Git

Git is a version control system that tracks files. Today, it is the standard tool for developers to write code and then push it to a repo. This allows many developers to work together on the same code base. It is also widely used by sysadmins and DevOps to store configuration files, scripts, or other documents.

Install **git** by running:

```
1. sudo apt-get install git
```

It is considered the best practice to use an SSH key when pushing and pulling code from your local computer to or from a Git Repo. For this to work, we need to create an SSH key that we can use. On your local Ubuntu, type the following command:

```
1. ssh-keygen
```

Accept the default values and set a password for your key.

No, we need to add the newly created ssh key to GitHub so that we can use it. Log in to your GitHub account and go to settings/SSH and GPG Keys. Now, create a new SSH key and add the public key we created before as follows:

```
2. cat .ssh/id_rsa.pub
```

Save your new key. By adding your SSH key to GitHub, we can run the command and use our GitHub user from the command line without logging in. This is the default way of using git and working with code. Read more about it from the following link, **https://docs. github.com/en/authentication/connecting-to-github-with-ssh.**

Check out the Git Repo for this book:

```
1. git clone https://github.com/bpbpublications/Ubuntu-Linux-in-30-
   days.git
```

To create a private Git Repo to store files and config. Navigate to github.com and create a new account. Under settings, add your newly created SSH key. You will get the key with the following command:

```
1. cat ~/.ssh/id_rsa.pub
```

Now, you can create a new repository in your GitHub account and clone it to your local Ubuntu. When ready, clone the empty repo to your local computer:

```
1. git clone REPO
```

In the folder, create a new file called **README.md** and add the following to the file:

```
1. #My test config
2. This is regular text
3.
4. ## This is a smaller heading
5.
6. ```
7. #!/bin/bash
8. echo "Script"
9.
```

Let us add this file to our Git Repo:

```
1. git add README.md
```

When the files are added to our Git Repo, we can commit the changes:

```
1. git commit -a -m "Our Readme File"
```

Files have been added and committed to our repo. Let us push the files back to the GitHub servers:

```
1. git push -u origin main
```

When you go to your repository page in GitHub, you will see our **README.md** files in the repo. You can do much more with Git, and if you are to work with Git, this book will help you master it:

https://github.com/bpbpublications/Ubuntu-Linux-in-30-days

Code

When working with code, scripts, or files, you need a good code editor. One of the best today for code is VS Code. It runs perfectly on Ubuntu and supports many different code languages. Later in this book, we will use VS Code to connect to the remote server, write scripts, and run them.

More info about VS Code can be found here:

https://code.visualstudio.com/

To install VS Code on Ubuntu, use the Snap Store or download the deb package from the website. Once you have downloaded the deb package, you can install it using the following command:

This command will also work from other apps that provide **.deb** files:

```
1. sudo dpkg -i <name of the file you downloaded>
```

PyCharm

PyCharm is another code editor to use, especially for Python programs. JetBrains, the company behind PyCharm, also has other IDEs for languages like Java and Rust. To install PyCharm, use their snap package and download the community version.

You can start it and select your first project when it is downloaded from:

https://www.jetbrains.com/pycharm/

About code editors

There are many different tools for writing code, and we must find the best one. An IDE that allows you to switch between different code languages and access server code will be a good choice. If you only use Python programming, PyCharm may be the tool for you.

If you want to install your first IDE code editor, start with VS Code.

Conclusion

By the end of this chapter, we learned to install and set up the i3 windows manager and change the windows manager. We have also installed and set up the tools to work with Ubuntu, including email chat tools, password manager, and encryption. You can also install and set up tools to stream video from sources to your computer and to make and stream video showing your desktop to streaming providers. We have also installed and set up tools to work as a developer using Ubuntu by installing IDE code editors like VS Code and version control systems like Git. You have also learned how to create your own Git repository, set up SSH, add files, and push back to GitHub.

In the next chapter, we will discuss and work on setting up multiple network devices.

Join our book's Discord space

Join the book's Discord Workspace for Latest updates, Offers, Tech happenings around the world, New Release and Sessions with the Authors:

https://discord.bpbonline.com

CHAPTER 4
Setting up Firewall, VPN, and Wi-Fi Networks

Introduction

Ubuntu has many powerful tools when it comes to network tools. Your regular Ubuntu Desktop has access to all the tools used in the Ubuntu Server that powers the network around the world. The Ubuntu Desktop also has default tools for setting up a **virtual private network (VPN)** and locking down Firewalls. In this chapter, we will look at some basic network tools. We will learn to connect to different types of networks and set up secure VPN connections.

Structure

In this chapter, we will cover the following topics:

- Network DHCP or static
- Connect to segment VLAN networks
- Connect to wireless networks
- Hide your computer by changing MAC address
- Secure your connections with VPN service
- Protect your traffic by using DNSS

- Protect your computer by applying a Firewall
- Detect and stop computer virus

Objectives

In this chapter, we will discuss network setup on your Ubuntu Desktop. We will look at connecting to networks over cable and wireless. We will then look at securing our connections using a VPN server and secure DNS. We will also look at locking down network traffic into and out of our Ubuntu Desktop.

By the end of this chapter, you will learn to set up different types of network connectivity with your Ubuntu Desktop, protect your Ubuntu using the Firewall, and connect securely using different VPN solutions.

Network DHCP or static

When connecting to a network, your computer needs an address. A router is where it can find other addresses and connect to the Internet. There are two ways to get an address. Your computer can ask the network for an address. This is called **Dynamic Host Configuration Protocol** (**DHCP**), and all routers and Wi-Fi access points have a DHCP server that provides addresses to the computers in the network.

This is also the default setting for network and Wi-Fi network cards in Ubuntu. However, you can also manually set your address to a network address. To do that, you need to have the range and router that are needed.

If you are connecting your computer to a new **Internet Protocol** (**IP**) camera and do not have a router or Wi-Fi point that hands out the address, you can set the network address on your network card to match the network on the camera.

Network static

In Ubuntu, setting your network to a static or manual IP address is easy. The mentioned steps can be followed to connect to a network using manual IP:

1. Open the network settings in Ubuntu by searching for `Advanced   Network Settings`. It will list all your network cards and bridges. It also lists all the WIFI access points.

2. When setting a network device to static, you only need to set the address for the selected wireless settings. So, if you have two wireless networks, v2 and v2-dmz, you can set the v2 wireless as manual. It will not affect the v2-dmz Wi-Fi.

3. If you select the network card and change the settings from DHCP to static (manual), it will affect every time you connect it with a cable.

4. Before you can set your network card to static (manual), there are some settings you need.

5. The address to use is usually in the range of 192.168.0-255.1-255. It is important that you use an address that is not already in use. So, if you set up an IP camera and in that IP camera manual, it is mentioned that the camera will default to the IP of 192.168.1.50, then you need to set your IP to 192.168.1.49.

6. The next setting is the netmask and that tells the network card the number of IPs that can be used. The default for home is 255.255.255.0 or 24.

7. The last setting is the router. The router will send all traffic to our computer that we cannot find in the local range. This will be the IP of your router or network device connected to the internet.

8. If you are only setting up two devices, like an IP camera, you can skip adding a router.

You will still be able to connect to devices that have an IP. So, without a router, if your camera is at 192.168.1.50 and you have set your computer to use 192.168.1.49, then you do not need to set a router to connect to the camera.

Connect to segment VLAN networks

Virtual Local Area Network (**VLAN**) is a way in the network cable to divide it into several layers. So, when you connect your computer with a network cable, you will get a default network.

However, if your switch has VLAN support, you can add multiple layers of network inside. VLAN is only supported by some switchers, and you need to have a management interface to configure the switch to set up a VLAN. You can look in your switch/router manual to learn if you device can handle VLANs.

This is handy if you have a server which you only want one other computer to access. Then, you can segment it into its own network segment and only add that segment to your computer.

In Ubuntu, we can create a new virtual network card connected to that segment.

Every VLAN has a number, which is the segment. So, before you can connect your Ubuntu to a VLAN, you first need to know the **Local Area Network** (**LAN**) ID. This is set up in the switch you are connecting to. Here, we are creating a new virtual interface for interface enp1s0. We give it the name **enp1s0.10** and set it to use VLAN id 10.

We set the base network card that it will be connected to. When the virtual device is added, you can configure it using DHCP or a static IP as a regular network card. As shown in the following command:

```
1. ip link add link enp1s0 name enp1s0.10 type vlan id 10
```

Connect to wireless network

Setting up a wireless network card is as easy as using a regular card. We first need to find the wireless network to connect to and then the correct authentication for the network.

There are two different wireless networks today, the old 2.4 G and the new 5 G. Today, most of the network Wi-Fi devices can use both, but if you are using older hardware, you need to verify that your wireless access point is using the same frequency as your computer. Otherwise, they will not be able to see the network.

Connecting to a wireless network is easy.

1. Select the network you want to connect to.
2. Then you will be asked for a password and asked to fill in the password for the wireless.

In Ubuntu network settings, you now have the wireless network. Under Wi-Fi, you can configure it as any other network card. The Wi-Fi network also has a security tab when connecting to the network.

Today, most wireless networks use one shared password when connecting, but you can also get access using other methods.

If you are required to use, for example, **Wi-Fi Protected Access** (**WPA**) Enterprise, it is on the security tab. You just need to configure it.

Hide your computer by changing MAC address

Every network device has a hardware address, and it is bound to an IP address. So, when packages are traveling in the network, in the end, they end up at the hardware address. Now in Ubuntu and most **operating system** (**OS**), you can change your MAC address to anything, even random. Now the network traffic will be connected to a MAC, but when you reconnect and change your MAC address. The network traffic will be connected to the new MAC address.

Let us install and set up a MAC change that will randomize your MAC addresses every time your network comes up:

```
1. apt-get install macchanger
```

In the folder **/etc/network/if-pre-up.d/**, create a file called **macchanger** and add the following content:

```
1. #!/bin/sh
2. # Radomize the mac address for the given interface
3. /usr/bin/macchanger -e "$IFACE"
```

To make it executable, run the following command:

```
1. chmod +x /etc/network/if-pre-up.d/macchanger
```

Change the **$IFACE** to match the network card you want to change the MAC address on. It can be on your Wi-Fi or a cable network card.

Note: This change can also cause problems in the network, so be ready to disable it at any time.

Secure your connections with VPN service

VPN is a way to connect our local computer to a network securely. If a company has a server on a local network and the server is not accessible from the internet, we can use a VPN to create a secure tunnel from your computer at home into the company network. Then, you will be able to connect to the servers in the local network.

It is used for developers to connect to databases that you do not want accessed from the internet.

The two most used VPN tools in Linux are OpenVPN and WireGuard. In Ubuntu, to set up a VPN client to a server we require the following steps:

1. Go to the network settings and add a new connection.

2. Select the VPN you want to add.

3. To install the package needed for **openvpn** and **wireguard** run the following command:

    ```
    1. sudo apt-get install openvpn wireguard
    ```

OpenVPN

The given steps can be followed to secure your connection with OpenVPN:

1. Start by visiting NordVPN and setting up a trial account, or if you have another OpenVPN service, you can use that.

    https://nordvpn.com/risk-free-vpn/

2. Now, in your Ubuntu, to set up an OpenVPN connection, you need to open the network settings tab. Then click on the + sign, and then add a new virtual OpenVPN config as shown in the following figure:

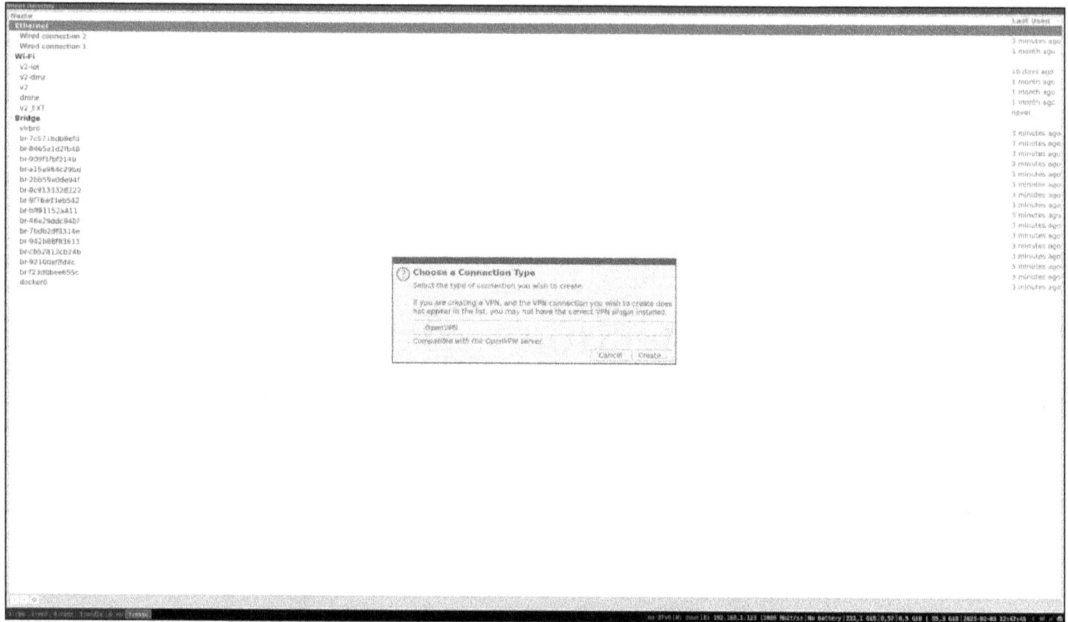

Figure 4.1: *Network settings and create an OpenVpn*

3. Add the settings from NordVPN and test your connection.

4. Add the settings you have received from NordVPN as shown in the following figure:

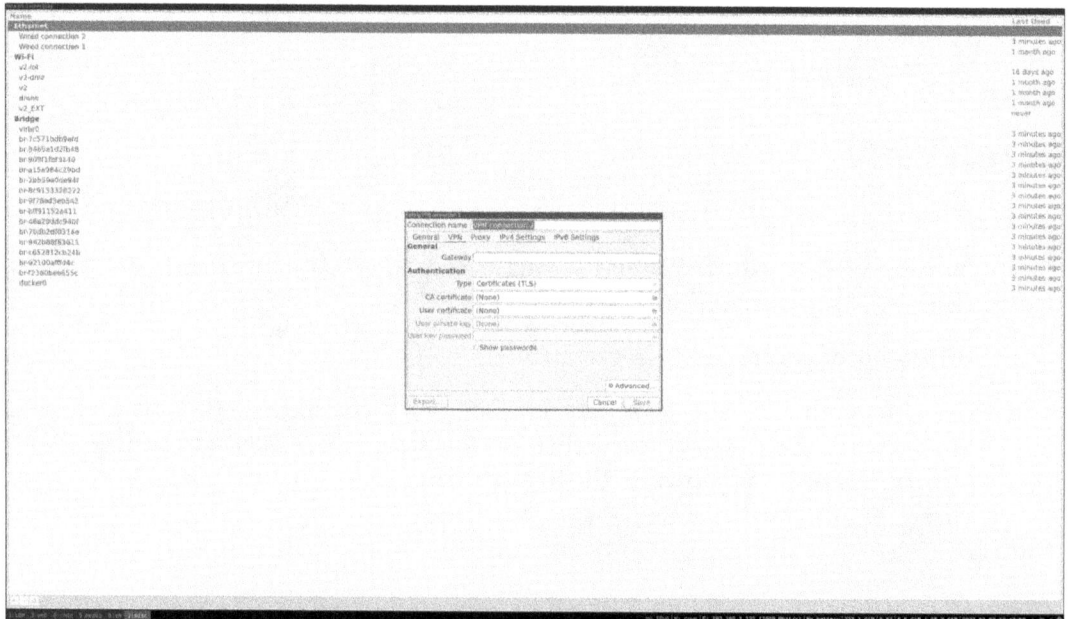

Figure 4.2: *Adding a new OpenVPN connection*

5. To verify that the VPN connections are working, browse with a web browser to the following site:

    https://www.whatsmyip.org/

    The IP should change when you turn the OpenVPN connection on and off.

WireGuard

WireGuard is a newer and much faster VPN than OpenVPN. To add a new WireGuard VPN, we use the same approach as we did with OpenVPN, as mentioned in the following steps:

1. Open the network settings for Ubuntu and click the + sign. Then, add a new Virtual WireGuard configuration.

2. There are many providers that offer a WireGuard VPN server to test your VPN. One example is **https://sshstores.net/wireguard**.

In *Chapter 9, Setup Advanced Network, Firewall, and VPN Servers* you will learn how to create both OpenVPN server and WireGuard Server.

Protect your traffic by using DNSS

When you are connected to the internet and visit a page like **google.com**, your computer needs to find the IP address of the domain **google.com**. This is done using a **Domain Name System** (**DNS**) request.

The problem that arises is that DNS requests are done in clear text traffic. The internet provider or other network devices that are between you and the DNS will be able to see the traffic.

You can set up your Ubuntu computer to start sending your DNS request to a DNS server over an encrypted channel.

There are different ways to set up DNS over HTTPS. The first and maybe the best way is setting up a DNS server in your network. The DNS server then receives request from the client in the network, then forwards the request to the public DNS server over HTTPS.

This will protect all the devices in your network.

The other way is to set up your Ubuntu to go directly to the public DNS server over HTTPS.

This is done by setting up a DNS demon on your Ubuntu computer. Then your local DNS request will be sent to the local DNS daemon on your computer, which will send the request. This will protect all DNS requests from your computer and outgoing as well. Still, access to the external DNS providers needs to be open. So, if you are at a public Wi-Fi point, this could stop working.

To install DNSS, run the following command:

```
1. sudo apt-get install dnss
```

To start DNSS, run the following command:

```
1. sudo dnss    --enable_dns_to_https --dns_listen_addr=:5553
```

Here, we are binding to port 5553 on your local computer. Now, let us test if it works by running **dig** and setting the DNS server to our DNS server.

```
 1. mattias@hrb:~$ dig google.se @127.0.0.1 -p5553
 2.
 3. ; <<>> DiG 9.18.1-1ubuntu1.2-Ubuntu <<>> google.se @127.0.0.1 -p5553
 4. ;; global options: +cmd
 5. ;; Got answer:
 6. ;; ->>HEADER<<- opcode: QUERY, status: NOERROR, id: 43953
 7. ;; flags: qr rd ra; QUERY: 1, ANSWER: 1, AUTHORITY: 0, ADDITIONAL: 1
 8.
 9. ;; OPT PSEUDOSECTION:
10. ; EDNS: version: 0, flags:; udp: 512
11. ;; QUESTION SECTION:
12. ;google.se.    IN A
13.
14. ;; ANSWER SECTION:
15. google.se.   300 IN A 142.250.147.94
16.
17. ;; Query time: 36 msec
18. ;; SERVER: 127.0.0.1#5553(127.0.0.1) (UDP)
19. ;; WHEN: Wed Jan 18 09:06:04 CET 2023
20. ;; MSG SIZE  rcvd: 63
```

Now that our DNSS server is working, we can update our network settings to use it.

Ubuntu starts its own resolver that listens on port 53, and we need to disable it before we can run our DNSS.

To open the file, run the following command:

```
1. sudo vi /etc/systemd/resolved.conf
```

To uncomment and change the settings:

```
1. DNSStubListener=no
```

Now, we need to reboot your Ubuntu computer.

Once rebooted, we can start our DNSS with the command:

```
1. sudo dnss    --enable_dns_to_https
```

When the **dnss** server is running, we can tell our system to resolve **dns** using it by updating the file **/etc/resolve.conf**:

```
2. nameserver 127.0.0.1
```

Let us add some configurations so that **dnss** gets auto-started:

```
1. systemctl start dnss
2. systemctl enable dnss
```

Protect your computer by applying a firewall

A firewall on a computer is like a door on a house. It allows traffic to be accepted only on the ports we configure. This will protect our computer, if we like, before installing a DNS server. We only want our computer to use the DNS server, not everyone on the network.

To protect ourselves, we can think of ports as doors. We want to keep the ports(doors) open for our friends and closed for everybody else.

A good setup could be having two different firewall settings:

- One default is when you lock everything out.

- And one for when you are more active on the network.

When you connect to a new network, your laptop's default profile should lock everything so nobody on the network can connect to your computer. The other profiles are more open and will allow outgoing traffic so that your computer can connect to network services like file shares and printers.

Let us start with the default to lock your laptop down. To use the firewall called *iptables*, we create a file with the **iptables** command. We then load the commands and can change the settings when we want.

This configuration will describe some open ports, but you may have other services. Then, you need to configure the Iptables file to match your settings.

Run this script to lock down your firewall for your computer. You can save this script in example **.config/fw** folder.

The following is the content of the bash file **lock-down.sh**:

```
1. #!/bin/bash
2. #
3. #
4. # This script will lock down the computer
5.
6. echo "Locking down fiewall"
7. #
8. #
```

```
 9.  #Lets flush the rules set so nothing is there
10. iptables -F
11. iptables -X
12.
13. # We are settings the defualt rule to deny all request !
14. iptables -P INPUT DROP
15. iptables -P OUTPUT DROP
16. iptables -P FORWARD DROP
17.
18. # Allow local traffick to 127.0.0.1 use
19. iptables -A INPUT -i lo -j ACCEPT
20. iptables -A OUTPUT -o lo -j ACCEPT
21.
22.
23. #Ping drop
24. iptables -A INPUT -p icmp -j DROP
25.
26.
27. #Allow DNS out
28. iptables -A OUTPUT -p udp -m udp --dport 53 -j ACCEPT
29. #Allow http
30. iptables -A OUTPUT -p tcp -m tcp --dport 80 -j ACCEPT
31. #Allow https
32. iptables -A OUTPUT -p tcp -m tcp --dport 443 -j ACCEPT
33.
34.
35. #allow related
36. iptables -A INPUT -m state --state RELATED,ESTABLISHED -j ACCEPT
37.
38.
39. #
40. # Some server we run on our computer add iptbales rules like Docker
    and need to be restarted when script is run
41. systemctl restart docker
```

The preceding script will not allow any traffic, except web and DNS traffic, to go out. If you want to connect to any other service, the script needs to be updated with more outgoing open ports. For example, if you want to connect to an SSH server, the following is the content of the bash file **lock-trusted.sh**:

```
1.  #!/bin/bash
2.  #
3.  #
```

```
4.  # This script will lock down the computer
5.
6.  echo "Locking down fiewall"
7.  #
8.  #
9.  #Lets flush the rules set so nothing is there
10. iptables -F
11. iptables -X
12.
13. # We are settings the defualt rule to deny all request !
14. iptables -P INPUT DROP
15. iptables -P OUTPUT ACCEPT
16. iptables -P FORWARD ACCEPT
17.
18. # Allow local traffick to 127.0.0.1 use
19. iptables -A INPUT -i lo -j ACCEPT
20. iptables -A OUTPUT -o lo -j ACCEPT
21.
22.
23. #Ping drop
24. iptables -A INPUT -p icmp -j DROP
25.
26.
27. #allow related
28. iptables -A INPUT -m state --state RELATED,ESTABLISHED -j ACCEPT
29.
30.
31. #
32. # Some server we run on our computer add iptbales rules like Docker
    and need to be restarted when script is run
33. systemctl restart docker
```

The previously mentioned firewall script will lock down all incoming traffic. However, it will allow any outgoing traffic. This allows you to find and connect to services on your local network, like network file shares and printers.

To activate the firewall, run the command with **sudo**:

```
1. mattias@laptop:~/.config/fw$ sudo ./lock-down.sh
2. [sudo] password for mattias:
3. Locking down fiewall
4. mattias@laptop:~/.config/fw$
```

Detect and stop computer virus

There are viruses today on all platforms. Additionally, we are integrating more with different people and OS. This means that Ubuntu can download a Windows virus, and if we send it along, we can infect others in the chain as well. To avoid this, using an antivirus is a good practice.

Start by installing *ClamAV*, the open-source antivirus tool:

https://www.clamav.net/

```
1. sudo apt-get install clamav clamtk
```

With ClamAV, the tool **clamscan** also comes installed. **Clamscan** can scan your folder for any virus. **clamscan** can be used to quickly scan any folder or file.

To scan files in your downloaded folder, run **clamscan** in the **Downloads** folder:

```
1.  mattias@laptop:~$ clamscan Downloads/
2.  /home/mattias/Downloads/818_1_Re-reviewed-1_MH.docx: OK
3.  /home/mattias/Downloads/balenaEtcher-1.13.3-x64.AppImage: OK
4.  /home/mattias/Downloads/NVIDIA-Linux-x86_64-525.85.05.run: OK
5.  /home/mattias/Downloads/818_2_Reviewed_mh_1.docx: OK
6.  /home/mattias/Downloads/Invoice.pdf: OK
7.  /home/mattias/Downloads/818_1_Re-reviewed_AS.docx: OK
8.  /home/mattias/Downloads/818_2_Reviewed_AS.docx: OK
9.  /home/mattias/Downloads/818_2_Reviewed_mh.docx: OK
10. /home/mattias/Downloads/4040_07 (1).pdf: OK
11. /home/mattias/Downloads/Book Outline_Ubuntu Linux in 30 days.pdf: OK
12. /home/mattias/Downloads/The Phoenix Project.epub: OK
13. /home/mattias/Downloads/rockpi-4b-ubuntu-focal-server-arm64-
        20220401-0346-gpt.img.xz: OK
14. /home/mattias/Downloads/The Wise Mans Fear.epub: OK
15. /home/mattias/Downloads/818_1_Re-reviewed (1)_AS.docx: OK
16. /home/mattias/Downloads/818_1_Re-reviewed_MH.docx: OK
17. /home/mattias/Downloads/4040_07.pdf: OK
18. /home/mattias/Downloads/Untitled Diagram.drawio.png: OK
19. /home/mattias/Downloads/fr24-raspberry-pi-latest.img.zip: OK
20. /home/mattias/Downloads/818_2_Reviewed_AS_1.docx: OK
21. /home/mattias/Downloads/.~lock.CGO3control_en.odt#: OK
22. /home/mattias/Downloads/Untitled Diagram.drawio: OK
23. /home/mattias/Downloads/The Name of the Wind.epub: OK
24. /home/mattias/Downloads/818_1_Reviewed_mh.docx: OK
25. /home/mattias/Downloads/CGO3control_en.odt: OK
26.
```

```
27. ----------- SCAN SUMMARY -----------
28. Known viruses: 8650933
29. Engine version: 0.103.6
30. Scanned directories: 1
31. Scanned files: 24
32. Infected files: 0
33. Data scanned: 61.22 MB
34. Data read: 1454.60 MB (ratio 0.04:1)
35. Time: 31.187 sec (0 m 31 s)
36. Start Date: 2023:02:02 16:02:44
37. End Date:   2023:02:02 16:03:15
```

Update virus database

For ClamAV to find a new virus, it needs to update the database with all the different new signatures if it is not updated. Then, if there is a new virus, ClamAV will not recognize the signature and will not be able to find it.

To update the ClamAV database, run **freshclam**:

```
1. sudo freshclam
```

ClamAV GUI

When we install ClamAV, we also install a small **graphical user interface** (**GUI**) so that we can easily use and set up ClamAV. Here, you can set up a scheduler for ClamAV to scan your home folder, regulate, and update the signature database.

The following figure showcases ClamAV interface to set up and schedule scans:

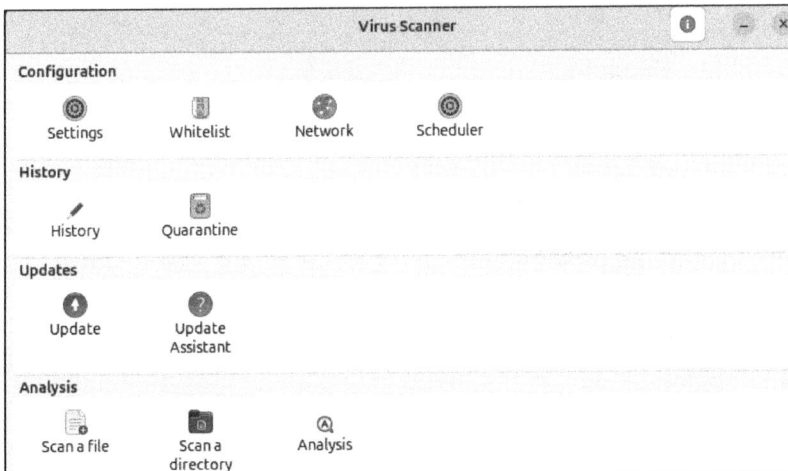

Figure 4.3: *ClamAV Gui to set up scheduled scans*

Conclusion

Through this chapter, you now have a basic knowledge of how the network in Ubuntu works, and you can connect your Ubuntu Desktop to different types of networks. We have also learned how to use VLAN and connect securely to the server using a VPN server. To protect our Ubuntu on the network, we also looked at generating a random MAC, using DNSS to hide our DNS traffic, setting up an iptables firewall to protect our own service on our Ubuntu computer, and installing and setting up Antivirus software.

Now, we are ready to use our Ubuntu computer connected to a network, and in the next chapter, we will connect our Ubuntu Desktop to the network and start using VPN.

Join our book's Discord space

Join the book's Discord Workspace for Latest updates, Offers, Tech happenings around the world, New Release and Sessions with the Authors:

https://discord.bpbonline.com

CHAPTER 5
Preparing Virtualization Environment

Introduction

Virtualization has changed the way we use computers, both desktop and server, by making it possible to run many OS on the same host. This helps in better using the resources on the host computer and distinguishing between the different OSs that are running. Virtualization is how cloud providers can use one physical server, and then you can add many virtual machines on top of that. There are also special OSs only built for virtualization that are used widely.

In this chapter, we will install KVM and set up and run virtual machines in KVM. We will then look at connecting our VM to the network and running common tasks. There are also other virtualization engines, and we will look at Vagrant, a virtual tool from *HashiCorp*.

Structure

In this chapter, we will cover the following topics:

- Overview of virtualization in Ubuntu
- KVM virtualization in Ubuntu
- Create bridge
- Installing our first VM

- Settings for your VM

- Snapshots

- Access to VM

- Using hardware devices directly in your VM

- Other virtualizations

- Build and run a Vagrant box inside KVM

- Converting images back and forth

Objectives

By the end of this chapter, we will understand how to set up a basic network to be used by our VM running on the host. We will also look at KVM, the default virtualization engine on Linux.

We will also look at some of the other virtualization engines, the use of Vagrant to share and use VM more flexibly, to move VM between different virtualization engines, how to migrate images, and how to test different virtualization engines.

Overview of virtualization in Ubuntu

When running a server or desktop, sometimes you want to run multiple versions of the same OS. If you work with many clients, you can have one Ubuntu Desktop for every client or many servers, and can reinstall one server many times. However, one is more stable. You can also share computer resources more effectively.

To achieve any of this, virtualization comes in. Virtualization allows you to install an OS and then install a different OS inside. The OSs share the same CPU and memory but are isolated and behave as stand-alone servers or desktops.

This is mostly used when you want to test a server, easily take a snapshot, and restore a state to test a command. Security is also a big concern when you want to isolate the different systems from each other. For example, you have many clients, and you want to have the clients' data separated from each other. If one virtual desktop gets infected with a virus, you can easily destroy that virtual machine desktop and create a new virtual machine to use.

All cloud providers use virtualization as a base for their servers. So, when you start a server in the AWS cloud server. The server you spin up is a virtual server.

There are many different vitalizing engines, and we will look at some of them. They all work the same way.

Your CPU needs to support full virtualization. You can run the following command to verify and boot your computer into BIOS mode and enable virtualization there. If your computer does not support virtualization, we can still run it. However, the performance will be slower.

Command to test if the computer supports virtualization:

```
1. mattias@laptop:~$ sudo kvm-ok
```

KVM virtualization in Ubuntu

KVM is the name of the standard virtualization engine in Ubuntu.

Let us install KVM as follows:

```
1. sudo apt install qemu-kvm libvirt-daemon-system libvirt-clients
   bridge-utils virt-manager
```

Add your username to the group **libvirt**. This will give you the correct permission to create and control VMs, as follows:

```
1. sudo adduser 'username' libvirt
```

Before we create our first VM, let us verify if we have hardware support on our host machine. Run the following command to test what kind of virtual system your computer supports:

```
1. mattias@laptop:~$ sudo apt install cpu-checker
2. mattias@laptop:~$ sudo kvm-ok
3. INFO: /dev/kvm exists
4. KVM acceleration can be used
5. mattias@laptop:~
```

If the **kvm-ok** command returns, **KVM acceleration can be used**, and then we have support. If the command output says acceleration cannot be used, we can still install VM, but the performance will be slower.

Now, we have all the tools and programs to start vitalizing, but first, let us create a bridge network. This makes it easy for us to connect from our host computer to our VM.

In virtualization, there are different types of networks we can use, as follows:

- **NAT network**: Here, the host computer acts as a router, and then your virtual server is located behind a separate subnet. This works if you want to isolate yourself from the big network, but you want your host computer to have access.

- **Bridge mode**: Here, we create a bridge on your host computer, and we then share the bridge with the VM. Then VM will have access to another computer on your network and will get an IP from your router as the host machine.

- **MAC Tap**: Here, the VM will add a top on your network card and get an IP from your network, which is the same network as the host machine. However, you will not be able to communicate with your host or your VM.

We only need to configure some settings when using bridge mode, and only if you plan to connect to your VM from both your host computer and other clients from the local IP.

You can also use a MAC Tap to get an IP from the local network and let other network clients connect to the VM using the MAC Tap interface. Then, you can also add a NAT network to your VM and connect to the VM from your host computer with the NAT IP.

Create bridge

When using a virtual server, you will need some sort of network connection to the server. There are several ways you can connect your virtual server to the network. We will set up bridge network access here. You can add using both the GUI for the network manager and the CLI. Here are the commands, but you can also open the GUI and see when the settings are applied.

Bridges can be hard to get to work and may need some more settings to get started.

Note: Having a bridge is not necessary to get started with VM on Ubuntu; feel free to skip this step and come back later if needed.

Let us see what network settings we have before we start. Run the following command to show the current network stats:

1. nmcli con show

Create a **bridge** and add our interface to the **bridge**, as follows:

1. sudo nmcli con add ifname br0 type bridge con-name br0
2. sudo nmcli con add type bridge-slave ifname ens3 master br0
3. sudo nmcli con mod br0 bridge.stp no
4. sudo nmcli con down ens3
5. sudo nmcli con up br0

Here, we are attaching the interface **ens3**, but that may not be the name of your interface. From the following command, we can see that the interface **enp45s0** is used. Then, replace **ens3** with **enp45s0**.

Run the command **ip a** as follows:

1. root@hrb:/# ip a
2. 1: lo: <LOOPBACK,UP,LOWER_UP> mtu 65536 qdisc noqueue state UNKNOWN group default qlen 1000
3.   link/loopback 00:00:00:00:00:00 brd 00:00:00:00:00:00
4.   inet 127.0.0.1/8 scope host lo

```
5.        valid_lft forever preferred_lft forever
6.     inet6 ::1/128 scope host
7.        valid_lft forever preferred_lft forever
8. 2: enp39s0: <NO-CARRIER,BROADCAST,MULTICAST,UP> mtu 1500 qdisc mq
   state DOWN group default qlen 1000
9.      link/ether d8:bb:c1:3b:92:3b brd ff:ff:ff:ff:ff:ff
10.3: enp45s0: <BROADCAST,MULTICAST,UP,LOWER_UP> mtu 1500 qdisc mq
   state UP group default qlen 1000
11.     link/ether 00:1b:21:ed:02:f4 brd ff:ff:ff:ff:ff:ff
12.     inet 192.168.1.115/24 brd 192.168.1.255 scope global dynamic
   noprefixroute enp45s0
```

Installing our first VM

The following steps can be used to install your first Ubuntu VM:

1. Go to the download page of Ubuntu, download the Ubuntu Desktop iso, and store it in your downloads folder.

    https://ubuntu.com/download/desktop

2. Start the KVM tool virtual manager and click the **add virtual machine** button. You will then be guided through setting up your first VM. Fill in your values or leave them as the default until you see the network settings.

3. In the network settings, select bridge and add the name of the bridge we created before as a network device. You can also add the new network nic and the NAT as a secondary network interface.

4. Start the VM and follow the guide to install Ubuntu. (We have walked through the installation of Ubuntu in *Chapter 2, Install, Upgrade, and Configure Ubuntu Desktop*)

5. When the installation is done, boot your VM and log in to it. The following figure shows the login screen running inside the virtual machine:

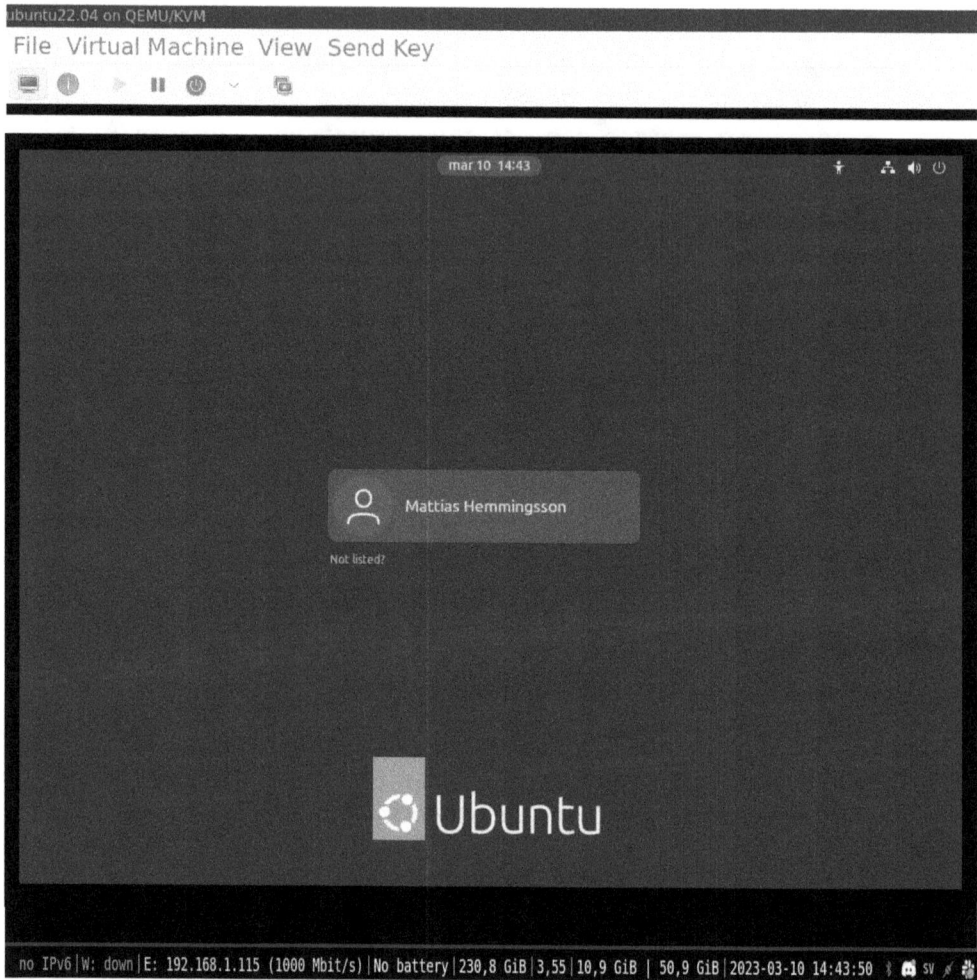

Figure 5.1: *Login screen inside KVM virtual machine*

Here, we have an Ubuntu VM desktop running inside my Ubuntu Desktop. With this, we can use the virtual server as a regular app and open and close it as a regular.

Settings for your VM

When you open the VM in the KVM manager, you can see in the top menu a blue circle with a small I in it. Clicking this will open the VM's settings page. Here, you can add new network cards, disks, and more. Some settings require you to stop and then start your VM, but some can be changed while the VM is running.

Figure 5.2 shows the settings page with the settings that can be altered. Here, you can add a disk or more network devices:

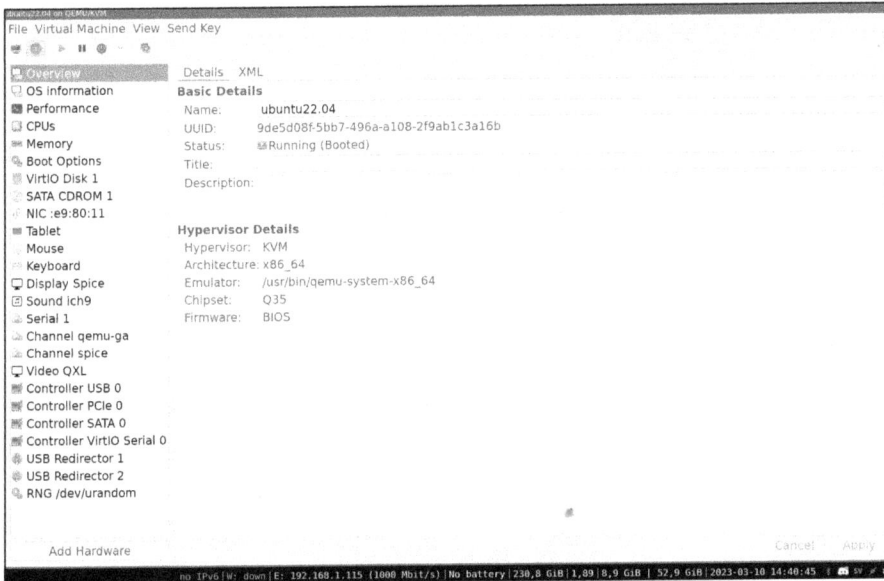

Figure 5.2: *Shows the settings page of the virtual machine*

Snapshots

A snapshot is a point in time in your VM. You can go back to this point if you need to check something, and can make a new VM from a snapshot. Now, when we have a clean installation of Ubuntu, this snapshot is a clean installation of Ubuntu and a great starting point if you would like to start a new Ubuntu Desktop.

Create a snapshot and call it **Stabil**.

The following figure shows the snapshot page of the VM with the snapshot **Stabil**:

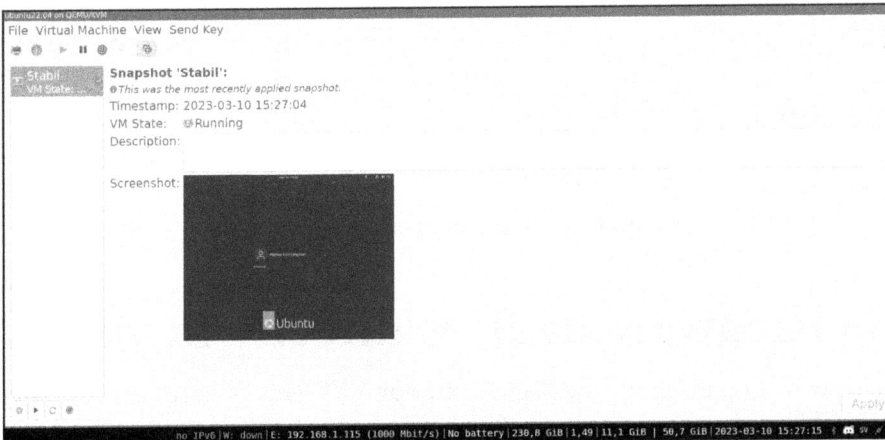

Figure 5.3: *Snapshot manager page of the VM*

Custom snapshot

With snapshots, we can also create our own custom Ubuntu and then start up a clean Ubuntu Desktop from there. Let us install some of the tools we are using for our daily work with Ubuntu. Then, we will create a new snapshot. We can now clone our new Ubuntu Desktop that already have some basic tools. This is an easy way to have a pre-ready desktop that you can use if you want a new, clean Ubuntu or if you are testing new tools and want to go back if something breaks.

Access to VM

There are several ways to access the VM. Use regular SSH access to have CLI access to the box. Use the desktop provided by KVM as you see it booting up, and you can also add desktop sharing tools to share the desktop using tools like VNC.

The following figure shows an Ubuntu VM that has openssh-server installed and then ssh access from the host computer into the VM:

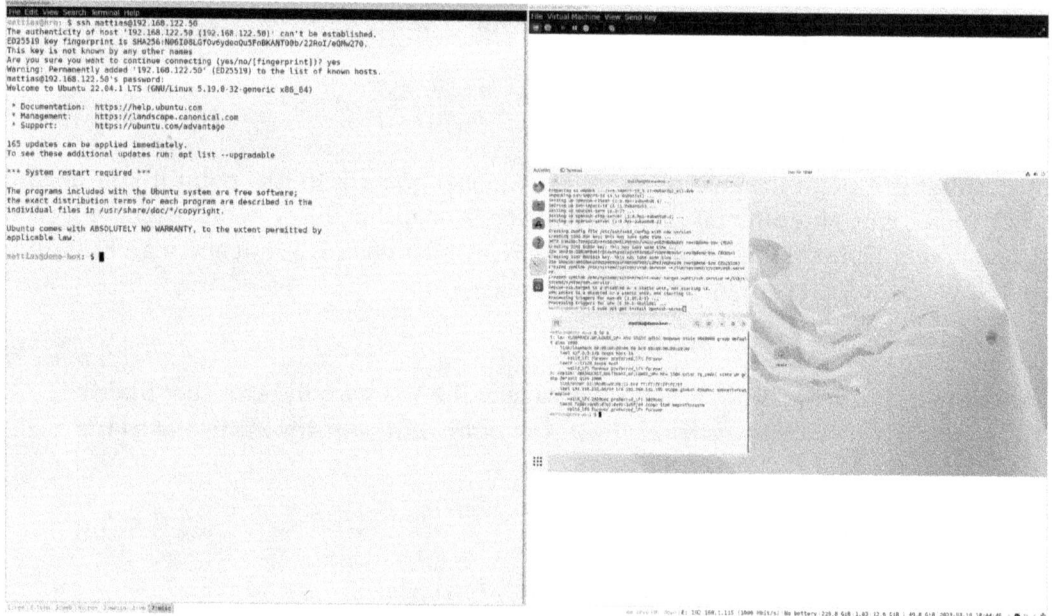

Figure 5.4: Access from the host computer to the VM

Using hardware devices directly in your VM

With KVM, we can pass devices directly into our VM. This is used, for example, when you have a GPU and want access to the GPU inside your VM. Many of us have Ubuntu as a daily OS; however, we may want to play video games. Then, you can easily pass your

GPU inside your Windows installation and use it there. You may also have USB devices or another hardware device that you need access to inside your VM. To set up pass-throw devices, look in the settings page for the VM.

Other virtualizations

KVM is the default VM engine for Linux, but there are many more. When you work in an environment with more OS, using a virtualization engine that works on more OS is a good idea.

Oracle's virtual box is a good tool and can be used on many different OS. It works and runs the same as KVM. To download VirtualBox, visit the link as follows:

https://www.virtualbox.org/

Another VM tool is *Vmware Player,* which can be found on the link as follows:

https://www.vmware.com/se/products/workstation-player.html

This is also a good tool and works similarly to VirtualBox.

If you have worked with one of the virtual tools, you will have the basic knowledge to work with all of them.

Note: If you have KVM running, it already has access to the kernel. If you try to run any other virtualization engine, you might see errors.

On VirtualBox, we will get the error, `VirtualBox can't enable the AMD-V extension`.

Build and run a Vagrant box inside KVM

Vagrant from HashiCorp is a way to make VMs and then upload them to their cloud storage. Then, others can download and run the VM. This makes it easy to build and share images with other examples. If you are a developer and want to share a VM with your colleagues, or you have a test server. There are also pre-made images for different services like WordPress and more.

A different VM is called **a box in vagrant**. So, in this guide, a box and a VM are the same thing.

Start by visiting the Vagrant homepage and downloading and setting up Vagrant.

https://www.vagrantup.com/

Run VirtualBox inside KVM

To be able to run tests with Vagrant and VirtualBox, we can install them inside a KVM host.

Here, we access the VM from the host computer with SSH and desktop; then, we run cli commands directly into the terminal and look at the VirtualBox GUI, as shown:

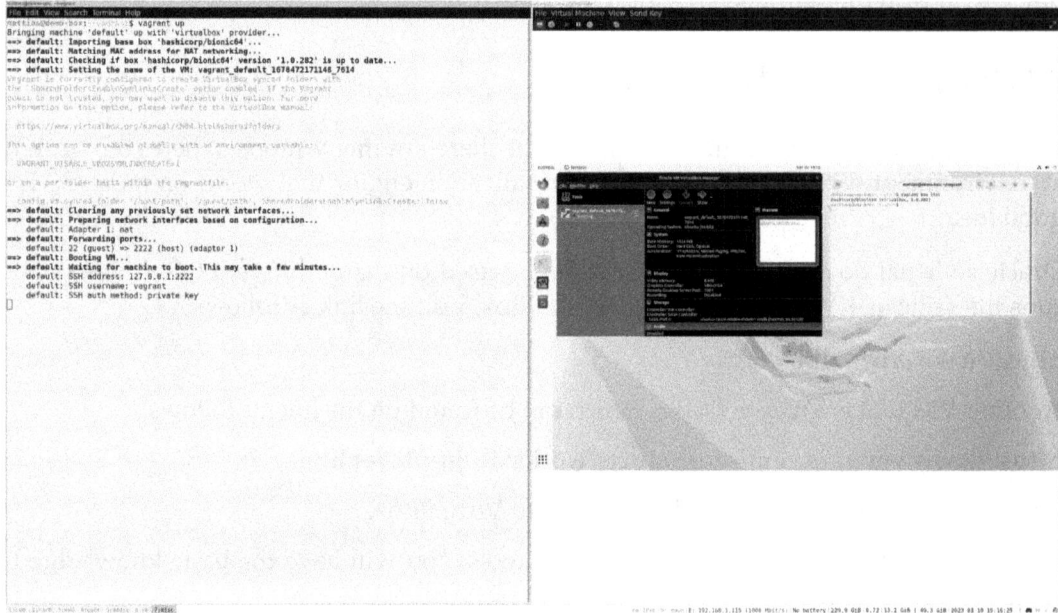

Figure 5.5*: KVM running VirtualBox and Vagrant*

Follow the guide on the given webpage to install Vagrant on your Ubuntu Desktop.

https://developer.hashicorp.com/vagrant

Make a folder, and in it, start up a Vagrant box:

1. `mkdir vagrant`
2. `cd vagrant`
3. `vagrant box add hashicorp/bionic64`
4. `vagrant init hashicorp/bionic64`
5. `vagrant up`

To find different boxes to run, visit:

https://app.vagrantup.com/boxes/search

Converting images back and forth

As discussed in the previous section, there are different tools for running VM. Each has its own image format. Luckily, we can convert our VM images between the other tools.

When running a VM, the image is like a hard drive and has all the information that you have installed. You can easily move the image to a new computer or virtualization engine. Add the image, give it resources like CPU and memory, and then boot.

There is an open format for VM images, but not all providers follow the format.

https://en.wikipedia.org/wiki/Open_Virtualization_Format

Here, files are located on the host computer. By default, KVM images are located in path **/var/liv/libvirt/images**.

```
1.  root@hrb:/var/lib/libvirt/images# ls
2.  ubuntu22.04-2.qcow2  ubuntu22.04.qcow2
3.  root@hrb:/var/lib/libvirt/images#
```

Let us convert one image to **vmdk** format:

```
1.  root@hrb:/var/lib/libvirt/images# qemu-img convert -p -f qcow2 -O
    vmdk ubuntu22.04-2.qcow2 ubuntu22.04.vmdk
2.     (100.00/100%)
3.  root@hrb:/var/lib/libvirt/images#
```

Now, move the images to the **qcow** format use:

```
1.  root@hrb:/var/lib/libvirt/images# qemu-img convert -f vmdk -O qcow2
    image.vmdk image.qcow2
```

Conclusion

By the end of this chapter, we will have discussed how virtualization can help you use a computer. In the next chapter, resources are defined more effectively, both for running servers and desktops. We have also used virtualization to test other virtualization tools and to migrate images between them. To connect our VM to the network, we have learned the difference between MAC Tap, NAT, and bridging network devices. Additionally, we understood how to install and set up an Ubuntu Desktop running inside the KVM virtualizing engine, take snapshots, and use them to create a new VM. We also discussed how to use Vagrant to create and share VM images with team members and migrate VMs between different engines.

In the next chapter, we will explore how to run Kubernetes and Docker.

Join our book's Discord space

Join the book's Discord Workspace for Latest updates, Offers, Tech happenings around the world, New Release and Sessions with the Authors:

https://discord.bpbonline.com

CHAPTER 6

Up and Running with Kubernetes and Docker

Introduction

When you are a developer or work with IT-related tools, you want to have the tools to help you run your product or other products locally so you can test them. You may not want to have to install extensive databases or BI tools locally to use them. This is where containers come in. It is based on the idea of shipping containers with many small similar containers on a ship. But the content inside the container can be anything.

This is the same when we talk about containers for computers. Your computer is the ship, and you can run many containers on it. So, the big difference between VMs and containers is size and speed. In the VM, we install the whole OS, and you virtualize the whole computer. So, the VM shares the CPU and sits beside your computer. Instead, the container shares some of your computer resources and sits inside your OS; this makes it smaller.

Although the concept of containers, or lightweight virtualization, has been around for a long time, it did not start to gain traction in the Linux world until the early 2000s.

Around the same time, a new container technology called *Docker* was being developed by *Solomon Hykes* and his team at *dotCloud* (now known as *Docker Inc.*). Docker was based on **Linux container** (**LXC**), but it introduced a new way of packaging and distributing container images, as well as a new set of tools and APIs for managing containers. Docker quickly gained popularity among developers and became the de facto standard for containerization in the Linux world.

Structure

In this chapter, we will cover the following topics:

- Docker and container
- Installing Docker
- Docker Hub
- Start your first Docker
- Adding Docker Compose
- Connecting service with Docker Compose
- Expanding Docker Compose
- Connecting two stacks
- Local development with Docker
- About Kubernetes

Objectives

In this chapter, we will understand how to install Docker on our Ubuntu Desktop. Start your first Docker image and run a Minecraft server.

We will then put more containers together and set up a WordPress blog and Metabase BI tool. When we have a working WordPress running, it is time to move over to Kubernetes. You will learn how to install Kubernetes on your Ubuntu. Deploy a MySQL server and a WordPress blog and do some basic commands using kubectl to communicate with your cluster.

We will also understand how to run containers as Docker images and in a Kubernetes cluster.

Docker and container

Docker is a software platform that allows developers to create, deploy, and run applications in containers. Container is a reference to container ships, where you pack your items in a standard format, and that format is supported by trucks, ships, and planes. The same idea is for software. You build your software and pack it into containers. Now your software can run on any platform that supports docker. So, if a Docker runs and works on one laptop, it should run on Google Cloud or on a regular server if it supports the Docker format.

Docker and containers consist of several components today, including:

- The engine are tools like CRI-O or Docker and the engine will take the container image and make it to a container running process.

- The image from the container start was only called Docker Image, but now we use **Open Container Image (OCI)**, which aims to make all the images in a standard way.

- Kubernetes uses CRI-O as the default way of running containers.

For example, replace docker with Podman and simply run the same command in docker but instead use the open-source tool Podman: **https://docs.podman.io/en/latest/**

Installing Docker

Installing Docker can be done from the regular source repo of Ubuntu. However, here we will look at installing it from the guide from the Docker webpage. We will add a Docker repo to our computer. Then, install the Docker engine and add our user to the Docker groups to have access to run Docker. Now, we can start our first Docker image.

Setting up Docker repos for Ubuntu

Let us start with installing the dependencies needed for Docker, as shown in the following code:

```
1.  sudo apt-get update
2.  sudo apt-get install \
3.      ca-certificates \
4.      curl \
5.      gnupg
```

We can add the Docker registry public key and repo by running the following code:

```
1.  sudo mkdir -m 0755 -p /etc/apt/keyrings
2.  curl -fsSL https://download.docker.com/linux/ubuntu/gpg | sudo gpg
    --dearmor -o /etc/apt/keyrings/docker.gpg
3.  echo \
4.  "deb [arch="$(dpkg --print-architecture)" signed-by=/etc/apt/
    keyrings/docker.gpg] https://download.docker.com/linux/ubuntu \
5.  "$(. /etc/os-release && echo "$VERSION_CODENAME")" stable" | \
6.  sudo tee /etc/apt/sources.list.d/docker.list > /dev/null
```

When the repos and key are added, we can update the package cache and install the Docker engine, as shown in the following command:

```
1.  sudo apt-get update
2.  sudo apt-get install docker-ce docker-ce-cli containerd.io docker-
    buildx-plugin docker-compose-plugin
```

Let us add our user to the Docker group so we can run Docker containers from our own user, as shown in the following command:

```
1. sudo usermod -aG docker $USER
```

You may have to close the terminal or log out and log in so that new group permission is added.

To verify everything is working, run the following command:

```
1. docker run hello-world
```

Docker Hub

To find Docker images and store them, Docker has a place called **Docker Hub**. In the hub, users and companies can upload their Docker images. All big companies upload their apps as images to the Docker Hub. You can find core Linux distributions like Ubuntu or open-source apps such as WordPress or Metabase.

By allowing a user to upload Docker images to the hub, Docker Hub is one of the default places for companies and opensource companies to share their apps and services.

There are also more places you, a developer or a software builder, can store your Docker images. For example, AWS, Google Cloud, and more.

Official images

In the Docker Hub, there are images called **official**. This means that it is the same as downloading software directly from the maker. For example, WordPress is the official Docker repository of WordPress (**mattiashem/WordPress** is the author's version of WordPress).

It is important to know the risk when downloading and running Docker images.

Start your first Docker

Let us start our first Docker container, and we will be using a Minecraft server as a test here. When we start our Docker, we need to pass some settings to it. Passing settings to the container is done using environment variables. We also need to tell Docker to open a port so that we can connect to the server.

This command will start our Minecraft server:

```
1. docker run -it -e EULA=true   -p --name mc itzg/minecraft-server
2.
3. [13:50:12] [Server thread/INFO]: Done (11.178s)! For help, type
   "help"
4. [13:50:12] [Server thread/INFO]: Starting remote control listener
5. [13:50:12] [Server thread/INFO]: Thread RCON Listener started
6. [13:50:12] [Server thread/INFO]: RCON running on 0.0.0.0:25575
```

```
7.
8. This shows the server is up and running
```

To stop the server, press *ctr+c*.

Expanding our Docker Compose to run services

When we start, the Minecraft server Docker gives us a generated port to use every time we start. However, we want our Minecraft server to bind to the ports used by Minecraft and always use the port. When we log in to the Minecraft server and play, all our world will be saved inside the Docker container. If we then stop the container, all the world will be lost.

To resolve this issue, let us add some more arguments to our Docker run command. Now, we are telling Docker to bind to port 25566 to be used for Minecraft. We will mount the folder **minecraft_data** into our container at **/data**.

You can add and configure the Docker to know all the different values. Go to the maker of the images page:

https://github.com/itzg/docker-minecraft-server/blob/master/README.md

Now, let us start Minecraft again with the following settings:

```
1. docker run -it -e EULA=true   -v minecraft_data:/data -p 25565:25565
   --name mc itzg/minecraft-server
2.
3. [13:50:12] [Server thread/INFO]: Done (11.178s)! For help, type
   "help"
4. [13:50:12] [Server thread/INFO]: Starting remote control listener
5. [13:50:12] [Server thread/INFO]: Thread RCON Listener started
6. [13:50:12] [Server thread/INFO]: RCON running on 0.0.0.0:25575
7.
8. This shows the server is up and running
```

Adding Docker Compose

The Docker command we use to start our Minecraft server will work if you have one server and you can remember the settings. We can also add our settings to a file called **docker-compose.yaml** and then the tool Docker Composes to start our Docker.

Create a file called **docker-compose.yaml** and add the following content to it:

```
1. version: "3"
2. services:
3.   mc:
4.     image: itzg/minecraft-server
5.     ports:
```

```
6.        - 25565:25565
7.      environment:
8.        EULA: "TRUE"
9.      tty: true
10.     stdin_open: true
11.     restart: unless-stopped
12.     volumes:
13.       # attach a directory relative to the directory containing this
     compose file
14.       - ./minecraft-data:/data
15.
```

Now, let us start our Minecraft server with Docker Compose by running the following command:

```
docker compose up
```

Note: Docker Compose was added as a separate project, and then the command docker-compose was used to start it. Now, Docker Compose is added with Docker and used with Docker Compose without the dash. However, it works the same.

If you want the Minecraft server to run in the background, we can use the command:

```
1. docker compose run
```

To verify the server is running, run the following command:

```
2. docker compose ps
```

To stop the server, run the following command:

```
3. docker compose stop
```

Connecting service with Docker Compose

Docker Compose is an easy way not only to start one container but also to put more containers together into a stack. Now, we will start a stack for a WordPress blog and the Metabase BI tool.

Let us begin by making a WordPress stack start-up.

Create a new folder called WordPress, and in the folder, create the file **docker-compose. yaml.**

Add the following content to the file, as shown:

```
1. services:
2.   db:
3.     # We use a mariadb image which supports both amd64 & arm64
     architecture
```

```
4.       image: mariadb:10.6.4-focal
5.       # If you really want to use MySQL, uncomment the following line
6.       #image: mysql:8.0.27
7.       command: '--default-authentication-plugin=mysql_native_password'
8.       volumes:
9.         - db_data:/var/lib/mysql
10.      environment:
11.        - MYSQL_ROOT_PASSWORD=somewordpress
12.        - MYSQL_DATABASE=wordpress
13.        - MYSQL_USER=wordpress
14.        - MYSQL_PASSWORD=wordpress
15.      expose:
16.        - 3306
17.        - 33060
18.      networks:
19.        - local
20.   wordpress:
21.      image: wordpress:latest
22.      ports:
23.        - 80:80
24.      environment:
25.        - WORDPRESS_DB_HOST=db
26.        - WORDPRESS_DB_USER=wordpress
27.        - WORDPRESS_DB_PASSWORD=wordpress
28.        - WORDPRESS_DB_NAME=wordpress
29.      networks:
30.        - local
31. volumes:
32.   db_data:
33. networks:
34.   local:
35.     external: true
```

In the docker-compose file, you can see that we are setting some values. When it starts, we set the user and password for our MySQL server. We also added the same user and password to our WordPress docker. This will first start the SQL server and create a user for WordPress to use.

Start the stack with docker-compose up to verify that all services start.

Then, verify your installation using your browser and go to the page to complete it.

Note: You will not need to enter any SQL user or password. If you have another service running on port 80, you will need to modify the `docker-compose.yaml` file.

Open the following link, it will open and point to your local computer, and when not setting a port, it will use the following port:

80.http://localhost

Figure 6.1 shows the WordPress installation page when the MySQL setting is already set:

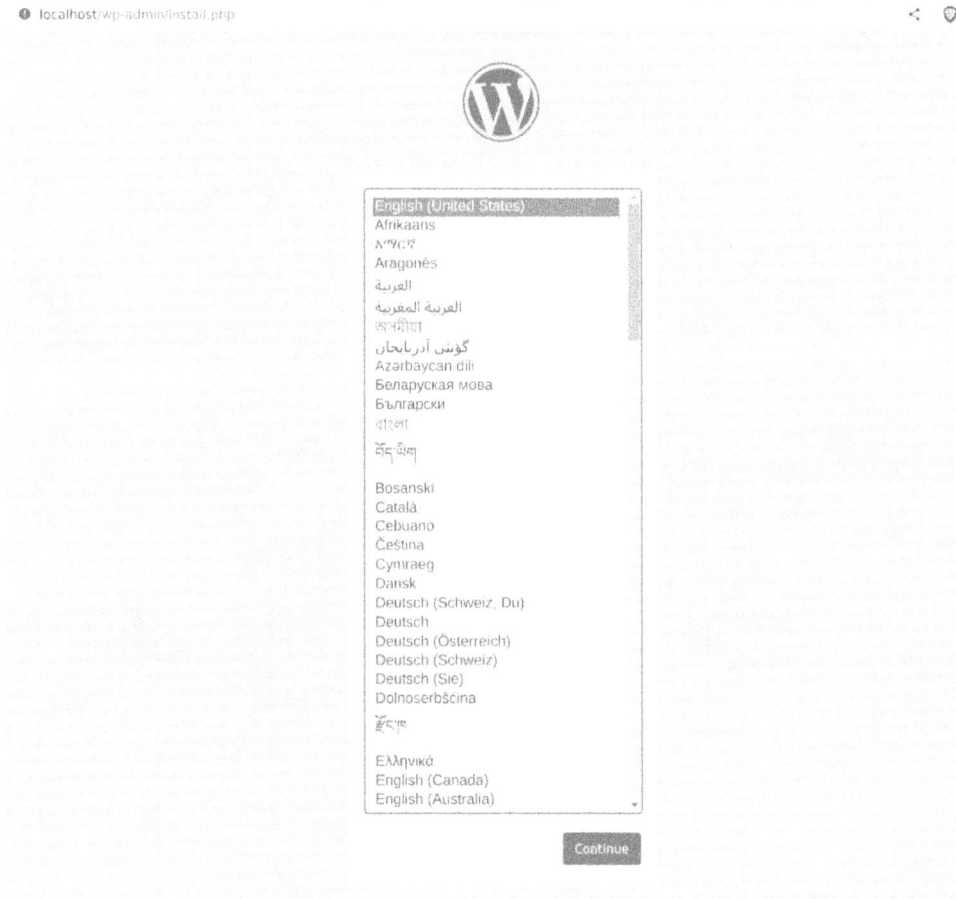

Figure 6.1: *WordPress installation*

Expanding Docker Compose

If you already have a WordPress blog and want to move your current one to it. You want to add a tool to access the MySQL server.

Let us create **phpmyadmin** and give it access to the MySQL used for WordPress.

Modify your docker-compose, as shown:

```
1.  services:
2.    db:
3.      # We use a mariadb image which supports both amd64 & arm64
        architecture
4.      image: mariadb:10.6.4-focal
5.      # If you really want to use MySQL, uncomment the following line
6.      #image: mysql:8.0.27
7.      command: '--default-authentication-plugin=mysql_native_password'
8.      volumes:
9.        - db_data:/var/lib/mysql
10.     environment:
11.       - MYSQL_ROOT_PASSWORD=somewordpress
12.       - MYSQL_DATABASE=wordpress
13.       - MYSQL_USER=wordpress
14.       - MYSQL_PASSWORD=wordpress
15.     expose:
16.       - 3306
17.       - 33060
18.     networks:
19.       - local
20.   wordpress:
21.     image: wordpress:latest
22.     ports:
23.       - 80:80
24.     environment:
25.       - WORDPRESS_DB_HOST=db
26.       - WORDPRESS_DB_USER=wordpress
27.       - WORDPRESS_DB_PASSWORD=wordpress
28.       - WORDPRESS_DB_NAME=wordpress
29.     networks:
30.       - local
31.   phpmyadmin:
32.     image: phpmyadmin
33.     ports:
34.       - 8080:80
35.     environment:
36.       - PMA_ARBITRARY=1
37.       - PMA_HOST=db
38.       - PMA_USER=wordpress
39.       - PMA_PASSWORD=wordpress
40.     networks:
```

```
41.      - local
42. volumes:
43.   db_data:
44. networks:
45.   local:
46.     external: true
```

Start the stack by using, as follows:

```
1. docker compose up
```

You can log in to **phpMyAdmin** by visiting the page. *Figure 6.1* shows **phpmyadmin** with access to the MySQL server for WordPress.

The following link will open a web browser on your local computer and use port :8080:

http://localhost:8080

In the following figure, we see that **phpMyAdmin** has started and logged in to the MySQL server:

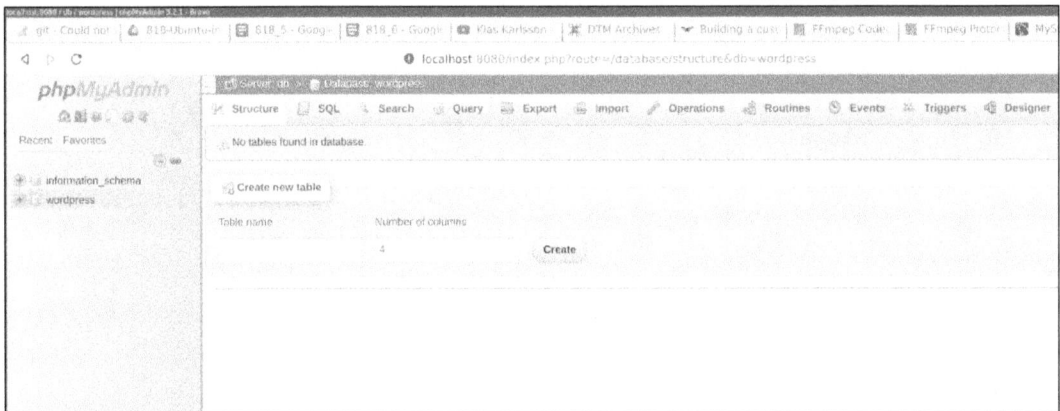

Figure 6.2: PhpMyAdmin

Connecting two stacks

When you start a docker-compose, Docker creates a separate network for it so that the container is isolated, with only the service listed in the docker-compose file. However, sometimes, you want to connect two stacks.

If you develop and have multiple services, they need to talk to each other.

Sometimes, when a developer uses a stack with a core service like a database, they can have a smaller Docker Compose of only the app they are working on.

In the following WordPress example, you can see that we use the network values:

```
1.              networks:
2.          - local
3.
4.
5.  networks:
6.    local:
7.      external: true
```

This tells us that we want our stack to run in a shared network setup.

Now, create a new folder called Metabase, and in that folder, create a **docker-compose.yaml** file with the following content:

```
1.  version: '3'
2.  services:
3.    metabase:
4.      image: metabase/metabase
5.      ports:
6.        - 3000:3000
7.      environment:
8.        MB_DB_TYPE: postgres
9.        MB_DB_DBNAME: metabase
10.       MB_DB_PORT: 5432
11.       MB_DB_USER: metabase
12.       MB_DB_PASS: metabase
13.       MB_DB_HOST: postgres
14.     networks:
15.       - local
16.   postgres:
17.     image: postgres:latest
18.     environment:
19.       POSTGRES_USER: metabase
20.       POSTGRES_DB: metabase
21.       POSTGRES_PASSWORD: metabase
22.     #command: tail -f /etc/fstab
23.     volumes:
24.       - ./pg:/var/lib/postgresql/data
25.     networks:
26.       - local
27. networks:
28.   local:
29.     external: true
```

We need to keep track of the names of containers in docker-compose that will be added to the **Domain Name Server (DNS)** of Docker. So that when we have more files, we cannot use the same name. For example, we cannot use DB as the name for the db in both the WordPress and Metabase docker-compose files.

We also need to keep track of ports. We can only open a port to one service. In the example, we have used WordPress for port 8080. Then, we cannot use port 8080 in any of the other services using the same docker network.

Now, let us start Metabase and our WordPress by starting both stacks using two terminals and **docker compose up**.

When Metabase is up, you can start the installation guide on Metabase by visiting **http://localhost:3000.**

During the Metabase installation, you are asked to add a DB. Choose MySQL and add the values from our WordPress installation.

Figure 6.3 shows how to add MySQL data to Metabase:

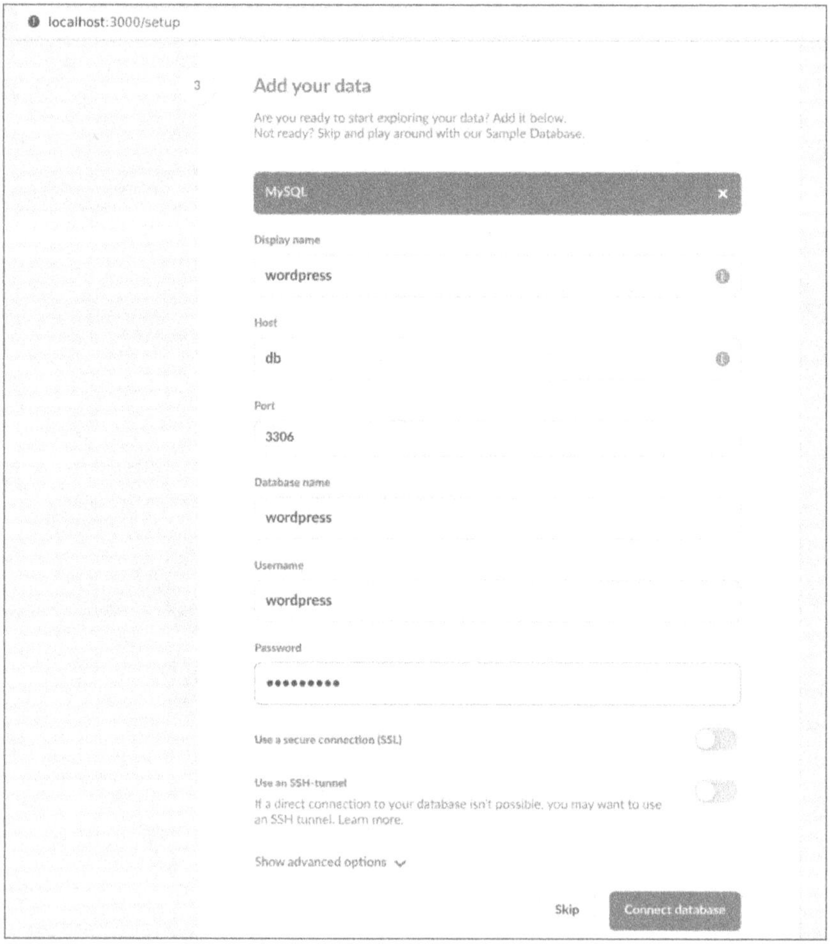

Figure 6.3: *Metabase adding data*

Local development with Docker

Docker is a tool for developing applications, and there are many different ways to get started. Here, we will make a new docker-compose with our code, and then add some simple HTML pages,

Create a new folder, and in that folder, make a **docker-compose.yaml** file.Add the following content to that file:

```
1. services:
2. dev:
3.     image: nginx
4.     volumes:
5.        - ./code:/usr/share/nginx/html
6.   ports:
7.     - 80:80
```

Now, besides the **docker-compose.yaml** file creates a folder called code.

In that folder, create a file called **index.html**. Then, add the following to that file, as shown:

```
1. <html>
2. <head>docker test</head>
3. <body><h2>Docker test</h2></body>
4. </html>
```

Start the Docker stack with the following **docker-compose up**:

```
1. docker compose up
```

Visit the page **http://localhost** to see the content of our **index.html** file

In our **docker-compose** file, start an NGINX container and then use a volume to mount the **index.html** file into the web folder of the NGINX server. The NGINX server will then read our **index.html** file and show the content. You can now edit the content in **index.html** and refresh your browser to see the new content. There is no need to stop and start the docker container to see the new content. We can develop locally using a docker container by mounting your code.

About Kubernetes

Kubernetes is a popular open-source container orchestration platform that automates the deployment, scaling, and management of containerized applications. It was originally developed by *Google* and is now maintained by the **Cloud Native Computing Foundation (CNCF)**.

Today, Kubernetes is becoming the standard way of running applications in containers.

You can get a Kubernetes cluster on almost all cloud providers today. With Kubernetes, you can easily deploy your applications and then let Kubernetes take care of scaling and deploying your applications.

Kubernetes also has a power API that can be expanded. So, different services can add their own endpoint and, in so, add new functions to the cluster. It can be from adding functions to creating **Transport Layer Security** (**TLS**) certificates to handling incoming and outgoing traffic.

In the *Server* section, we will go over how you can set up your own Kubernetes cluster. First, we will start up a small local cluster and test some applications on it. There are several tools that can help you spin up a local Kubernetes cluster. We will focus on using a tool called **Minkube**.

https://minikube.sigs.k8s.io/docs/

Now, follow the guide and start our local **minikube** cluster as shown:

```
1. curl -LO https://storage.googleapis.com/minikube/releases/latest/
   minikube-linux-amd64
2. sudo install minikube-linux-amd64 /usr/local/bin/minikube
```

This will get the **minikube** binary and install it into your Ubuntu. When you start your **minikube**, choose how you want to run **minikube** as a virtual machine or as a docker. Start Minikube as follows:

```
1. minikube start <--- default will bring up minikube with docker
2. minikube start --driver=kvm2  <-- Will start minikube as Virtual
   Server
```

To connect to our Kubernetes cluster, we use a tool called **kubectl**. Install **kubectl** using the following command from the install page **https://kubernetes.io/docs/tasks/tools/install-kubectl-linux/**, as follows:

```
1. curl -LO "https://dl.k8s.io/release/$(curl -L -s https://dl.k8s.io/
   release/stable.txt)/bin/linux/amd64/kubectl"
2. curl -LO "https://dl.k8s.io/$(curl -L -s https://dl.k8s.io/release/
   stable.txt)/bin/linux/amd64/kubectl.sha256"
3. sudo install -o root -g root -m 0755 kubectl /usr/local/bin/kubectl
```

Now, we can run a **kubectl** command to connect to our **minikube** cluster and get all our nodes as shown:

```
1. mattias@hrb:~$ kubectl get nodes
2. NAME        STATUS    ROLES                AGE    VERSION
3. minikube    Ready     control-plane,master  3m6s   v1.22.3
4. mattias@hrb:~$
```

Deploy app on Kubernetes

Let us deploy the WordPress app that we used in docker-compose into our Kubernetes cluster. We will create two namespaces and deploy MySQL into one and WordPress into the other. Then, we will open a local port so that we can access our WordPress.

MySQL

Start by creating a file called **mysql.yaml** and pass the following content:

```
 1. mattias@hrb:~/kubernetes$ cat mysql.yaml
 2. apiVersion: v1
 3. kind: Service
 4. metadata:
 5.   name: mysql
 6.   namespace: mysql
 7.   labels:
 8.     app: wordpress
 9. spec:
10.   ports:
11.     - port: 3306
12.   selector:
13.     app: mysql
14. ---
15. apiVersion: apps/v1
16. kind: Deployment
17. metadata:
18.   name: mysql
19.   namespace: mysql
20.   labels:
21.     app: mysql
22. spec:
23.   selector:
24.     matchLabels:
25.       app: mysql
26.   strategy:
27.     type: Recreate
28.   template:
29.     metadata:
30.       labels:
31.         app: mysql
32.     spec:
```

```
33.        containers:
34.        - image: mysql:5.7
35.          args: ["--default-authentication-plugin=mysql_native_
    password"]
36.          name: mysql
37.          env:
38.          - name: MYSQL_ROOT_PASSWORD
39.            value: "myrootpassword"
40.          - name: MYSQL_DATABASE
41.            value: wordpress
42.          - name: MYSQL_USER
43.            value: wordpress
44.          - name: MYSQL_PASSWORD
45.            value: password
46.          ports:
47.          - containerPort: 3306
48.            name: mysql
```

You can think of the namespace as a separate folder that separates what we run in Kubernetes. Now, we will create a namespace to hold our deployments as follows:

```
1. mattias@hrb:~/kubernetes$ kubectl create namespace mysql
2. namespace/mysql created
```

The namespace is created. Now, we can apply our YAML to Kubernetes, as shown:

```
1. mattias@hrb:~/kubernetes$ kubectl apply -f mysql.yaml
2. service/mysql created
3. deployment.apps/mysql created
```

Let us verify if everything is running by running the following code:

```
1.  mattias@hrb:~/kubernetes$ kubectl get all -n mysql
2.  NAME                        READY   STATUS    RESTARTS   AGE
3.  pod/mysql-5b74979c5d-4b575  1/1     Running   0          4m57s
4.
5.  NAME            TYPE        CLUSTER-IP       EXTERNAL-IP   PORT(S)
    AGE
6.  service/mysql   ClusterIP   10.105.243.103   <none>        3306/TCP
    4m57s
7.
8.  NAME                    READY   UP-TO-DATE   AVAILABLE   AGE
9.  deployment.apps/mysql   1/1     1            1           4m57s
10.
11. NAME                              DESIRED   CURRENT   READY   AGE
12. replicaset.apps/mysql-5b74979c5d  1         1         1       4m57s
```

We tell Kubernetes to create a deployment. Then, Kubernetes creates a new **replicaset** that holds data on the current deployment. If you update the deployment, a new replica set will be created, which will create a Pod. The Pod is for the container that is running. The service is essentially a port that provides access to the MySQL server.

For more information, we can describe our pod, or any of the other, like deployment and service.

The following is the description of the MySQL Pod:

```
 1. mattias@hrb:~/projects/hrb/book/818/6/kubernetes$ kubectl describe
    pod -n mysql
 2. Name:              mysql-5b74979c5d-4b575
 3. Namespace:         mysql
 4. Priority:          0
 5. Service Account:   default
 6. Node:              minikube/192.168.49.2
 7. Start Time:        Mon, 08 May 2023 22:03:13 +0200
 8. Labels:            app=mysql
 9.                    pod-template-hash=5b74979c5d
    {DATA REMOVED FOR VISIBILITY}

10.                                node.kubernetes.io/
    unreachable:NoExecute op=Exists for 300s
11. Events:
12.   Type     Reason     Age     From              Message
13.   ----     ------     ----    ----              -------
14.   Normal   Scheduled  8m34s   default-scheduler Successfully assigned
    mysql/mysql-5b74979c5d-4b575 to minikube
15.   Normal   Pulling    8m33s   kubelet           Pulling image
    "mysql:5.6"
16.   Normal   Pulled     8m29s   kubelet           Successfully pulled
    image "mysql:5.6" in 4.49632388s
17.   Normal   Created    8m28s   kubelet           Created container
    mysql
18.   Normal   Started    8m28s   kubelet           Started container
    mysql
```

WordPress

Setting up WordPress is very similar to how we set up MySQL. We create the namespace and apply the YAML. Provided is the YAML for WordPress and the commands to apply it, as follows:

```
 1. mattias@hrb:~/kubernetes$ cat wordpress.yaml
 2. apiVersion: v1
```

```
 3. kind: Service
 4. metadata:
 5.   name: wordpress
 6.   namespace: wordpress
 7.   labels:
 8.     app: wordpress
 9. spec:
10.   ports:
11.     - port: 80
12.   selector:
13.     app: wordpress
14.     tier: frontend
15.   type: LoadBalancer
16. ---
17. apiVersion: apps/v1
18. kind: Deployment
19. metadata:
20.   name: wordpress
21.   namespace: wordpress
22.   labels:
23.     app: wordpress
24. spec:
25.   selector:
26.     matchLabels:
27.       app: wordpress
28.       tier: frontend
29.   strategy:
30.     type: Recreate
31.   template:
32.     metadata:
33.       labels:
34.         app: wordpress
35.         tier: frontend
36.     spec:
37.       containers:
38.       - image: wordpress:6.2.0-apache
39.         name: wordpress
40.         env:
41.         - name: WORDPRESS_DB_HOST
42.           value: mysql.mysql.svc
43.         - name: WORDPRESS_DB_USER
44.           value: wordpress
45.         - name: WORDPRESS_DB_NAME
```

```
46.          value: wordpress
47.        - name: WORDPRESS_DB_PASSWORD
48.          value: password
49.        ports:
50.        - containerPort: 80
51.          name: wordpress
52.
53. mattias@hrb:~/kubernetes$ kubectl create namespace wordpress
54. namespace/wordpress created
55. mattias@hrb:~/kubernetes$ kubectl apply -f wordpress.yaml
56. service/wordpress created
57. deployment.apps/wordpress created
```

Let us verify if our WordPress has been deployed and is running, as follows:

```
1.  mattias@hrb:~/projects/hrb/book/818/6/kubernetes$ kubectl get all -n
    wordpress
    NAME                              READY   STATUS    RESTARTS   AGE
2.  pod/wordpress-769b78779-lmwrx     1/1     Running   0          4m21s
3.
4.  NAME                 TYPE           CLUSTER-IP      EXTERNAL-IP
    PORT(S)        AGE
5.  service/wordpress    LoadBalancer   10.104.110.191  <pending>
    80:31352/TCP    4m46s
6.
7.  NAME                        READY   UP-TO-DATE   AVAILABLE   AGE
8.  deployment.apps/wordpress   1/1     1            1           4m21s
9.
10. NAME                                    DESIRED   CURRENT   READY
    AGE
11. replicaset.apps/wordpress-769b78779     1         1         1
    4m21s
```

Access your service

When we deployed MySQL and WordPress, we deployed two different services. If you examine the YAML, you should notice the various types of services we use. In MySQL, we use the type ClusterIP. This will make the service accessible in the Kubernetes cluster.

For WordPress, we use the type LoadBalancer. This type accepts traffic from outside the cluster into the cluster, as follows:

```
1. minikube service wordpress -n wordpress
```

The preceding command opens your browser and displays the port for you. This is a **minikube** command and will not work on other Kubernetes clusters.

Figure 6.4 shows the WordPress installation page that opens after running the `minikube` command:

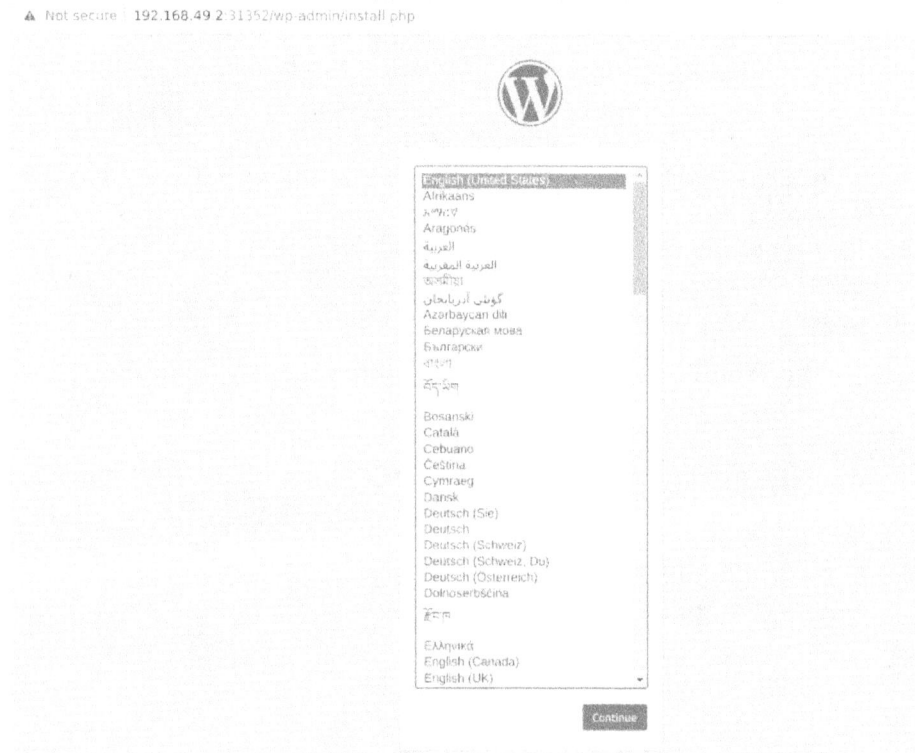

Figure 6.4: *WordPress installation*

Conclusion

In this chapter, we understood how to work with containers and a docker container and then add more to build a full stack of containers together into a working application. Then, we covered working on Kubernetes using minikube, installing Kubernetes on our Ubuntu Desktop, and deploying our first app, a WordPress blog with MySQL, into our Kubernetes cluster.

Now, we have basic knowledge of how to start and run containers in docker and into a Kubernetes cluster.

In the next chapter, we will use an Ubuntu Server with no GIU. We will start by understanding how to install and configure Ubuntu Servers. From one server to a fleet of servers with standard tools.

Install Ubuntu Server on Metal, Cloud, and Network

Introduction

Ubuntu can be installed and run from cloud providers, regular computers, servers, and small microcomputers like the Raspberry Pi. The installation approach is different from where you install one server to many, and several hundreds.

Structure

This chapter will cover the following topics:

- Cattle vs. pets
- Using SSH to connect to your server
- Install Ubuntu Server with USB
- Using Ubuntu in VM
- Ubuntu Server in Google Cloud and Hetzner
- Large Ubuntu installation made easy

Objectives

In this chapter, we will learn how to install an Ubuntu Server, from setting up a single server, such as a virtual machine or a physical computer.

We will also examine the installation and setup of an Ubuntu Server, both on Google Cloud and Hetzner, to understand how easily you can set up and utilize your Ubuntu Server within a cloud provider. We will then move over to large Ubuntu installations and provision your Ubuntu Server from one to many using the Ubuntu tool, **machine as a service (MAAS)**.

The new Ubuntu Server provides SSH access, allowing you to start administering your server. To use SSH safely, we will create secure SSH keys for use when accessing your Ubuntu Server.

Cattle vs. pets

When we talk about servers, we use the terms cattle and pets and treat them differently. When you have a server, and you treat it as a pet, you are taking care of the server for a long time. We log in to the server and upgrade it, install our software, and perform other tasks. When we use our servers as cattle, it takes some more time to set the tools up. Then, instead of keeping our server for a long time, we delete and reinstall the server. We have the same software running, but instead of logging into our pet server and upgrading, we destroy our cattle server and reinstall it with the updated service.

This approach to treating servers is good practice. To ensure servers are running smoothly in a company for any production purpose, it is recommended to handle them as cattle. If you have your home server with your media on it, then you should be treating it with care

In this chapter, we will understand how to treat our servers more like cattle.

Using SSH to connect to your server

When connecting to your server as an administrator, we use SSH. SSH is a client on your computer that connects to an SSH server on the server. It then creates a secure tunnel between the client and server and lets you run CLI commands on the server. This is the default way of administering your Ubuntu Server. To secure this communication, the default is to use a username and password to log in.

However, a more secure way is to create an SSH key on the computer where you work.

This key is made of two parts:

- The private part that you do not want to share.

- The public part you can share with others.

When we use SSH keys, we install our public key on the server, and then we connect to the SSH server. You can only let people in if they have the matching private key.

This has now become the default way of accessing your server in the cloud.

You should always aim to use SSH keys when you can. To generate the keys and run the following command:

```
1.  mahe@hrb-demo:~$ ssh-keygen
2.  Generating public/private rsa key pair.
3.  Enter file in which to save the key (/home/mahe/.ssh/id_rsa):
4.  Enter passphrase (empty for no passphrase):
5.  Enter same passphrase again:
6.  Your identification has been saved in /home/mahe/.ssh/id_rsa
7.  Your public key has been saved in /home/mahe/.ssh/id_rsa.pub
8.  The key fingerprint is:
9.  SHA256:J/cau5OkIIcYMOIYnyYW/5bl3m5S37aFezCIJk5jRik mahe@hrb-demo
10. The key's randomart image is:
11. +---[RSA 3072]----+
12. |                 |
13. |=.               |
14. |+=o.        .    |
15. |oo=.  E +        |
16. |.o o..* S + .    |
17. |  . o+oB B.o o.  |
18. |    .o*.*oo.o.o. |
19. |      +.oo= oo.  |
20. |        +.+o.oo  |
21. +-----[SHA256]-----+
22. mahe@hrb-demo:~$
```

The command generates both keys for you and to retrieves the public key for you to run the following command:

```
1.  mahe@hrb-demo:~$ cat ~/.ssh/id_rsa.pub
2.  ssh-rsa AAAAB3NzaC1yc2EAAAADAQABAAABgQDISm
    /S/ztzr2tmNHYjZcmYpCy9jSQyEGuGP7VwQ2f/PAJZxcKRRUhjDoXt/XqE4gYpgd
    PAz7PaaV+zQzTobySit3aaGeAhLa54jhk8D7BevlSNbWwXXlmkeV5X7UdffoNB0vr
    XKriNw1Pcz6P1kUcOXhJkYuztM3IJ4d5WgsvD2JcrdtKUX6ckFZp9uR1FR8Jvx3rz
    POZznC8lAef0z1c35MdjEN4mMJIXs7LCL1tY9MjDB1lsanirVaKzvxTAdYqTi4Gn8S
    IyAit5QWQjepd7zJcww6dUFqvW+a3++UbKDEDtnBgK9aUgjicnopjYnyYaWn6hUg
    /+ACC/brl6l8pF181TfOn71M68344Wnj7ZNziZ6mHFmBTPoNs3lkoCzUUAHVpSgx+z
    GlqMuneMhvzvL5mhvXJHBjPIs/GWD3jaf6hySHJrRbGshQhM30fInpFtxZUEsq1eROQn
    AU0Gw9DhaFjIqYuTGsNEmrDT/e+THpRLwJRXQOzMio67+NK3DhM= mahe@hrb-demo
mahe@hrb-demo:~$
```

The output is what you want to add to your cloud provider. For example, GitHub when they ask for an SSH key.

To copy your key to a server and start using the key instead of the password, run the following command:

```
1.  mahe@hrb-demo:~$ ssh-copy-id mahe@192.168.122.27
2.  /usr/bin/ssh-copy-id: INFO: Source of key(s) to be installed: "/home/
    mahe/.ssh/id_rsa.pub"
```

3. The authenticity of host '192.168.122.27 (192.168.122.27)' can't be established.
4. ED25519 key fingerprint is SHA256:xSOoPXxVNmiVS1FHWn0nWj5kg5VGVUOc/RSLrd5Fw7Q.
5. This key is not known by any other names
6. Are you sure you want to continue connecting (yes/no/[fingerprint])? Yes
7. /usr/bin/ssh-copy-id: INFO: attempting to log in with the new key(s), to filter out any that are already installed
8. /usr/bin/ssh-copy-id: INFO: 1 key(s) remain to be installed – *if you are prompted now it is to install the new keys*
9. mahe@192.168.122.27's password:
10. Number of key(s) added: 1
11. Now try logging into the machine, with: "ssh 'mahe@192.168.122.27'"
12. and check to make sure that only the key(s) you wanted were added.
13. mahe@hrb-demo:~$

Now, you can ssh into the server without using your password.

Install Ubuntu Server with USB

We will install our Ubuntu Server in the same way we install our Ubuntu Desktop. First, download the Ubuntu Server image, and then, by using balenaEtcher, burn the image to a USB device. You can then start your computer and choose boot on USB. You will receive a guide similar to the Ubuntu Desktop and follow the guide until the end.

During the installations, you can choose two different versions of the Ubuntu Server.

The regular installation is best if you log in and use the server regularly. The minimal installation is smaller and does not include many programs, such as office tools. This installation will be apt if you only plan to run an example Docker on your server. The default is the regular Ubuntu, as shown in *Figure 7.1*:

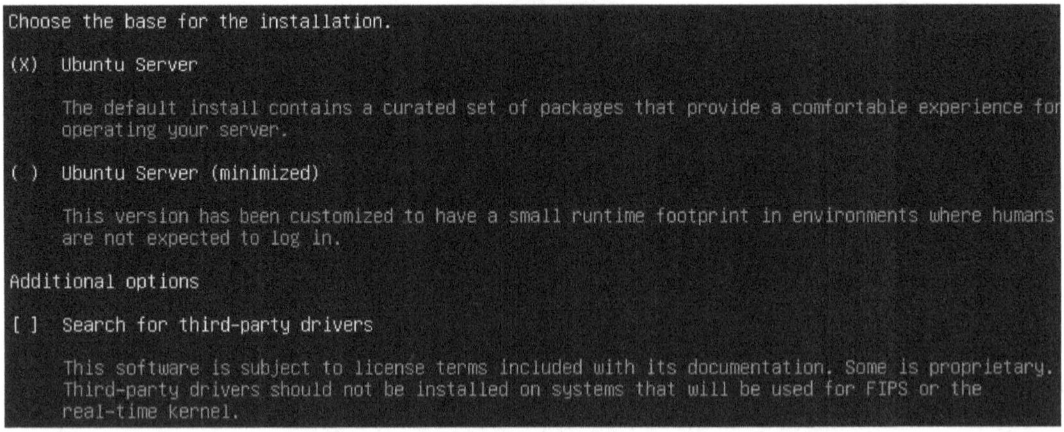

Figure 7.1: Show the different Ubuntu Server versions

During the installation, you also need to set up the disk used for Ubuntu. When using a server, you may want to set up extra disks and partitions based on what you will run on the server. However, for us here, we will use the default disk configurations as shown in *Figure 7.2*:

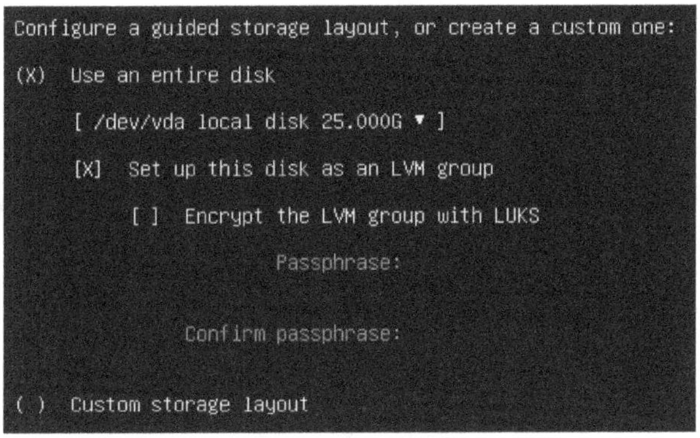

```
Configure a guided storage layout, or create a custom one:

(X)  Use an entire disk

     [ /dev/vda local disk 25.000G ▼ ]

     [X]  Set up this disk as an LVM group

          [ ]  Encrypt the LVM group with LUKS

                       Passphrase:

                  Confirm passphrase:

( )  Custom storage layout
```

Figure 7.2: *Ubuntu Server disk setup*

During the installation, you want to connect your new server to a network. The Ubuntu Server now features a **graphical user interface** (**GUI**), and we will manage it using a **command line interface** (**CLI**) over SSH. You can use a regular Ubuntu Desktop as your server, as there are no differences in core between the Ubuntu Server and the Ubuntu Desktop. So, all packages can be installed in both.

So, if you only have one computer and want that on all the time, all the server commands we will run will also work for the Ubuntu Desktop.

During the installation, you are asked to install the **OpenSSH server**. Select this option to connect to our new server when installation is completed. *Figure 7.3* shows the screen where OpenSSH is requested to be installed:

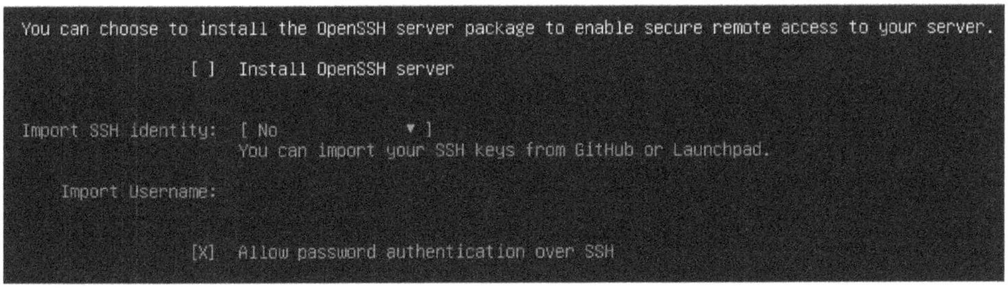

```
You can choose to install the OpenSSH server package to enable secure remote access to your server.

          [ ]  Install OpenSSH server

Import SSH identity:  [ No           ▼ ]
                      You can import your SSH keys from GitHub or Launchpad.

   Import Username:

          [X]  Allow password authentication over SSH
```

Figure 7.3: *Select to install the OpenSSH server*

Ubuntu Server can also install some pre-installed packages for you, and the last installation steps show some of the packages you can install.

If you know what you want, you can choose it here. *Figure 7.4* shows which package you can select from:

```
These are popular snaps in server environments. Select or deselect with SPACE, press ENTER to see
more details of the package, publisher and versions available.

[ ] microk8s              canonical             Kubernetes for workstations and appliances        ►
[ ] nextcloud             nextcloud✓            Nextcloud Server - A safe home for all your data   ►
[ ] wekan                 xet7                  The open-source kanban                             ►
[ ] kata-containers       katacontainers✓       Build lightweight VMs that seamlessly plug into the►
[ ] docker                canonical✓            Docker container runtime                           ►
[ ] canonical-livepatch   canonical✓            Canonical Livepatch Client                         ►
[ ] rocketchat-server     rocketchat✓           Rocket.Chat server                                 ►
[ ] mosquitto             mosquitto✓            Eclipse Mosquitto MQTT broker                      ►
[ ] etcd                  canonical✓            Resilient key-value store by CoreOS                ►
[ ] powershell            microsoft-powershell✓ PowerShell for every system!                       ►
[ ] stress-ng             cking-kernel-tools    tool to load and stress a computer                 ►
[ ] sabnzbd               safihre               SABnzbd                                            ►
[ ] wormhole              snapcrafters          get things from one computer to another, safely    ►
[ ] aws-cli               aws✓                  Universal Command Line Interface for Amazon Web Serv►
[ ] google-cloud-sdk      google-cloud-sdk✓     Google Cloud SDK                                   ►
[ ] slcli                 softlayer             Python based SoftLayer API Tool.                   ►
[ ] doctl                 digitalocean✓         The official DigitalOcean command line interface   ►
[ ] conjure-up            canonical✓            Package runtime for conjure-up spells              ►
[ ] postgresql10          cmd✓                  PostgreSQL is a powerful, open source object-relatio►
[ ] heroku                heroku✓               CLI client for Heroku                              ►
[ ] keepalived            keepalived-project✓   High availability VRRP/BFD and load-balancing for Li►
[ ] prometheus            canonical✓            The Prometheus monitoring system and time series dat►
[ ] juju                  canonical✓            Juju - a model-driven operator lifecycle manager for►
```

Figure 7.4: Ubuntu Server package to install

Connect to your Ubuntu Server

Now, it is time to connect from your Ubuntu Desktop or other computer to your Ubuntu Server. To do that, we are using a tool called SSH and making a secure connection between your computer and your server. This is also the standard way to get access to any Ubuntu Server in the cloud.

First, get the IP of your Ubuntu Server. If you have a screen and keyboard connected to it, you can log in and then type:

```
1. ip a
```

This will show the IP of the Ubuntu Server. Now, from your desktop, run the following command:

```
1. ssh USERNAME@IP
```

Replace the **USERNAME** with your username and the IP with the IP of your server. The first thing that comes back is that you need to approve the host key. Every SSH server generates a hostkey; before you can connect, you need to approve it. This will also protect you and will not let you SSH into a server with the same IP as your home server. The hostkey will differ, and your SSH client will show an error message.

After entering your password, you should have a CLI connection to your Ubuntu Server.

Using Ubuntu in VM

Let us install the Ubuntu Server into a VM using the libvirt we used before. When we have our Ubuntu Server up and running, we can use the tools in the VM tool. To clone our Ubuntu Server, make more Ubuntu Servers. This is a great way of setting up new servers easily, and it is the same way many cloud providers use today. You have one base installation that you keep updated, and then create a new version from that base image.

Install an Ubuntu Server like we install a Ubuntu Desktop into your VM. In the following figure, we use KVM, as done before. When we have our Ubuntu Server running, we can make a clone of the server, as shown:

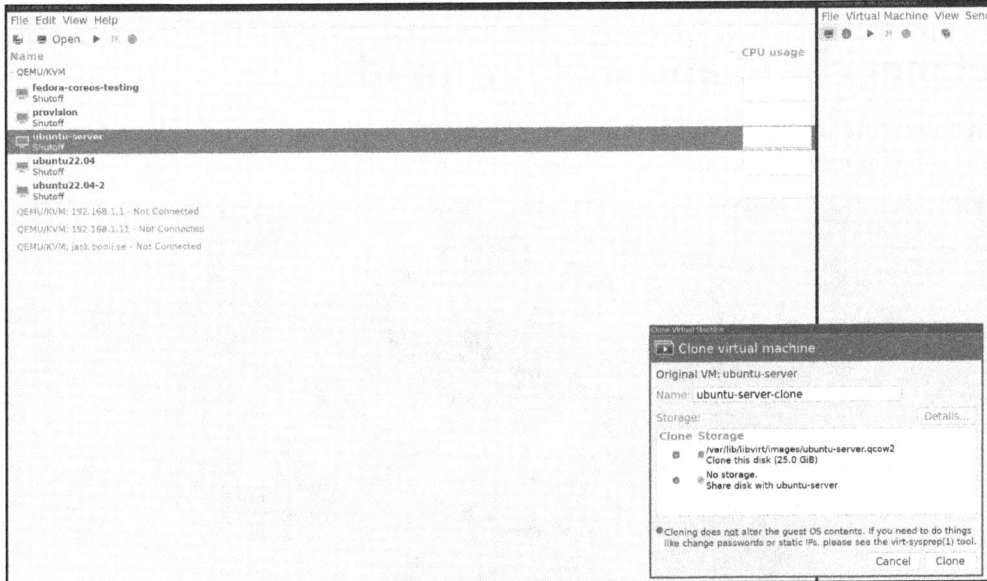

Figure 7.5: Clone Ubuntu Server

Now, from our newly created clone, we can make a new Ubuntu Server, as shown in the following figure:

Figure 7.6: Cloned Ubuntu Server

Ubuntu Server in Google Cloud and Hetzner

All cloud providers today offer to run an Ubuntu Server. If you are looking for a small server, there are producers like Digital Ocean or Linode. There are enormous cloud providers such as AWS, Google Cloud, and Azure as well.

A provider also gives you a physical server, but it runs in their datacenter like Hetzner. They all work the same way. In this chapter, we will explore setting up an Ubuntu Server in Google Cloud and at Hetzner. You can then connect to that server over ssh and control your server. This setup we are doing now is more for simple usage, and if you plan to run some production load on that server, you need to learn more about the provider and set up the server in best practice using their guides.

Hetzner cloud and metal provider

In the following figure, we logged in to the Hetzner cloud control and ordered an Ubuntu Server. As you can see in the figure, there are many configuration options:

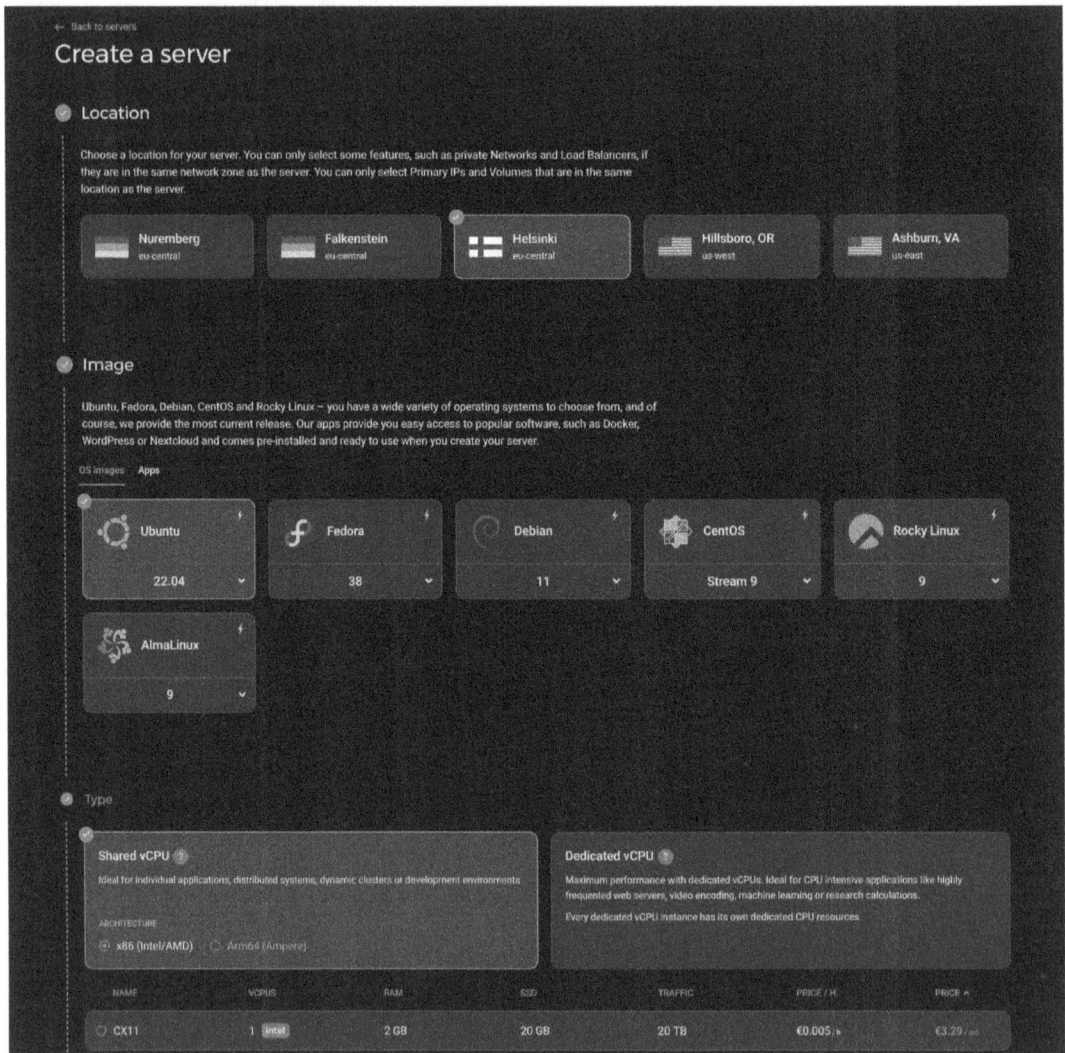

Figure 7.7: Select Linux server Hetzner

You need to add your SSH key to the server to connect to it later. In the following figure, you can see that we have added my SSH key:

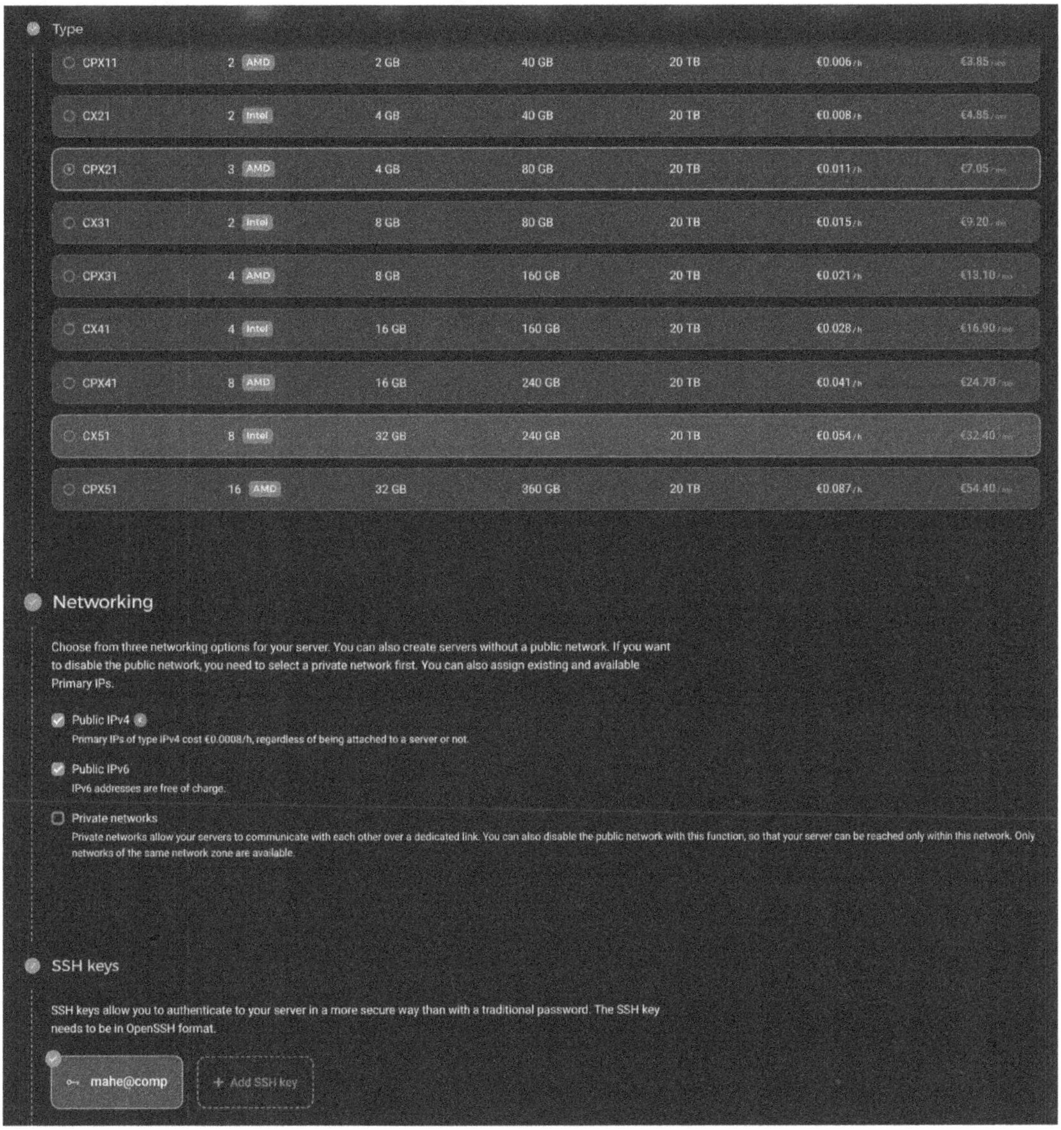

Figure 7.8: Hetzner Linux with SSH key added

When your server has been deployed and is ready, you can see some details in the web console as graphs and settings, as shown in the following figure:

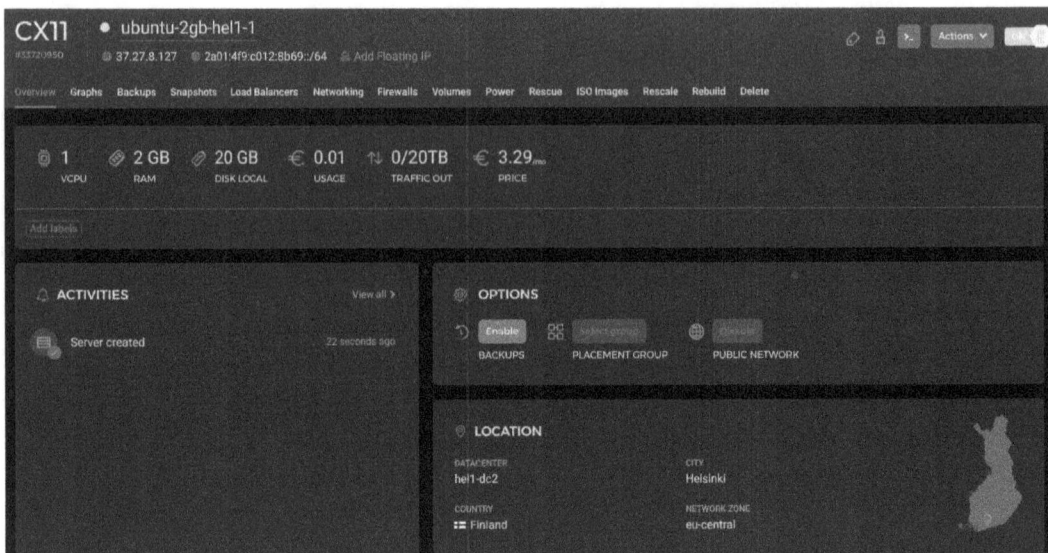

Figure 7.9: Server settings in Hetzner cloud

In the preceding figure, you can see the external IP of the server and to login with SSH. You can run the following command from your computer that has the SSH key we installed:

```
1.  mattias@hrb:~$ ssh root@37.27.8.127
2.  Welcome to Ubuntu 22.04.2 LTS (GNU/Linux 5.15.0-73-generic x86_64)
3.
4.  * Documentation:  https://help.ubuntu.com
5.  * Management:     https://landscape.canonical.com
6.  * Support:        https://ubuntu.com/advantage
7.
8.  System information as of Wed Jun 14 03:46:18 PM UTC 2023
9.
10.  System load:  0.0                    Processes:              92
11.  Usage of /:   10.0% of 18.45GB       Users logged in:         0
12.  Memory usage: 7%                     Ipv4 address for eth0:
     37.27.8.127
13.  Swap usage:   0%                     Ipv6 address for eth0:
     2a01:4f9:c012:8b69::1
14.
15. Expanded Security Maintenance for Applications is not enabled.
16.
17. 0 updates can be applied immediately.
18.
19. Enable ESM Apps to receive additional future security updates.
```

20. See https://ubuntu.com/esm or run: sudo pro status
21.
22.
23. root@ubuntu-2gb-hel1-1:~#

Creating an Ubuntu Server in Google cloud

In Google Cloud, the setup is similar, but Google Cloud has so many different services. So, before we can start our Ubuntu Server, we need to go to **Compute Engine** then, we can create a new server. We select Ubuntu by changing the boot disk and then choose the desired Ubuntu version. The following figure shows a setup of an Ubuntu Server ready to be created:

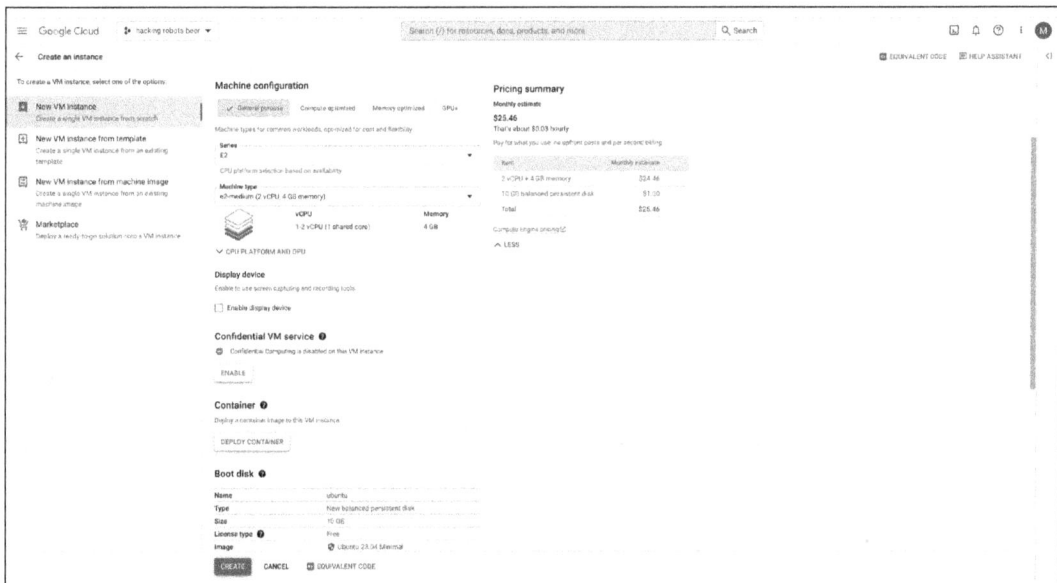

Figure 7.10: Google Cloud create Ubuntu Server

When our server is created, we can open the settings for the server, and on the top, there are settings to connect to your server, as shown in the following figure:

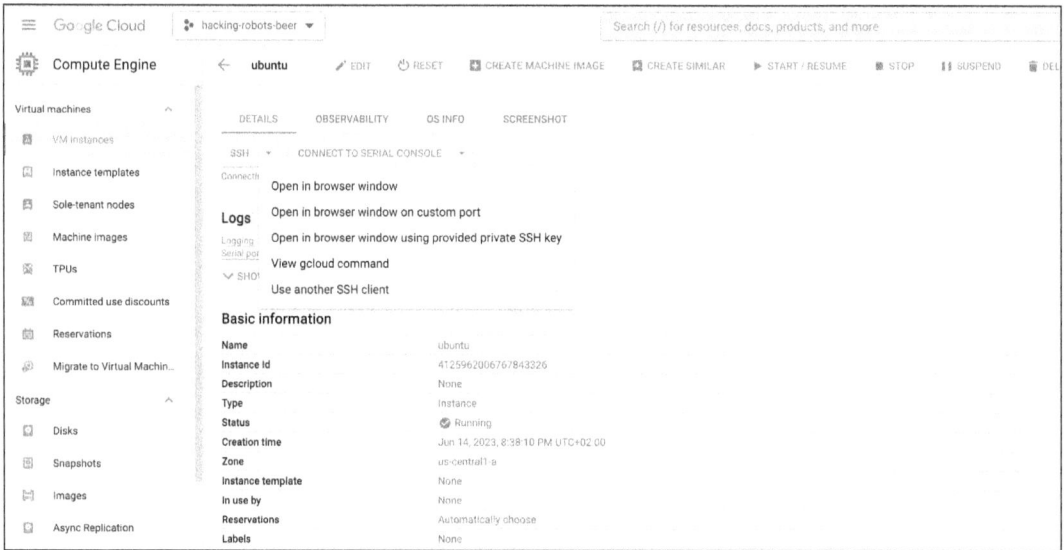

Figure 7.11: *Connect to Google Cloud server*

When the server has been deployed, you can open an SSH screen in your browser. From there, we can add our SSH key to the server, as shown in *Figure 7.12*:

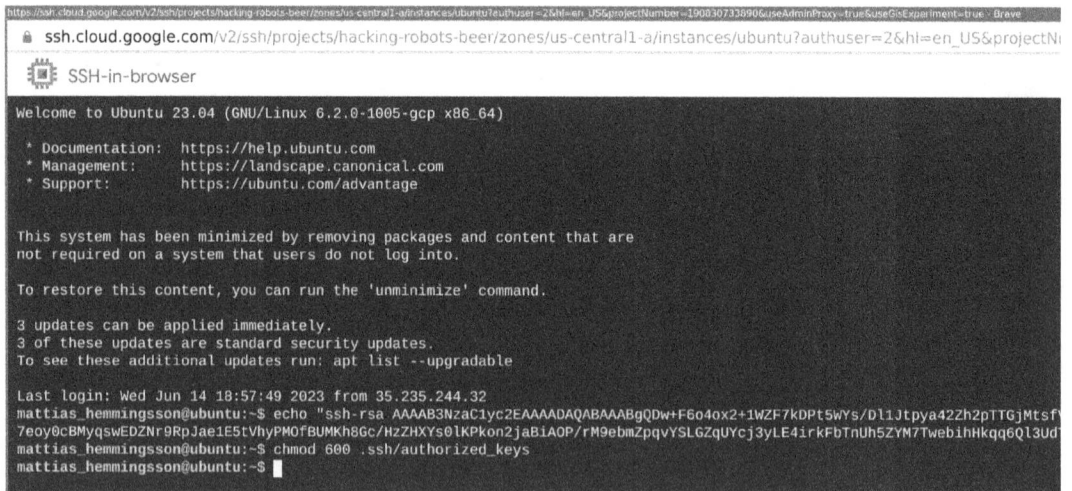

Figure 7.12: *Adding SSH pub key to Google Cloud server*

Then, log in from our computer, as shown in *Figure 7.13*. Notice the username that we use and then you will find the external IP in the server list.

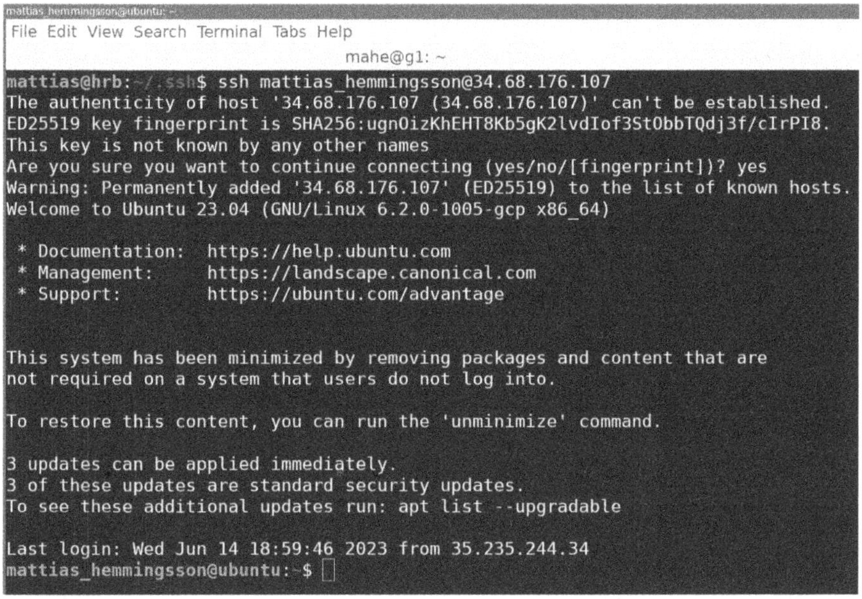

Figure 7.13: SSH into the Google Cloud server from a local computer

As you can see, deploying an Ubuntu Server in a cloud provider is easy and fast. You can, when your Ubuntu Server is running, use SSH to log into the server and control it in the same way as you would SSH and control your local server or even your Ubuntu Desktop.

Large Ubuntu installations made easy

To install a larger number of Ubuntu or other Linux servers, you can use many different tools. One of the tools is called MAAS, and it is from Ubuntu: (**https://maas.io/**). MAAS is made so that you can easily install and set up a large number of servers, such as a data center. However, they also work well for smaller installations and for keeping good practice in reinstalling and updating the server regularly.

PXE booting

The installation is done by using the options that the server and regular computer can boot from the network. When the computer boots, instead of booting from a local drive, USB, or CD, it asks the network for a boot image. In your DHCP server, which gives out the DHCP address to the computer, you can specify which server the clients can get boot images from. Now, when a server boots, it gets a boot image and starts that image. It is similar to when we installed Ubuntu Desktop and started the Ubuntu live image from a USB drive. You had your Ubuntu running, but you had not installed anything.

Now, when the PXE Ubuntu is started on your server over the network. We can send it some commands.

Typically, when installing, Ubuntu adds the user's key and sets some network settings. When the installation is complete, the computer is restarted. This time, when it tries to pxe boot, our provision tools do not give the computer any image to boot from. Then, it falls back to boot from the hard drive we installed Ubuntu on before, and your freshly installed Ubuntu is started.

Provision VM with MAAS

Let us try installing some VMs using MAAS, as shown in the following steps:

1. We will set up an Ubuntu Server and then install MAAS on that server

2. When MAAS is installed, we can boot up a new VM and install Ubuntu on the new server using MAAS

3. Start by creating a Ubuntu Server in a VM. You can also use this on a regular computer at home, but it will not work in a cloud provider.

4. Log in to your Ubuntu Server using SSH to begin the installation of MAAS. Use the following command:

```
1. sudo snap install –channel=3.3 maas
```

This command will start installing MAAS into your Ubuntu Server. When the installation is complete, we can init the MAAS by running the **maas init** command with **–help** and then run the command listed from the help section, as shown:

```
 1. root@hrb-demo:/home/mahe# maas init --help
 2. usage: maas init [-h] {region+rack,region,rack} ...
 3.
 4. Initialise MAAS in the specified run mode.
 5.
 6. options:
 7.   -h, --help              show this help message and exit
 8.
 9. run modes:
10.   {region+rack,region,rack}
11.     region+rack           Both region and rack controllers
12.     region                Region controller only
13.     rack                  Rack controller only
14.
15. When installing region or rack+region modes, MAAS needs a
16. PostgreSQL database to connect to.
17.
18. If you want to set up PostgreSQL for a non-production deployment on
19. this machine, and configure it for use with MAAS, you can install
```

20. the `maas-test-db` snap before running 'maas init':
21.
22.   sudo snap install maas-test-db
23.   sudo maas init region+rack --database-uri maas-test-db:///

Install the demo database for **MAAS** by running the following command:

1. root@hrb-demo:/home/mahe# *sudo snap install maas-test-db*
2. maas-test-db (3.3/stable) 14.2-29-g.ed8d7f2 from Canonical✓ installed

Now, **init** the **MAAS** against the demo database with the following command:

1. root@hrb-demo:/home/mahe# *sudo maas init region+rack --database-uri maas-test-db:///*
2. MAAS URL [default=http://192.168.122.27:5240/MAAS]:
3. MAAS has been set up.
4.
5. If you want to configure external authentication or use
6. MAAS with Canonical RBAC, please run
7.
8.   sudo maas configauth
9.
10. To create admins when not using external authentication, run
11.
12.   sudo maas createadmin
13.
14. To enable TLS for secured communication, please run
15.
16.   sudo maas config-tls enable
17.
18. root@hrb-demo:/home/mahe#

Create our first admin user by running the following command:

1. root@hrb-demo:/home/mahe# *sudo maas createadmin*
2. Username: matte
3. Password:
4. Again:
5. Email: xxxx.xxxxxxx@gmail.com
6. Import SSH keys [] (lp:user-id or gh:user-id): n
7. SSH import protocol was not entered. Using Launchpad protocol (default).
8. Unable to import SSH keys. There are no SSH keys for launchpad user n.
9. root@hrb-demo:/home/mahe#

Now, we can log into our MAAS deployment by browsing to **http://${SERVER_IP}:5240/ MAAS**.

The first screen is to set up some basic settings for MAAS. You can go ahead and add your SSH key.

When the setup is complete, you are shown the MAAS home screen. Now it is time to set up our network for MAAS.

Setting up our network

When running MASS in **Kernel-based Virtual Machine** (**KVM**), we want to set up a network. By default, KVM will have a DHCP server in the range of 192.168.122.0-255, which we are currently using. However, we want to create a new network for our new server and make our MAAS server the default DHCP server here. If you run your MAAS in your own network, you can disable your current DHCP server and activate the MAAS DHCP server, or you can configure your current DHCP server to point to your MAAS.

In your virtual manager, go to the network and create a new network called provision.

The following figure shows a network with an IP range of 10.33.33.0, and it has the DHCP server off:

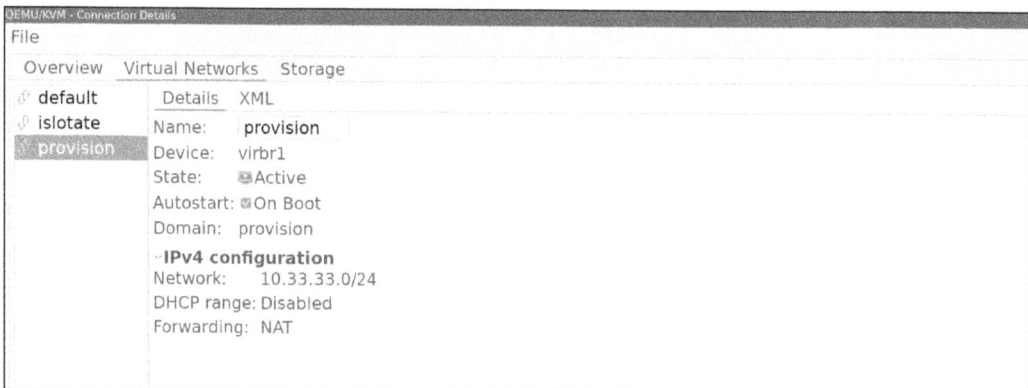

Figure 7.14: KVM new network without provision

Now, we can add this network to our VM host, as shown in the following figure. First, add a new device, and then save. For the change to take effect, turn your VM off and then on again.

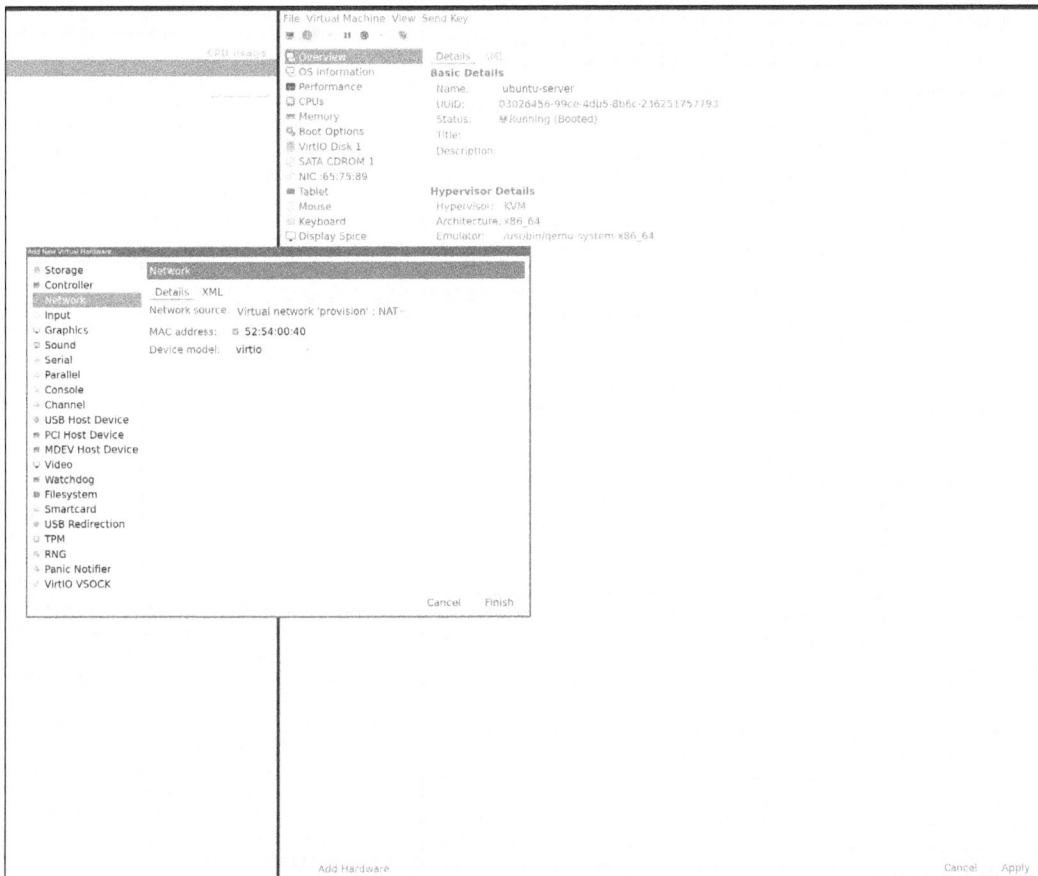

Figure 7.15: New network device for virtual host

When our server has rebooted, let us give our new network device an IP. First, get the name of the new IP by listing all the network devices, then, run the following command.

```
1.  mahe@hrb-demo:~$ ip a
2.  1: lo: <LOOPBACK,UP,LOWER_UP> mtu 65536 qdisc noqueue state UNKNOWN
    group default qlen 1000
3.      link/loopback 00:00:00:00:00:00 brd 00:00:00:00:00:00
4.      inet 127.0.0.1/8 scope host lo
5.         valid_lft forever preferred_lft forever
6.      inet6 ::1/128 scope host
7.         valid_lft forever preferred_lft forever
8.  2: enp1s0: <BROADCAST,MULTICAST,UP,LOWER_UP> mtu 1500 qdisc fq_codel
    state UP group default qlen 1000
9.      link/ether 52:54:00:65:75:89 brd ff:ff:ff:ff:ff:ff
10.     inet 192.168.122.27/24 metric 100 brd 192.168.122.255 scope
    global dynamic enp1s0
```

```
11.        valid_lft 3589sec preferred_lft 3589sec
12.     inet6 fe80::5054:ff:fe65:7589/64 scope link
13.        valid_lft forever preferred_lft forever
14. 3: enp7s0: <BROADCAST,MULTICAST> mtu 1500 qdisc noop state DOWN
    group default qlen 1000
15.     link/ether 52:54:00:40:b1:16 brd ff:ff:ff:ff:ff:ff
```

The preceding command shows the name of the new network device is **enp7s0**.

We can now open our network config and set the IP off our NIC by running the following command:

```
1. mahe@hrb-demo:~$ cat /etc/netplan/00-installer-config.yaml
2. # This is the network config written by 'subiquity'
3. network:
4.   ethernets:
5.     enp1s0:
6.       dhcp4: true
7.     enp7s0:
8.       dhcp4: no
9.       addresses: [10.33.33.2/24]
10.  version: 2
11. mahe@hrb-demo:~$
```

This is the **netplan** config, where the settings for the network card are added. Now, activate your config with the following command:

```
1. mahe@hrb-demo:~$ sudo netplan apply
```

You can verify it works with the following command:

```
1. mahe@hrb-demo:~$ ip a
2. 1: lo: <LOOPBACK,UP,LOWER_UP> mtu 65536 qdisc noqueue state UNKNOWN
   group default qlen 1000
3.     link/loopback 00:00:00:00:00:00 brd 00:00:00:00:00:00
4.     inet 127.0.0.1/8 scope host lo
5.        valid_lft forever preferred_lft forever
6.     inet6 ::1/128 scope host
7.        valid_lft forever preferred_lft forever
8. 2: enp1s0: <BROADCAST,MULTICAST,UP,LOWER_UP> mtu 1500 qdisc fq_codel
   state UP group default qlen 1000
9.     link/ether 52:54:00:65:75:89 brd ff:ff:ff:ff:ff:ff
10.    inet 192.168.122.27/24 metric 100 brd 192.168.122.255 scope
   global dynamic enp1s0
11.       valid_lft 3599sec preferred_lft 3599sec
12.    inet6 fe80::5054:ff:fe65:7589/64 scope link
13.       valid_lft forever preferred_lft forever
```

```
14. 3: enp7s0: <BROADCAST,MULTICAST,UP,LOWER_UP> mtu 1500 qdisc fq_codel
    state UP group default qlen 1000
15.    link/ether 52:54:00:40:b1:16 brd ff:ff:ff:ff:ff:ff
16.    inet 10.33.33.2/24 brd 10.33.33.255 scope global enp7s0
17.       valid_lft forever preferred_lft forever
18.    inet6 fe80::5054:ff:fe40:b116/64 scope link
19.       valid_lft forever preferred_lft forever
```

We have created a new virtual network and connected our MAAS server to the new network. Now, it is time to set up MAAS to start using our network, so that we can install a server from the network.

Let us start by setting up the network range we want to use in our MAAS. Go to subnets and select the new subnet for 10.33.33.0 and create a new dynamic range. The dynamic part is essential, so MAAS can use the IP address for its DHCP server.

The following figure shows the settings for the range:

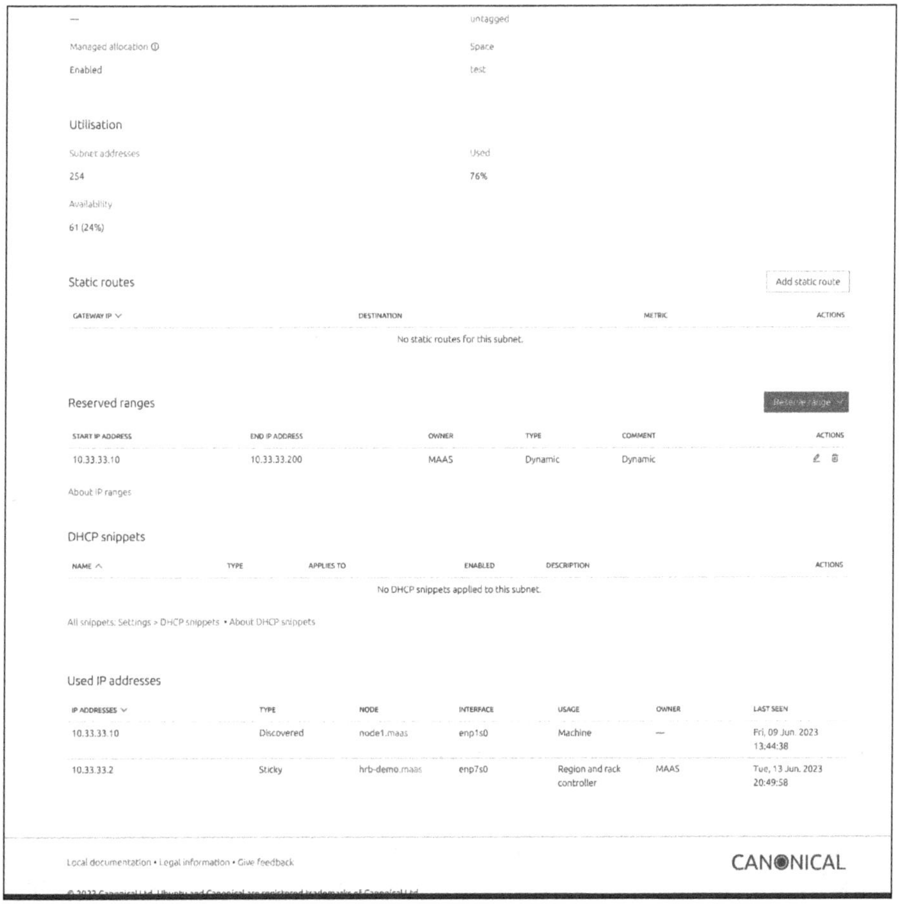

Figure 7.16: *MAAS Setup IP range in subnets*

Now, when we have the range, we can enable the internal MAAS DHCP server by going to the VLAN untagged and enabling the DHCP server. The following figure shows the enabled DHCPD server:

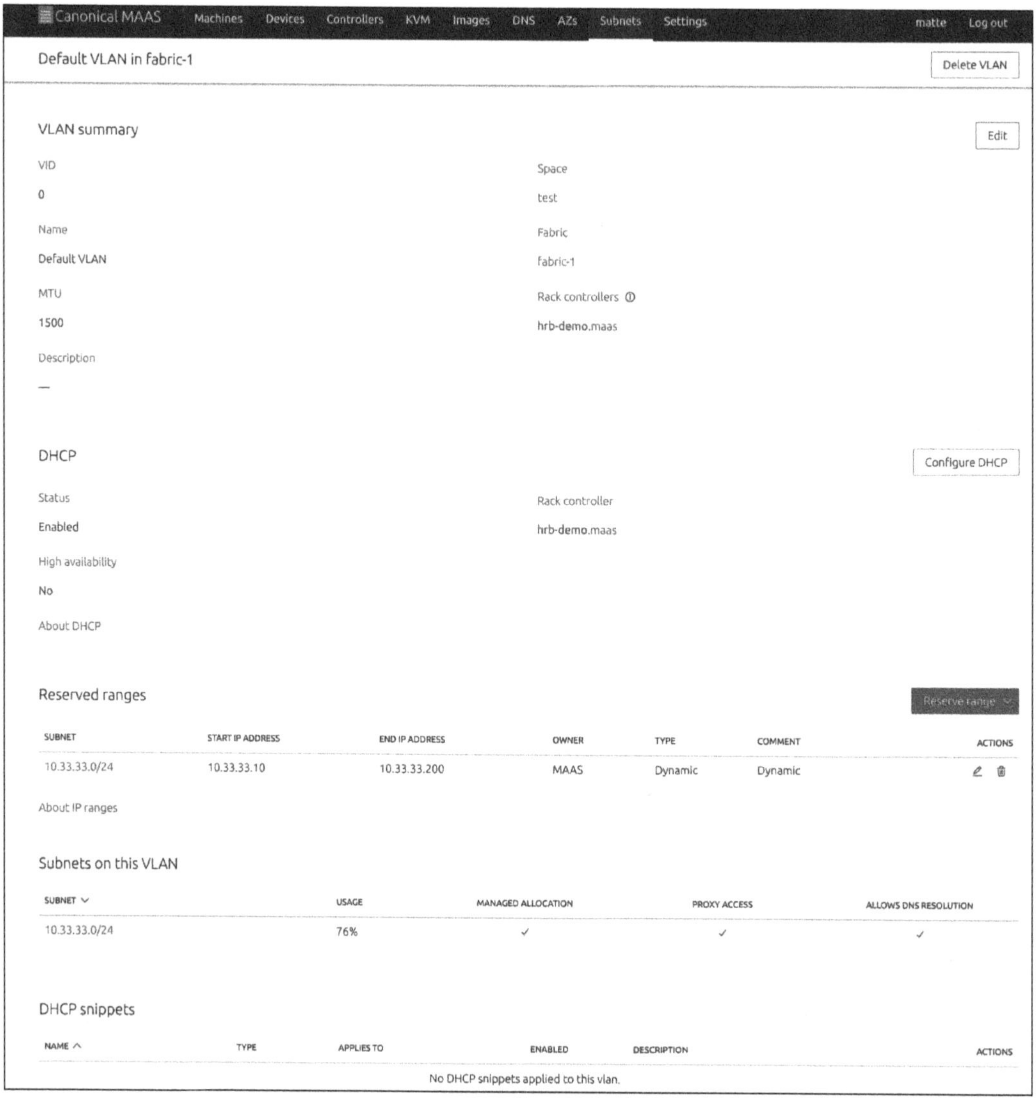

Figure 7.17: *MAAS VLAN default DHCP settings*

PXE installation on our server

To install our server, we first need to create our VM in KVM and set it to use our newly created KVM network. Then, we need to update the boot settings so that it will boot from the network. When we have our VM ready, we can log in to MAAS and register our VM by using the network, MAC.

The following figure shows our VM settings using KVM:

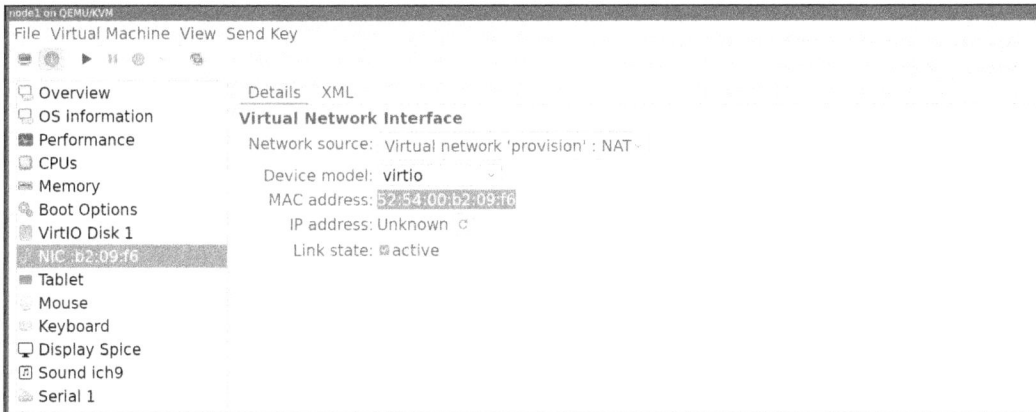

Figure 7.18: KVM network and MAC address marked

With the MAC address from our VM server, we create a new machine and add our MAC address to our server. Also, notice the power settings. Here, we set it to manual when we are controlling the power, as shown in the following figure:

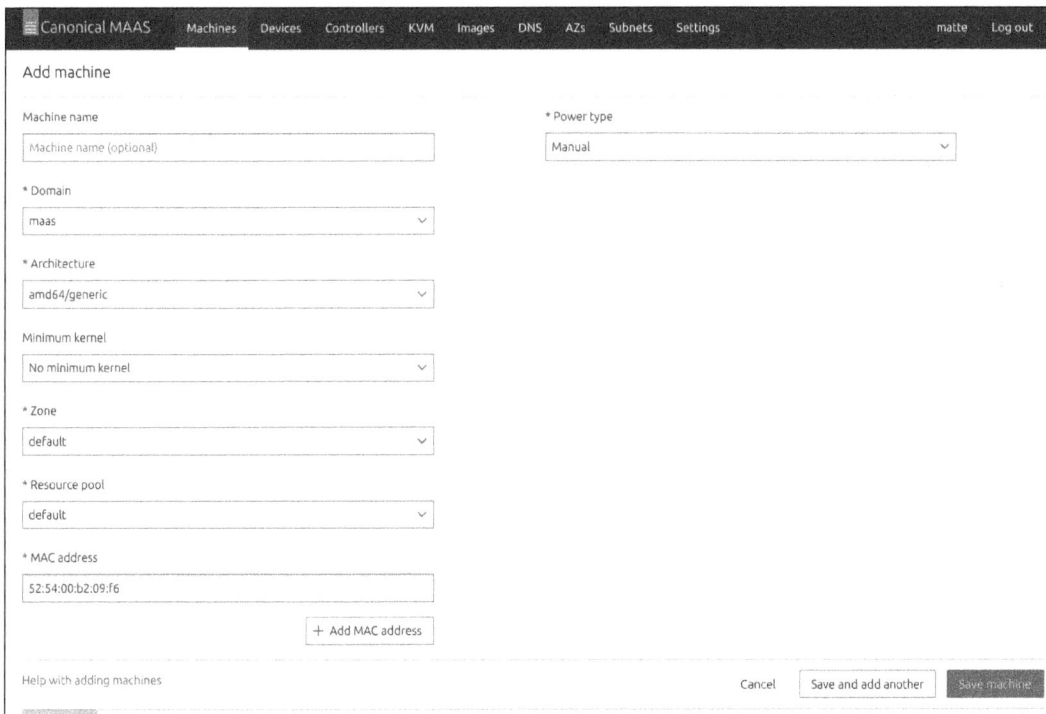

Figure 7.19: MAAS create new machine

Time to boot

Now you can boot your VM and follow the console log. When the installations are done, the VM will power off, and you will see the status for the machine changed to Ready. Take a look at the IP, and login into your new server. The default user can be different, but a good guess to start is Ubuntu. For more info, visit the MAAS webpage **https://maas.io/**.

More control

To control the power state, you can connect your MAAS to your KVM host. Then, MAAS can boot and prevent the server from the MAAS interface.

Conclusion

By the end of this chapter, we will understand how to install Ubuntu Server from a single server, using a USB drive or in a VM. You have also learned how to set up an Ubuntu Server in a cloud provider and large deployments of Ubuntu using the tool MAAS. With this, you now have the knowledge to plan and act on how and where you want to run your Ubuntu Server.

With this knowledge of how to install your server optimally, we can now proceed to setting up the server to maximize the benefits of our Ubuntu Server.

In the next chapter, we will understand how to monitor our Ubuntu Servers and collect and store logs.

Join our book's Discord space

Join the book's Discord Workspace for Latest updates, Offers, Tech happenings around the world, New Release and Sessions with the Authors:

https://discord.bpbonline.com

Keeping Check on Your Ubuntu Server

Introduction

When running your Ubuntu Server, it is essential to keep an eye on what is going on inside the server. We want to know if we have some issues with performance, so our memory or CPU goes up way high, monitor network performance to understand how much traffic our Ubuntu Server uses.

We also want to monitor our logs from our server to know everything is working as it should. Lastly, we want to look for any security issues. Any bad logins or processes that run on our server?

In this chapter, we will install different monitoring tools so that you can take control over a single Ubuntu Server or a farm of Ubuntu Servers. Monitor them to verify they all work as they should.

Structure

In the following chapter, we will cover the following topics:

- Commands for monitoring a Linux server
- Monitoring Ubuntu Server using Cockpit
- Monitoring Ubuntu Server data at scale
- Logs command

- Collecting and storing logs together
- Detecting hacking on your server

Objectives

By the end of this chapter, we will understand how to set up tools to monitor our server both as a single server and as a cluster. When we monitor our server, we will learn how to deploy tools that will read and send server metrics that we can then analyze and look at to verify our server status.

We will start by monitoring a single server but then move to a larger scale of deployments to understand how you can monitor many servers. Additionally, we will also look at collecting the logs from our server and storing them in a better way to be able to read logs from multiple servers at one location.

We will also understand how to deploy security tools and monitor server behavior so that we can detect and act on different security concerns that will happen.

Lastly, when our tools collect our data, we will set up alarms and notify us if our tools find any problems in our system.

Commands for monitoring a Linux server

Let us start with the most used command. You can type in your SSH shell on your server. It will be a good starting point when troubleshooting or monitoring.

However, we will not discuss the commands in detail.

Top

Top will print out the current state, and you can see the load and what process is eating the resources. The following is how the command is written:

```
1. top
```

Netstat

Netstat shows what connections are being used by the bean. There are many different arguments you can pass to **Netstat**; the following can be used first:

```
1. Netstat -anp
```

lsof

It shows you what files are used in the system at the moment.

```
1. lsof
```

du

There are times the server runs out of disk. The command to get the size of the folder and resolve the issue is as follows:

1. *Du-h —max-depth=1*

Monitoring Ubuntu Server using Cockpit

Cockpit is a web-based tool that can help you monitor and administrate your Ubuntu Server from a web page. You can install Cockpit on the server, and then we can log in and control it from our browser.

Install the **cockpit** using our CLI, with the following command:

```
. /etc/os-release
sudo apt install -t ${VERSION_CODENAME}-backports cockpit
```

Let the installation go, and then you will find the Cockpit WebGUI at the following website, **https://IP:9090**.

You can log in with the username on the server. From here, you can now see metrics and data on how your server will behave. You can also see logs.

Cockpit can also connect to more servers, and you can add them so it can configure the vm and container instances for you.

For all the settings, visit the Cockpit home page to find out more:

https://cockpit-project.org/

Monitoring Ubuntu Server data at scale

When we have more servers or want more visibility, we can install other tools that can combine metrics and logs. Now, we will have one or several Ubuntu Servers and then will all send the metrics and logs into one central place.

This gives us one single pane where we can monitor our server pool. Several tools can do this, but we will specifically work on the Grafana stack.

We will set up a Grafana instance on one of our servers. Then, we will deploy collector nodes on the server we want to monitor. The collector nodes will get metrics and logs and send them to our Grafana instance.

From there, we can see all our data, and we can also trigger alarms if something goes wrong.

Installing Grafana on Ubuntu

Grafana is our tool to search and visualize data. It has a small database for users and Graf, but the big thing with Grafana is that it can connect to several different backends and databases, and we can then use Grafana to visualize our data.

We will start by installing Grafana on our server, and we will move back out to our other server and install the tools we need to send data to be shown in Grafana.

The following command is used to install Grafana into our Ubuntu Server:

1. `#Adding grafana key`
2. `sudo wget -q -O /usr/share/keyrings/grafana.key https://apt.grafana.com/gpg.key`
3. `#Adding grafana repos`
4. `echo "deb [signed-by=/usr/share/keyrings/grafana.key] https://apt.grafana.com stable main" | sudo tee -a /etc/apt/sources.list.d/grafana.list`
5. `#Update our repo to get the grafana packeges`
6. `apt update`
7. `#Install grafana`
8. `apt install grafana`
9.

When Grafana is installed, we may need to restart it by using the following command:

1. `systemctl restart grafana-server`

Now you can login into Grafana by visiting **http://IP:3000** and use the username admin and password admin.

The first thing you need to do is change your password.

Visualizing your metrics with Grafana

Grafana is a tool to show data from several databases, and for us to display our metrics from our Ubuntu Server. We need a database to store the server's data in.

There are several to pick from, and it can be good to look around and find the database for your needs.

For us now, we will use Prometheus for storing our metrics.

Prometheus has no Ubuntu package, so we need to take some steps before we can start it.

Note: Remember the scripts are located in this book's Git Repo.

Another good idea is to install Prometheus with Docker, which is covered in Docker on the server section in this book.

Let us get started installing Prometheus by running the following code:

```
1.  #Adding user and group
2.  sudo groupadd --system prometheus
3.  sudo useradd -s /sbin/nologin --system -g prometheus prometheus
4.  #Making folders
5.  sudo mkdir /var/lib/prometheus
6.  sudo mkdir /etc/prometheus/
7.  sudo mkdir /etc/prometheus/rules
8.  sudo mkdir /etc/prometheus/rules.d
9.  sudo mkdir /etc/prometheus/files_sd
10. #Now lets download and install prometheus
11. cd /tmp
12. curl -s https://api.github.com/repos/prometheus/prometheus/releases/
    latest | grep browser_download_url | grep linux-amd64 | cut -d '"'
    -f 4 | wget -qi -
13. tar xvf prometheus*.tar.gz
14. cd prometheus*/
15. sudo mv prometheus promtool /usr/local/bin/
16. sudo mv prometheus.yml /etc/prometheus/prometheus.yml
17. sudo mv consoles/ console_libraries/ /etc/prometheus/
```

We now installed the default config and moved the correct binaries to the right location. Now, we want to make a start file so that when Ubuntu starts, Prometheus also starts. We also need to control it using our **systemd** tool.

For that, we create a Prometheus file and add it to the **systemd** folder, shown as follows:

```
1.  sudo tee /etc/systemd/system/prometheus.service<<EOF
2.  [Unit]
3.  Description=Prometheus
4.  Documentation=https://prometheus.io/docs/introduction/overview/
5.  Wants=network-online.target
6.  After=network-online.target
7.
8.  [Service]
9.  Type=simple
10. User=prometheus
11. Group=prometheus
12. ExecReload=/bin/kill -HUP \$MAINPID
13. ExecStart=/usr/local/bin/prometheus \
14.    --config.file=/etc/prometheus/prometheus.yml \
15.    --storage.tsdb.path=/var/lib/prometheus \
16.    --web.console.templates=/etc/prometheus/consoles \
17.    --web.console.libraries=/etc/prometheus/console_libraries \
```

```
18.    --web.listen-address=0.0.0.0:9090 \
19.    --web.external-url=
20.
21. SyslogIdentifier=prometheus
22. Restart=always
23.
24. [Install]
25. WantedBy=multi-user.target
26. EOF
```

Let us activate our startup file and set some permission, and then we are ready to start Prometheus, shown as follows:

```
1. #Set some permissions
2. for i in rules rules.d files_sd; do sudo chown -R
   prometheus:prometheus /etc/prometheus/${i}; done
3. for i in rules rules.d files_sd; do sudo chmod -R 775 /etc/
   prometheus/${i}; done
4. sudo chown -R prometheus:prometheus /var/lib/prometheus/
5. #Enable prometeus
6. sudo systemctl daemon-reload
7. sudo systemctl start prometheus
8. sudo systemctl enable prometheus
```

Note: Prometheus Lissen on port 9090, that are the same port as the Cockpit that we installed before, are listed. If you have them on separate servers, then its ok else we need to turn Cockpit off.

You can disable **cockpit** with the following command:

```
1. systemctl stop cockpit.socket
2. systemctl disable cockpit.socket
```

Now, you can browse to Prometheus using your browser by visiting the following:

http://IP:9090.

Pushing data vs. pulling data

When we have our time series database (Prometheus) running, we need to add data to it. To add data, there are two different ways. One way is that the client pushes data into the database. This is an example of the default way when sending logs or metrics from one server to another. It is also easy if the client's example is behind a gateway. Then, you only need to open traffic out, and the client can send data.

The other way is that you have clients with an endpoint showing data. Your database goes to the clients, scrapes that client data, and then adds them into it. This is how Prometheus works.

You can setup Prometheus to collect and then send data also but that's outside our setup.

Installing Node Exporter to export server data

Node Exporter is a tool from the same company as Prometheus, and the installation is the same as with Prometheus. Node Exporter will then connect to the Linux system and export metrics on an endpoint. We will, then, set up Prometheus to scrape the Node Exporter on a regular basis.

The installations are done in a similar way to Prometheus. During the capture on containers, you will learn how to install node exporter with the container. Now, let us install using this way

Go to your **/tmp** folder and download Node Exporter. We will then unpack it and move it to the right places, shown as follows:

```
1.  #Download and unpack nodeexporter
2.  https://github.com/prometheus/node_exporter/releases/download/
    v1.6.0/node_exporter-1.6.0.linux-amd64.tar.gz
3.  tar zxvf node_exporter-1.6.0.linux-amd64.tar.gz
4.
5.  #Copy the nodeexporter to bin
6.  cd node_exporter-1.6.0.linux-amd64
7.  sudo cp node_exporter /usr/local/bin
8.  #Create a user and set permissions
9.  sudo useradd --no-create-home --shell /bin/false node_exporter
10. sudo chown node_exporter:node_exporter /usr/local/bin/node_exporter
```

When we have the bin in the right place and have set up the user, we can make our startup script and enable it by following the given steps:

1. Create a **systemd** service file by running the following command:

    ```
    1.  sudo nano /etc/systemd/system/node_exporter.service
    ```

2. Now, add the following content to the file, shown as follows:

    ```
    1.  [Unit]
    2.  Description=Node Exporter
    3.  Wants=network-online.target
    4.  After=network-online.target
    5.
    6.  [Service]
    7.  User=node_exporter
    8.  Group=node_exporter
    9.  Type=simple
    10. ExecStart=/usr/local/bin/node_exporter
    11.
    12. [Install]
    13. WantedBy=multi-user.target
    ```

3. Now, we can enable the service and start it by running the following command:

```
1. systemctl daemon-reload
2. systemctl start node_exporter
3. systemctl enable node_exporter
```

Now, when we have it tested, we can verify that we have some values. As we were using a pull service here, we can use **curl** to fetch data from the Node Exporter, shown as follows:

```
1.  root@g1:/# curl -v http://127.0.0.1:9100/metrics
2.  *   Trying 127.0.0.1:9100...
3.  * Connected to 127.0.0.1 (127.0.0.1) port 9100 (#0)
4.  > GET /metrics HTTP/1.1
5.  > Host: 127.0.0.1:9100
6.  > User-Agent: curl/7.81.0
7.  > Accept: */*
8.  >
9.  * Mark bundle as not supporting multiuse
10. < HTTP/1.1 200 OK
11. < Content-Type: text/plain; version=0.0.4; charset=utf-8
12. < Date: Wed, 28 Jun 2023 20:16:15 GMT
13. < Transfer-Encoding: chunked
14. <
15. # HELP go_gc_duration_seconds A summary of the pause duration
    of garbage collection cycles.
16. # TYPE go_gc_duration_seconds summary
17. go_gc_duration_seconds{quantile="0"} 0
18. go_gc_duration_seconds{quantile="0.25"} 0
19. go_gc_duration_seconds{quantile="0.5"} 0
20. go_gc_duration_seconds{quantile="0.75"} 0
21. go_gc_duration_seconds{quantile="1"} 0
22. go_gc_duration_seconds_sum 0
```

It will print a lot more data from your server.

Combining tools to visualize the data

Now, we have the tools we need, and Grafana will show the graphs. Prometheus will collect and store our metrics. We have Node Exporter that will find and expose our metrics. Now, we need to connect them all. Let us start getting Prometheus to get data from our Node Exporter.

Open the Prometheus config file and add a scraper for our new Node Exporter, as shown in the following code:

```
1.  root@g1:/# vi /etc/prometheus/prometheus.yml
2.
3.    - job_name: "g1"
```

```
4.        # metrics_path defaults to '/metrics'
5.        # scheme defaults to 'http'.
6.        static_configs:
7.           - targets: ["localhost:9100"]
8.
9.  root@g1:/# systemctl restart prometheus
10.
```

Here, we tell Prometheus to add a new job getting data from a target. We set the target to localhost:9100. Here, we will be running a known Node Exporter on the same host as Prometheus. If you have installed the Node Exporter on another host, then update it to match the node.

When the installation is done, you can reload Prometheus, and go to the Prometheus webpage to verify the targets are connected by going to the following web page:

http://IP:9090/targets?search=

Now, we can connect our Grafana to our Prometheus and get the metrics. Let us login into Grafana and add a new data source. Choose Prometheus as kind and save as shown in following figure:

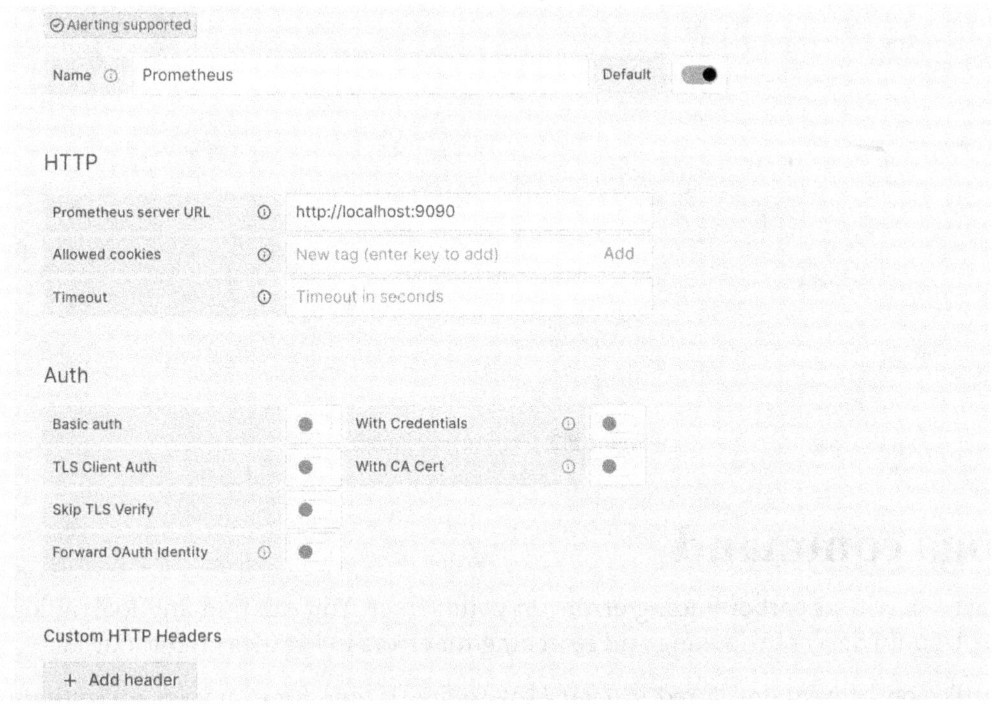

Figure 8.1: Grafana data source Prometheus

Grafana will test the connection and then save the data source. We have now connected our tree components.

Grafana dashboards

Grafana has an online service where you can upload your own set of dashboards and also download others.

For the most common tools, like the Node Exporter, there are premade dashboards.

So, in our Grafana, we will now set up the premade dashboard for Node Exporter and use the data source of Prometheus.

To do so, go to and import dashboards we can now past the id if 1860 found from **https:// grafana.com/grafana/dashboards/**.

Now, Grafana will download the dashboard and set all up for you.

When the dashboard is downloaded, you will see graphs showing up at once, as shown in the following figure:

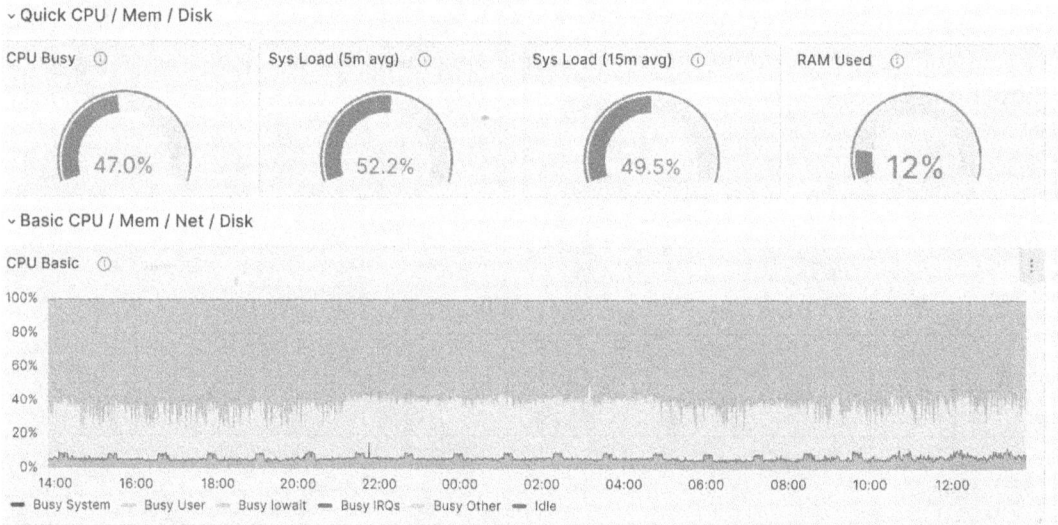

Figure 8.2: Grafana host metrics

Logs command

Logs are a critical part of finding errors on your server. You can find and look at logs on your Ubuntu Server by looking and searching for errors in log files on the journal.

Log files on Ubuntu are stored in **/var/log** folder. If you, for example, are setting up a web server that will have a lot of traffic and you want to save all the access logs.

During the installation giving the path **/var/log** its disk can be a good choice.

You can run the following command to search in the log files:

```
tail -f /var/log/syslog
```

This will follow and file and print all the events from the file

If you combined the **tail** command with a **grep** you can also get all the errors, as shown in the following command:

```
tail -f /var/log/syslog | grep "error"
```

Collecting and storing logs together

When you take a look at logs, you would want all logs in one place to easily place them. There are many tools that can help you set up logs in this way.

Loki is one tool that can be used, together with Grafana, to see logs and metrics on Grafana. The setup is similar but uses other components. Elasticsearch and Kibana is another tool set that can be used.

For this, we will show how to set up Filebeat, Elasticsearch, and Kibana.

Let us add the repos from Elasticsearch and install the tools. Then, run the following commands:

1. `sudo apt-get install apt-transport-https`
2. `wget -qO - https://artifacts.elastic.co/GPG-KEY-elasticsearch | sudo gpg --dearmor -o /usr/share/keyrings/elasticsearch-keyring.gpg`
3. `echo "deb [signed-by=/usr/share/keyrings/elasticsearch-keyring.gpg] https://artifacts.elastic.co/packages/8.x/apt stable main" | sudo tee /etc/apt/sources.list.d/elastic-8.x.list`
4. `sudo apt-get update && sudo apt-get install elasticsearch kibana filebeat`

This will install the tools we need. When the installation is done, we can connect the tool as we did before. However, here we are using a push service, and we will start by pushing logs and metrics to Elasticsearch from Filebeat. Then, connect Kibana to visualize the data for us.

Let us start setup Elasticsearch and Kibana before we start sending logs.

Now, let us update the **elastic** password using the following command:

1. `/usr/share/elasticsearch/bin/elasticsearch-reset-password -u elastic`

Then, we can visit the **elasticsearch** page at **https://IP:9200**.

You will only see a JSON output. Let us start Kibana, and to connect Kibana with Elasticsearch, we need to make some changes. First, let us set Kibana to listen on all interfaces so we can connect from our laptop to our server by following the given steps:

1. Open the file by running the following command:

    ```
    1. vi /etc/kibana/kibana.yml
    ```

2. Now, set server to the IP of your server and the path to **elasticsearch**. The server host is such that **kibana** starts to listen on all IP and not only localhost. This is so that you can connect from any host to your **kibana** by changing the following values in the config file:

    ```
    1. server.host: 192.168.1.11
    2. elasticsearch.hosts: ['https://10.0.0.3:9200']
    ```

3. Then, restart **kibana**. Get the token from **elasticsearch** and paste it into **kibana**, shown as follows:

    ```
    1. /usr/share/elasticsearch/bin/elasticsearch-create-enrollment-
       token -s kibana
    ```

4. Now, **kibana** wants to add a auth number and you can add that into your **kibana** to verify we have access to our **kibana** server, shown as follows:

    ```
    1. /usr/share/kibana/bin/kibana-verification-code
    ```

5. When Kibana gets the verification number, it will restart, and you will get to a login page. Now, login with your elastic server we reset the password for earlier.

You should now have access and can look around in **kibana** when it is connected to Elasticsearch. However, we do not have any data in there now, so let us add our Filebeat to read the logs from our server and send them to Elasticsearch.

When Filebeat sends logs to Elasticsearch, it sends the logs over TLS. However, here we do not have a valid certificate. So, before we can start, we need to setup Filebeat to use our Elasticsearch certificate.

We will set Filebeat to listen for syslog server on UDP and TCP port. We will use this later to connect other appliances, like a firewall or switch to sending logs into our Filebeat. Then, the logs will be transferred to Elasticsearch.

We also set up **filebeat** to get all the logs from our journal in Ubuntu. This will pick up any logs and send them on to Elasticsearch.

The following code snippet is how our **filebeat** input looks like:

```
1. filebeat.inputs:
        - type: syslog
2. format: rfc3164
3. protocol.udp:
4. host: "192.168.1.11:514"
        - type: syslog
5. format: rfc3164
6. protocol.tcp:
```

```
7.  host: "192.168.1.11:514"
8.  # Each - is an input. Most options can be set at the input level, so
9.  # you can use different inputs for various configurations.
10. # Below are the input specific configurations.
        - type: journald
11. id: journal
12. # filestream is an input for collecting log messages from files.
        - type: filestream
13. # Unique ID among all inputs, an ID is required.
14. id: logfiles
15. # Change to true to enable this input configuration.
16. enabled: false
17. # Paths that should be crawled and fetched. Glob based paths.
18. paths:
        - /var/log/*.log
19. #- c:\programdata\elasticsearch\logs\*
```

Note: The https and the ssl cert. As you see we are using the elastic user, which is not the most secure.

We now need an output that sends data to our **elasticsearch**, shown as follows:

```
1.  output.elasticsearch:
2.  # Array of hosts to connect to.
3.  hosts: ["192.168.1.11:9200"]
4.  # Protocol - either `http` (default) or `https`.
5.  protocol: "https"
6.  # Authentication credentials - either API key or username/password.
7.  #api_key: "id:api_key"
8.  username: "elastic"
9.  password: "uJg_KlBcreLc_vP-"
10. ssl.certificate_authorities: ["/etc/elasticsearch/certs/http_ca.crt"]
```

Let us start our **filebeat**. The first step is to setup Elasticsearch by running the following command:

```
1.  filebeat setup -e
```

Then, we can verify our **filebeat** is working by running the following command:

```
1.  filebeat setup -e
```

When everything looks good, and **filebeat** does not crash we can start it with the following command:

```
1.  systemctl restart filebeat.
```

Now, **filebeat** is sending logs into our **elasticsearch**, before we can see the logos, we need to set up a **kibana** view. In **kibana**, go to **Stack Management** | **Data View**, and create a new view, as shown in the following figure:

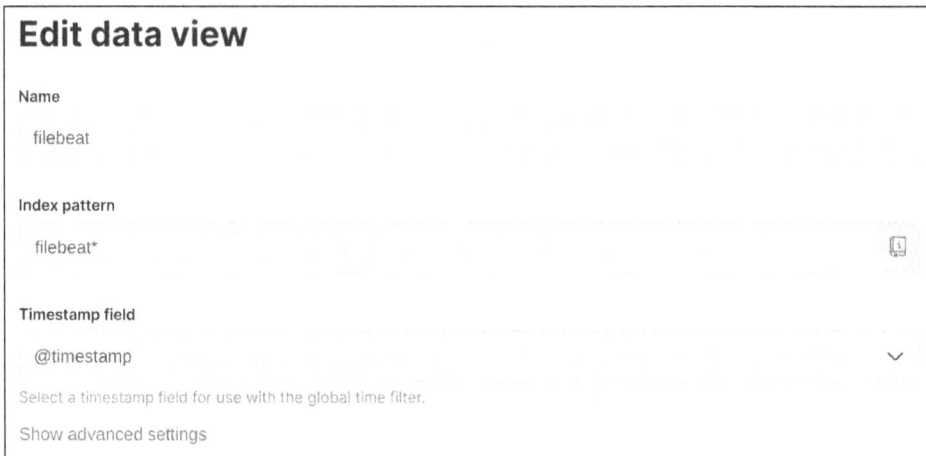

Figure 8.3: *Kibana data view for filebeat index*

Now, when we have an index, we can see and search in our logs in the following figure. We have searched for **error** in my stack, as follows:

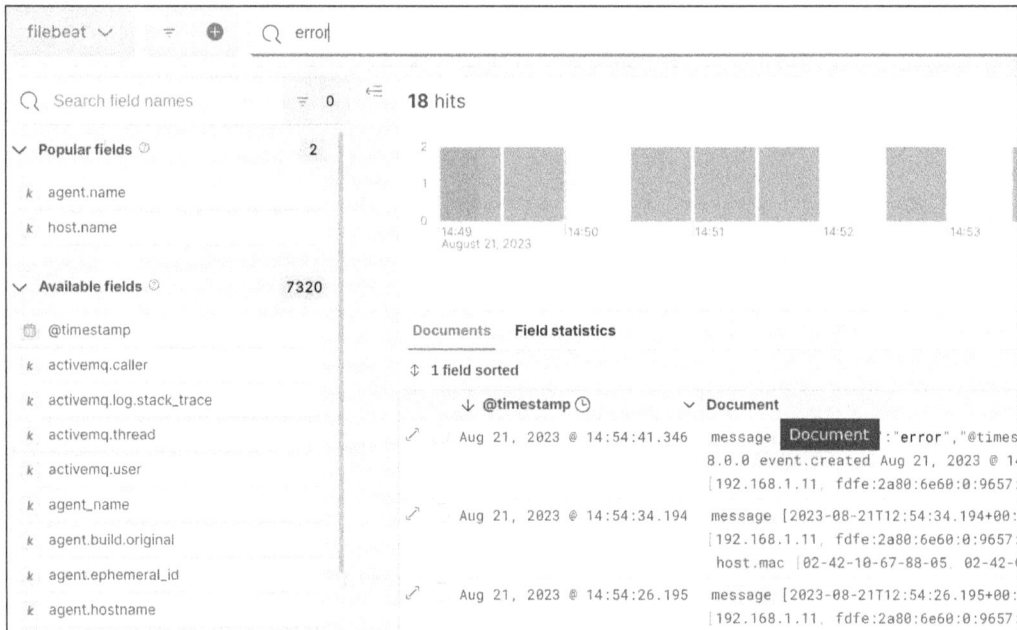

Figure 8.4: *Show Kibana search for error*

Detecting hacking on your server

Securing your Ubuntu Server is important. We want to detect if someone is trying to ssh into our server or if some unexpected programs start to run. To do this, we will use different tools. The first is the ssh brute tool (**fail2ban**). It will detect if there are many fault logins on ssh and then take actions like blocking the source IP of the attacker.

We will then move on to a more advanced tool called **Host Intrusion Detecting System** (**HIDS**) called **OSSEC**. OSSEC is both a server and a client. The clients report to the server, which can then take actions. You can build custom responses to actions. We will also pass all the logs from our OSSEC server to our Elasticsearch.

Fail2Ban

We can install **fail2ban** using our package manager, as shown in the following command:

```
1. apt install fail2ban
```

Then, enable and start **fail2ban** by following the given code snippets:

```
1. root@g1:/etc/fail2ban# systemctl enable fail2ban
2. Synchronizing state of fail2ban.service with SysV service script
   with /lib/systemd/systemd-sysv-install.
3. Executing: /lib/systemd/systemd-sysv-install enable fail2ban
4. Created symlink /etc/systemd/system/multi-user.target.wants/
   fail2ban.service → /lib/systemd/system/fail2ban.service.
5. root@g1:/etc/fail2ban# systemctl start fail2ban
```

Let us now configure **fail2ban**. First, copy the **fail jail.conf** to **jail.local**, shown as follows:

```
1. cp jail.conf jail.local
```

Now, we can set our **fail2ban** to use **systemd** to open the file **jail.local** and edit the backend, shown as follows:

```
1. backend = system
```

Then, we can restart **fail2ban** and tail the logs, shown as follows:

```
1. root@g1:/etc/fail2ban# systemctl restart fail2ban
2. root@g1:/etc/fail2ban# tail -f /var/log/fail2ban.log
3. 2023-08-14 13:19:49,374 fail2ban.jail          [282357]: INFO
   Creating new jail 'sshd'
4. 2023-08-14 13:19:49,393 fail2ban.jail          [282357]: INFO
   Jail 'sshd' uses systemd {}
5. 2023-08-14 13:19:49,394 fail2ban.jail          [282357]: INFO
   Initiated 'systemd' backend
6. 2023-08-14 13:19:49,396 fail2ban.filter        [282357]: INFO
   maxLines: 1
7. 2023-08-14 13:19:49,426 fail2ban.filtersystemd [282357]: INFO    [sshd]
   Added journal match for: '_SYSTEMD_UNIT=sshd.service + _COMM=sshd'
8. 2023-08-14 13:19:49,426 fail2ban.filter        [282357]: INFO
   maxRetry: 5
```

9. `2023-08-14 13:19:49,426 fail2ban.filter          [282357]: INFO`
   `findtime: 600`

10. `2023-08-14 13:19:49,426 fail2ban.actions         [282357]: INFO`
   `banTime: 600`

11. `2023-08-14 13:19:49,426 fail2ban.filter          [282357]: INFO`
   `encoding: UTF-8`

12. `2023-08-14 13:19:49,430 fail2ban.jail             [282357]: INFO`
   `Jail 'sshd' started`

Now, from a client, do not use a computer that needs access to the server to log in using the wrong password. When trying to log in after entering the wrong password, your IP will be blocked for a time.

It is good practice to test **fail2ban** to verify its working as follows:

```
[mattias@base:~/projects/hrb/book/images$ tail -f /var/log/fail2ban.log
2025-05-16 11:24:20,959 fail2ban.jail        [3245506]: INFO    Creating new jail 'sshd'
2025-05-16 11:24:21,026 fail2ban.jail        [3245506]: INFO    Jail 'sshd' uses pyinotify {}
2025-05-16 11:24:21,030 fail2ban.jail        [3245506]: INFO    Initiated 'pyinotify' backend
2025-05-16 11:24:21,030 fail2ban.filter      [3245506]: INFO      maxLines: 1
2025-05-16 11:24:21,039 fail2ban.filter      [3245506]: INFO      maxRetry: 5
2025-05-16 11:24:21,039 fail2ban.filter      [3245506]: INFO      findtime: 600
2025-05-16 11:24:21,039 fail2ban.actions     [3245506]: INFO      banTime: 600
2025-05-16 11:24:21,039 fail2ban.filter      [3245506]: INFO      encoding: UTF-8
2025-05-16 11:24:21,039 fail2ban.filter      [3245506]: INFO    Added logfile: '/var/log/auth.log' (pos = 0, hash =
2025-05-16 11:24:21,041 fail2ban.jail        [3245506]: INFO    Jail 'sshd' started


2025-05-16 11:25:12,736 fail2ban.filter      [3245506]: INFO    [sshd] Found 192.168.1.20 - 2025-05-16 11:25:12
2025-05-16 11:25:18,883 fail2ban.filter      [3245506]: INFO    [sshd] Found 192.168.1.20 - 2025-05-16 11:25:18
2025-05-16 11:25:22,574 fail2ban.filter      [3245506]: INFO    [sshd] Found 192.168.1.20 - 2025-05-16 11:25:22
2025-05-16 11:25:27,310 fail2ban.filter      [3245506]: INFO    [sshd] Found 192.168.1.20 - 2025-05-16 11:25:26
2025-05-16 11:25:28,160 fail2ban.filter      [3245506]: INFO    [sshd] Found 192.168.1.20 - 2025-05-16 11:25:28
2025-05-16 11:25:28,261 fail2ban.actions     [3245506]: NOTICE  [sshd] Ban 192.168.1.20
```

Figure 8.5: fail2ban detect fail to login and blocks ip

Setting up a HIDS

OSSEC is a HIDS that will keep your Ubuntu Server secure. It is based on a server and clients. The client reports data to the server, which then can take action. Here, we will install both the client and the server on the same server. However, if you have more servers, you can install one server and then add only the client part to your other server. We will then send the OSSEC logs to our Elasticsearch using Filebeat to visualize them. If you are running many servers, it also may be good to look at the tool **Wazuh** (**https://wazuh.com/**).

When we install OSSEC using **apt-get**, we cannot have both the server and the client running at the same time.

To resolve this and have both the client and server on the same, we will download and set up an OSSEC manual, as shown in the following code snippet:

Note: Observe how we select Local as the installation type. This will set up both the server and agent for me.

1. apt-get install build-essential make zlib1g-dev libpcre2-dev libevent-dev libssl-dev libsystemd-dev # we need some deps on our server so we can build ossec
2. cd /opt
3. mkdir ossec
4. cd ossec
5. wget https://github.com/ossec/ossec-hids/archive/3.7.0.tar.gz
6. tar -zxvf 3.7.0.tar.gz
7. cd ossec-hids-3.7.0/
8. ./install.sh
9. OSSEC HIDS v3.7.0 Installation Script - http://www.ossec.net
10.
11. You are about to start the installation process of the OSSEC HIDS.
12. You must have a C compiler pre-installed in your system.
13.
14.   - System: Linux g1 5.15.0-78-generic
15.   - User: root
16.   - Host: g1
17.
18.
19.   -- Press ENTER to continue or Ctrl-C to abort. --
20.
21.
22. 1- What kind of installation do you want (server, agent, local, hybrid or help)? local
23.
24.   - Local installation chosen.
25.
26. 2- Setting up the installation environment.
27.
28. - Choose where to install the OSSEC HIDS [/var/ossec]:
29.
30.   - Installation will be made at /var/ossec .
31.
32. 3- Configuring the OSSEC HIDS.
33.
34.   3.1- Do you want e-mail notification? (y/n) [y]:
35.   - What's your e-mail address? matte.hemmingsson@gmail.com
36.
37.   - We found your SMTP server as: alt1.gmail-smtp-in.l.google.com.
38.   - Do you want to use it? (y/n) [y]:
39.
40.   --- Using SMTP server: alt1.gmail-smtp-in.l.google.com.

```
41.
42.    3.2- Do you want to run the integrity check daemon? (y/n) [y]:
43.
44.     - Running syscheck (integrity check daemon).
45.
46.    3.3- Do you want to run the rootkit detection engine? (y/n) [y]:
47.
48.     - Running rootcheck (rootkit detection).
49.
50.    3.4- Active response allows you to execute a specific
51.         command based on the events received. For example,
52.         you can block an IP address or disable access for
53.         a specific user.
54.         More information at:
55.         http://www.ossec.net/docs/docs/manual/ar/index.html
56.
57.     - Do you want to enable active response? (y/n) [y]:
58.
59.       - Active response enabled.
60.
61.     - By default, we can enable the host-deny and the
62.       firewall-drop responses. The first one will add
63.       a host to the /etc/hosts.deny and the second one
64.       will block the host on iptables (if linux) or on
65.       ipfilter (if Solaris, FreeBSD or NetBSD).
66.     - They can be used to stop SSHD brute force scans,
67.       portscans and some other forms of attacks. You can
68.       also add them to block on snort events, for example.
69.
70.     - Do you want to enable the firewall-drop response? (y/n) [y]:
71.
72.       - firewall-drop enabled (local) for levels >= 6
73.
74.      -
75.        - 127.0.0.53
76.
77.     - Do you want to add more IPs to the white list? (y/n)? [n]:
78.
79.    3.6- Setting the configuration to analyze the following logs:
80.     -- /var/log/dpkg.log
81.     -- /var/log/nginx/access.log (apache log)
82.     -- /var/log/nginx/error.log (apache log)
```

83.
84. - If you want to monitor any other file, just change
85.   the ossec.conf and add a new localfile entry.
86.   Any questions about the configuration can be answered
87.   by visiting us online at http://www.ossec.net .
88.
89.
90.   --- Press ENTER to continue ---

If you only plan to run the agent or the server, you can install OSSEC using **apt**, shown as follows:

1. wget -q -O - https://updates.atomicorp.com/installers/atomic | sudo bash
2. *# Update apt data*
3. sudo apt-get update
4. *# Server*
5. sudo apt-get install ossec-hids-server
6. *# Use this if you only want to have the agent Agent*
7. #sudo apt-get install ossec-hids-agent

OSSEC comes with its own command that you can control OSSEC. In the folder **/var/ossec/bin** you can find them.

Now, we restart our OSSEC server using the following command in the OSSEC **bin** folder:

1. root@g1:/var/ossec/bin# *./ossec-control restart*
2. Deleting PID file '/var/ossec/var/run/ossec-syscheckd-1504.pid' not used...
3. Deleting PID file '/var/ossec/var/run/ossec-analysisd-1413.pid' not used...
4. Killing ossec-monitord ..
5. Killing ossec-logcollector ..
6. ossec-remoted not running ..
7. ossec-syscheckd not running ..
8. ossec-analysisd not running ..
9. ossec-maild not running ..
10. Killing ossec-execd ..
11. OSSEC HIDS v3.7.0 Stopped
12. Starting OSSEC HIDS v3.7.0...
13. 2023/08/16 11:50:29 ossec-maild: INFO: E-Mail notification disabled. Clean Exit.
14. Started ossec-maild...
15. Started ossec-execd...
16. Started ossec-analysisd...

```
17. Started ossec-logcollector...
18. Started ossec-remoted...
19. Started ossec-syscheckd...
20. Started ossec-monitord...
21. Completed.
22. root@g1:/var/ossec/bin#
```

To list all connected agents, run the following command:

```
1. root@g1:/var/ossec/bin# ./agent_control -L
2. OSSEC HIDS agent_control. List of available agents:
3.    ID: 000, Name: g1 (server), IP: 127.0.0.1, Active/Local
4. List of agentless devices:
5. root@g1:/var/ossec/bin#
```

As shown in the preceding command, the local agents are connected.

OSSEC logs its action into two logs, the **ossec.log**, and then if it does an active response in the active-response.log. Both these logs are located in the **/var/ossec/logs** folder. All alerts are logged to the alerts.log file in **/var/ossec/logs/alerts**.

Sending OSSEC logs with Filebeat to Elasticsearch

To detect and monitor our OSSEC, we can set up a Filebeat to read logs from our OSSEC server and send them to our Elasticsearch.

First, let us set our OSSEC server to log into JSON format by adding the following in the command:

```
1. <global>
2.   <jsonout_output>yes</jsonout_output>
3. </global>
```

In our **/var/ossec/etc/ossec.conf**, restart the OSSEC server to activate.

Then, edit our Filebeat config file and add using the following command:

```
1. - input_type: log
2.   paths:
3.     - /var/ossec/logs/alerts/alerts.json
4.   json.keys_under_root: true
5.   fields: {log_type: osseclogs}
```

Then, restart your Filebeat.

Now, we need to watch the file to see if any alerts will come up. Then, we can find them in our Elasticsearch.

Search for **ossec** in your Kibana to find the logs.

Conclusion

In this chapter, we understood how to monitor and secure one or many Ubuntu Servers.

We have set up tools to send metrics from our server to a central place where we can visualize and add alerts. We have also set up to collect logs from our server and store them in a time-series database so that we can see logs from all our servers in a timely order.

When we monitor, we want to have all the data in one place to track and monitor movements between servers or services. Monitoring for security is also important, and we have, during this chapter, set up tools that not only will alert us when it detects bad behavior but also fight back the attacker.

We now have a good base to stand on to monitor our Ubuntu Server going forward.

In the next chapter, we will work with the Ubuntu firewall and network. We will set up our Ubuntu Server as a router and use services like DHCP and DNS. We will also look at setting up our own VPN servers so that we can connect from our Ubuntu Desktop to our server and local network from the Internet.

Join our book's Discord space

Join the book's Discord Workspace for Latest updates, Offers, Tech happenings around the world, New Release and Sessions with the Authors:

https://discord.bpbonline.com

CHAPTER 9

Setup Advanced Network, Firewall, and VPN Servers

Introduction

Ubuntu Server can be used as a regular firewall. Additionally, in some cases, it performs better than any shell firewall.

In this chapter, we will use Ubuntu as the primary firewall to control what traffic can come in and out of the network. We will set up our own DHCP server and control what IP addresses clients will get and where they will go to get out on the internet. With a DNS server, we will set up and point domain names to the IP we want. Ubuntu also has the tools to set up secure tunnels between servers and clients to create a private network over the internet.

Structure

In this chapter, we will cover the following topics:

- Using Ubuntu as the main firewall
- Network clients with DHCP and DNS
- Securing communications
- VPN troubleshooting

Objectives

In this chapter, we will learn how to configure our Ubuntu Server as a firewall and control the traffic that can enter and exit our network. We will set up basic network tools, such as DHCP and DNS, to create a complete network that clients can use on both servers and desktops. We will also learn how to set up secure tunnels between our server and clients, creating our own private network.

Using Ubuntu as the main firewall

During the ten years of working at Fareoffice, we used a Linux firewall with iptables as our primary firewall for all traffic to our high-load sites. This would give us the ability to run a simple server with Linux to control our network, and when we needed any more tools and services, we could easily integrate them into our Linux server.

Now, let us set up our Ubuntu Server to have a public IP and then route traffic to our private network.

For this, we need two network devices, one for our external traffic and one for our private network.

On our server, we have one NIC connected using the IP 192.168.122.27, as shown by running the command IP, as follows:

```
1.  2: enp1s0: <BROADCAST,MULTICAST,UP,LOWER_UP> mtu 1500 qdisc fq_codel
    state UP group default qlen 1000
2.      link/ether 52:54:00:65:75:89 brd ff:ff:ff:ff:ff:ff
3.      inet 192.168.122.27/24 metric 100 brd 192.168.122.255 scope
    global dynamic enp1s0
4.         valid_lft 3291sec preferred_lft 3291sec
5.      inet6 fe80::5054:ff:fe65:7589/64 scope link
6.         valid_lft forever preferred_lft forever
```

Here, we will make a new virtual NIC with a new IP range to use for our network.

Ubuntu virtual NIC and VLAN

In Ubuntu, if we only have one network card on our server, we can add virtual NICs on that network card and clone it to a new one.

When we do an alias network card, it is a raw clone of the network card.

VLAN

VLAN is a network protocol that many switches support. Here, we can create new layers inside the network. Only the network card in the same layer can talk. If you are using

VLAN number 10, then only the network card connected to the same VLAN number 10 can communicate.

Setup network for routing

On our server, we have two physical network cards. Let us create one more, so we have three networks.

One is our public network, where we get an IP from, for example, our internet provider. The other NIC is our private one. Let us create one with a VLAN tag on that NIC.

Now, we have three networks that we can use on our setup. To set up the network, we use the Netplan tool. Then, we edit the file, be aware that the file can have different names on different installations, so look in the **netplan** folder:

/etc/netplan/ generated the name of the network config file. The file will have a different name depending on the Ubuntu and the network card (the name was **/etc/netplan/00-installer-config.yaml**), as shown:

```
1.  network:
2.    ethernets:
3.      enp1s0:
4.        dhcp4: true
5.      enp7s0:
6.        dhcp4: no
7.        addresses: [10.33.33.2/24]
8.    vlans:
9.        vlan.10:
10.           id: 10
11.           link: enp7s0
12.           addresses: [10.33.34.2/24]
13.   version: 2
14. ~
```

This is how the **netplan** config looks. We have a network card named enp1s0 using DHCD so we get an IP from our internet provider. On the network card **enp7s0** we have set a network of 10.33.33.2, and on that same network, we have set up a VLAN with tag 10 that has the IP of 10.33.34.2.

Let us apply our changes, as shown in the following code:

```
1.  root@hrb-demo:/home/mahe# netplan apply
2.  root@hrb-demo:/home/mahe# ip a
3.  1: lo: <LOOPBACK,UP,LOWER_UP> mtu 65536 qdisc noqueue state UNKNOWN
    group default qlen 1000
4.      link/loopback 00:00:00:00:00:00 brd 00:00:00:00:00:00
```

```
 5.     inet 127.0.0.1/8 scope host lo
 6.        valid_lft forever preferred_lft forever
 7.     inet6 ::1/128 scope host
 8.        valid_lft forever preferred_lft forever
 9. 2: enp1s0: <BROADCAST,MULTICAST,UP,LOWER_UP> mtu 1500 qdisc fq_codel
    state UP group default qlen 1000
10.     link/ether 52:54:00:65:75:89 brd ff:ff:ff:ff:ff:ff
11.     inet 192.168.122.27/24 metric 100 brd 192.168.122.255 scope
    global dynamic enp1s0
12.        valid_lft 3596sec preferred_lft 3596sec
13.     inet6 fe80::5054:ff:fe65:7589/64 scope link
14.        valid_lft forever preferred_lft forever
15. 3: enp7s0: <BROADCAST,MULTICAST,UP,LOWER_UP> mtu 1500 qdisc fq_codel
    state UP group default qlen 1000
16.     link/ether 52:54:00:40:b1:16 brd ff:ff:ff:ff:ff:ff
17.     inet 10.33.33.2/24 brd 10.33.33.255 scope global enp7s0
18.        valid_lft forever preferred_lft forever
19.     inet6 fe80::5054:ff:fe40:b116/64 scope link
20.        valid_lft forever preferred_lft forever
21. 4: vlan.11@enp7s0: <BROADCAST,MULTICAST,UP,LOWER_UP> mtu 1500 qdisc
    noqueue state UP group default qlen 1000
22.     link/ether 52:54:00:40:b1:16 brd ff:ff:ff:ff:ff:ff
23.     inet 10.33.34.2/24 brd 10.33.34.255 scope global vlan.11
24.        valid_lft forever preferred_lft forever
25.     inet6 fe80::5054:ff:fe40:b116/64 scope link
26.        valid_lft forever preferred_lft forever
27. root@hrb-demo:/home/mahe#
```

Now that we have our base network set up, we can start adding services like iptables, DHCPD, and DNS, which we will use later in this chapter.

Controlling traffic with iptables

Iptables is a tool we use to control traffic coming in and out of our server. There are three basic chains, the input/forward and output chains.

Now, we need to add rules to them all for setting up our router.

To set up our Ubuntu Server as a basic router and route traffic from our private network to our public, first, we need to set up our server to forward packages between our network cards. This is done by running the following code:

```
1. echo "1" > /proc/sys/net/ipv4/ip_forward
```

Now, we can make a simple script that sets up our router. If you search the internet, you will find that many firewall scripts for Ubuntu set up the same configuration. Here, we will give a simple example. If you plan to run this in production, search for a good script as a base on the internet.

Keeping you safe

Before you start editing firewall rules, set up a backup path to get access. It can be as simple as a screen, keyboard, or virtual console.

If you cannot set up a screen, a crontab rule that clears the iptables rules can be added.

The command, **iptables -F**, will clear all the rules, and adding that to a **crontab** will save you if you lock yourself out.

Add the following to **/etc/crontab**, as shown:

```
1. 00 1    * * *    root    iptables -F
```

Let us set up our firewall, create a new file called **fw.sh**, and add the following commands to that script. Then, you can simply apply them.

First, we need to add rules to forward the traffic from our different network cards.

```
1. iptables -t nat -A POSTROUTING -s 10.33.33.0/24 ! -d 10.33.33.0/24
   -j MASQUERADE
2. iptables -t nat -A POSTROUTING -s 10.330.34.0/24 ! -d 10.33.34.0/24
   -j MASQUERADE
3. iptables -A FORWARD -d 10.33.33.0/24 -o enp7s0 -m state --state
   RELATED,ESTABLISHED -j ACCEPT
4. iptables -A FORWARD -d 10.33.34.0/24 -o vlan.11@enp7s0 -m state
   --state RELATED,ESTABLISHED -j ACCEPT
5. iptables -A FORWARD -s 10.33.33.0/24 -i enp7s0 -j ACCEPT
6. iptables -A FORWARD -s 10.33.34.0/24 -i vlan.11@enp7s0 -j ACCEPT
```

It is essential that the IP and interfaces are correct when running the scripts.

The small script aforementioned is all that is needed to set up so that traffic can now go from your private network and out. However, now we also need to lock down our server so we cannot access any ports, for example, SSH, from the public network.

First, set the **INPUT** chain to block any traffic by default. Then, we can add the rules to allow incoming. (If you plan to ssh into your server, add the allow rules to allow ssh as the first row and then the following default block command)

The following code shows the rules that will allow traffic to some example ports:

```
1. #lo
2. iptables -A INPUT -i lo -j ACCEPT
3. #ssh
4. iptables -A INPUT -p tcp -m tcp --dport 22 -j ACCEPT
```

```
 5. #http
 6. iptables -A INPUT -p tcp -m tcp --dport 80 -j ACCEPT
 7. #https
 8. iptables -A INPUT -p tcp -m tcp --dport 443 -j ACCEPT
 9. # SSH from subnet
10. iptables -A INPUT -p tcp --dport 22 -s 192.168.0.0/16 -j ACCEPT
```

As you can see, you need to add the ports to be open. If you have any tools running on a different port, you can update the command with the port you need.

In the last line, you can also see a rule where we have added a subnet, so only clients from that subnet can access the port.

To use ssh inside your server, you also need to add some ports for traffic going out, as shown in the following code:

```
1. iptables -A OUTPUT -o lo -j ACCEPT
2. iptables -A OUTPUT -p tcp --sport 22 -m state --state ESTABLISHED -j
   ACCEPT
```

Some like to keep all output traffic open, and you can choose however you would like to move forward.

Now that we have our rules, we can set the default rule for the chains, as shown in the following code:

```
1. iptables -P INPUT DROP
2. iptables -P OUTPUT DROP
```

Now you should be able to set your Ubuntu Server or Desktop as a router and send traffic from a private network to a public network.

Network clients with DHCP and DNS

Now, when we have our router set up, it can transfer traffic from our private network out to our public network and can set up clients that can use the network. To set up the private network, we require two services. One is our HCPD server, which will hand out DHCP (IP address) to clients and connect them. The other service is a DNS server, allowing our clients in the network to resolve DNS names (such as **ubuntu.com**) and access the internet.

Many different tools perform this, however, here we use the tool **dnsmasq**. It can work both as a DHCPD server and a DNS server. This is why it is easy to use.

Let us start with installing **dnsmasq** on our Ubuntu Server by running the following code:

```
1. apt install dnsmasq
```

To set up our DNS server, we need some data to use. First, we need to have a network to which we will give our IP address. It needs to be a network we have set up a network card for.

You cannot send out IP on a range that you have no network card connected to.

When we configure our network card, we are using the range 10.33.33.0/24 and we sat our server that we will use as a router on the IP 10.33.33.2. We also plan to run our DNS server on the same host, so the DNS server for the network client will also be the same IP as the router 10.33.33.2.

When you set up your own network, you will need to update the address to match your setup.

To set up our **dnsmasq** server, open the file and run the following code:

```
1. vi /etc/dnsmasq.conf
```

In the config file aforementioned, notice the following settings:

```
1.  # Set the interface on which dnsmasq operates.
2.  # If not set, all the interfaces is used.
3.  #interface=vlan.11@eno1
4.
5.  # To disable dnsmasq's DNS server functionality.
6.  #port=0
7.
8.  # To enable dnsmasq's DHCP server functionality.
9.  dhcp-range=10.33.33.10,10.33.34.200,255.255.255.0,12h
10.
11. # Set static IPs of other PCs and the Router.
12. dhcp-host=3C:98:72:F9:14:D8,server,10.33.33.12,infinite
13.
14. # Set gateway as Router. Following two lines are identical.
15. dhcp-option=3,10.33.33.2
16.
17. # Set DNS server as Router.
18. dhcp-option=6,10.33.33.2
19.
20. #enable-tftp
21. #tftp-root=/var/lib/tftpboot
22. dhcp-match=set:bios,option:client-arch,0
23. dhcp-boot=tag:bios,undionly.kpxe
24. dhcp-match=set:efi32,option:client-arch,6
25. dhcp-boot=tag:efi32,ipxe.efi
26. dhcp-match=set:efibc,option:client-arch,7
27. dhcp-boot=tag:efibc,ipxe.efi
28. dhcp-match=set:efi64,option:client-arch,9
29. dhcp-boot=tag:efi64,ipxe.efi
30. dhcp-userclass=set:ipxe,iPXE
```

```
31. dhcp-boot=tag:ipxe,http://10.33.33.2:8081/boot.ipxe
32.
33. # Logging.
34. log-facility=/var/log/dnsmasq.log    # Logfile path.
35. log-async
36. log-queries # log queries.
37. log-dhcp     # log dhcp related messages.
```

In the config file aforementioned, notice the following settings:

```
1.  dhcp-range=10.33.33.10,10.33.34.200,255.255.255.0,12h
```

This is the range that tells **dnsmasq** to send out an IP address between 10.33.33.20 and 10.22.22.200. We leave some IPs for the server and others for my setup. However, it is up to you, as shown in the following command:

```
1.  dhcp-host=3C:98:72:F9:14:D8,server,10.33.33.12,infinite
```

We have one server that uses DHCP. However, we want it to have the same IP of 10.33.33.12 every time.

So, we can add this value and set a static host, as follows:

```
1.  # Set gateway as Router. Following two lines are identical.
2.  dhcp-option=3,10.33.33.2
3.
4.  # Set DNS server as Router.
5.  dhcp-option=6,10.33.33.2
```

These two lines will set the router to the server we had before setting up the router and to our DNS server. You do not need to add your own DNS server; instead, you can use a third-party DNS server, such as a Google or Cloudflare DNS server.

If we set up PXE to boot and install many servers, we need to set our the PXE settings in our DHCP Server, as shown. If not, we can skip the lines as follows:

```
1.  dhcp-match=set:bios,option:client-arch,0
2.  dhcp-boot=tag:bios,undionly.kpxe
3.  dhcp-match=set:efi32,option:client-arch,6
4.  dhcp-boot=tag:efi32,ipxe.efi
5.  dhcp-match=set:efibc,option:client-arch,7
6.  dhcp-boot=tag:efibc,ipxe.efi
7.  dhcp-match=set:efi64,option:client-arch,9
8.  dhcp-boot=tag:efi64,ipxe.efi
9.  dhcp-userclass=set:ipxe,iPXE
10. dhcp-boot=tag:ipxe,http://10.33.33.2:8081/boot.ipxe
```

Before we can start our DNS server, we need to disable Ubuntu's own DNS server and restart our own. The following are the commands to stop and disable it:

```
 1. # Disable ubuntu own dns server
 2. systemctl stop systemd-resolved
 3. systemctl disable systemd-resolved
 4. systemctl mask systemd-resolved
 5.
 6. # Restart dnsmasq
 7. systemctl restart dnsmasq
 8.
 9. # If error fix resolve.conf
10. rm /etc/resolv.cont
11. vi /etc/resolv.conf
12. cat /etc/resolv.con
13. #manual setup dns
14. namserver 1.1.1.1
```

DNS settings

Adding your own DNS record to your server is easy. Say that we want to direct the DNS name of **portal.com** to our server and router, we need to run the following code:

```
 1. root@g1:/home/mahe# cat /etc/hosts
 2. 127.0.0.1 localhost
 3. 127.0.1.1 g1
 4. 10.100.0.40 sidero-cp
 5. # The following lines are desirable for IPv6 capable hosts
 6. ::1     ip6-localhost ip6-loopback
 7. fe00::0 ip6-localnet
 8. ff00::0 ip6-mcastprefix
 9. ff02::1 ip6-allnodes
10. ff02::2 ip6-allrouters
11.
12.
13. 1.1.1.1 google.com
14. root@g1:/home/mahe#
```

In the file above, we can see that we have added our resolve file to point to **google.com** to the IP of 1.1.1.1. However, this is wrong.

When the connection was tested, it asked for the **google.com** IP address, and the reply indicated that **google.com** is located at IP 1.1.1.1, which is wrong, and the answer was read from my local DNS server, as shown in the following code:

```
 1. root@g1:/home/mahe# dig google.com @127.0.0.1
 2.
```

```
3. ; <<>> DiG 9.18.12-0ubuntu0.22.04.2-Ubuntu <<>> google.com
   @127.0.0.1
4. ;; global options: +cmd
5. ;; Got answer:
6. ;; ->>HEADER<<- opcode: QUERY, status: NOERROR, id: 13530
7. ;; flags: qr aa rd ra; QUERY: 1, ANSWER: 1, AUTHORITY: 0, ADDITIONAL:
   1
8.
9. ;; OPT PSEUDOSECTION:
10. ; EDNS: version: 0, flags:; udp: 1232
11. ;; QUESTION SECTION:
12. ;google.com.    IN A
13.
14. ;; ANSWER SECTION:
15. google.com.   0 IN A 1.1.1.1
16.
17. ;; Query time: 4 msec
18. ;; SERVER: 127.0.0.1#53(127.0.0.1) (UDP)
19. ;; WHEN: Mon Sep 11 12:13:18 UTC 2023
20. ;; MSG SIZE  rcvd: 55
```

Our server replies that google.com is located at 1.1.1.1:

```
1. root@g1:/home/mahe# dig google.com @127.0.0.1
```

The preceding command is a good tool to test the DNS server at the **@** point to your server, so you can update that to test the reply of your server and example offers. We can use it when changing the DNS server to validate that it gives the same responses.

This is the last bit for setting up a local network. We now have an Ubuntu Server that routes traffic from a private network to a public (Internet). We have set up a DHCPD server and DNS to help the clients in our private network use our router and go only to the Internet.

Securing communications

This section will examine how we can utilize security communications between two Ubuntu Linux systems. When we set up the VPN, we will have one server and then one or more clients connecting to that server. The communications are secure between the client and the server, and we can set up so that all the client traffic goes through the server. You can also use a VPN to connect to multiple locations over the public internet.

We will explore two solutions. First, OpenVPN, and then WireGuard VPN. They are both good VPNs. However, WireGuard is comparatively newer. We will connect a server with one or many clients. Depending on what you will use, pick the VPN that best suits your needs and has support for the devices you use.

OpenVPN

OpenVPN is the oldest of the two and can be found as a standard tool in many applications, both on servers and desktops. In *Chapter 4, Setting Up Firewall, VPN, and Wi-Fi Networks*, we understood how to set up an OpenVPN client to connect to a server.

Now, we will set up our OpenVPN server and then connect the client to that server. The server needs to be accessed over the internet, but for testing, you can run this in a local network as well.

OpenVPN is found in the standard Ubuntu repo and can be installed by running the following command:

```
1. apt install openvpn easy-rsa
```

When we set up the OpenVPN server and client, we use TLS certs to verify the client and the user. For that, we need to create certs that we can use. To make it easier, we will use the tool **easy-rsa** to generate the certs.

Let us create a folder in **/etc/pki** for **easy-rsa** and link the files we need into it by running the following code:

```
1. root@hrb-1 /etc/pki # mkdir easy-rsa
2. root@hrb-1 /etc/pki # cd easy-rsa/
3. root@hrb-1 /etc/pki/easy-rsa # ln -s /usr/share/easy-rsa/* .
4. root@hrb-1 /etc/pki/easy-rsa # ls
5. easyrsa  openssl-easyrsa.cnf  vars.example  x509-types
6. root@hrb-1 /etc/pki/easy-rsa #
```

Now, we have a folder where we can host our certs. Let us set up our first cert for the server.

Create a file called vars and add the following to that file:

```
1. root@hrb-1 /etc/pki/easy-rsa # vi vars
2. root@hrb-1 /etc/pki/easy-rsa # cat vars
3. set_var EASYRSA_ALGO "ec"
4. set_var EASYRSA_DIGEST "sha512"
5. root@hrb-1 /etc/pki/easy-rsa #
```

Now, we can set up our PKI server. We will use this base of certs to generate both server and client certs. Set up the **pki** with the command **./easyrsa init-pki** and build the CA, as shown in the following code:

```
1. root@hrb-1 /etc/pki/easy-rsa # ./easyrsa init-pki
2.
3. init-pki complete; you may now create a CA or requests.
4. Your newly created PKI dir is: /etc/pki/easy-rsa/pki
5.
6. root@hrb-1 /etc/pki/easy-rsa #
```

After the **init-pki** we can create our CA and remember that password, as shown in the following code:

```
1.  root@hrb-1 /etc/pki/easy-rsa # ./easyrsa build-ca
2.  Using SSL: openssl OpenSSL 3.0.2 15 Mar 2022 (Library: OpenSSL 3.0.2
    15 Mar 2022)
3.
4.  Enter New CA Key Passphrase:
5.  Re-Enter New CA Key Passphrase:
6.  You are about to be asked to enter information that will be
    incorporated
7.  into your certificate request.
8.  What you are about to enter is what is called a Distinguished Name
    or a DN.
9.  There are quite a few fields but you can leave some blank
10. For some fields there will be a default value,
11. If you enter '.', the field will be left blank.
12. -----
13. Common Name (eg: your user, host, or server name) [Easy-RSA CA]:
14.
15. CA creation complete and you may now import and sign cert requests.
16. Your new CA certificate file for publishing is at:
17. /etc/pki/easy-rsa/pki/ca.crt
18.
19. root@hrb-1 /etc/pki/easy-rsa #
```

Our PKI is now ready, and we can make our first cert for our OpenVPN server, as shown in the following code:

```
1.  root@hrb-1 /etc/pki/easy-rsa # ./easyrsa gen-req server nopass
2.  Using SSL: openssl OpenSSL 3.0.2 15 Mar 2022 (Library: OpenSSL 3.0.2
    15 Mar 2022)
3.  ..+.....+...+...+.............+.+.....+.+...+..+....++++++++++++++++++++++
    ++++++++++++++++++++++++++++++++++++++++++++++*..+.+.........++++++++++
    ++++++++++++++++++++++++++++++++++++++++++++++++++++++*.+.+.........
    ....+...+.............+....+.....+....+.......+......+..+.....
    ....+.......+....+......+........+.+.+....+....+......+.............
    .....+....+......+....+.+..+../.....+.............+....+......
    .......+...+......+.+......+.+....................+...+..+...+.....
    .+....+..+.+....+...+.....+.+....+......+.....+.+.....+.+...+....+.
    .+......+....+......+.......+..+......+....+......+....+..
    +.+.....+....+......+...+.....+.+.....+..+.....+.
    ....+...+.....+....+.+............+....+...............
    ...+.............+..+..+.............+...+.....+......+...+......+.
    .....+....++++++++++++++++++++++++++++++++++++++++++++++++++++++++++++
    +++++++
```

4.  ```
    .....+...+....+...++++++++++++++++++++++++++++++++++++++++++++
    ++++++++++++++*....,++++++++++++++++++++++++++++++++++++++++++++
    ++++++++++++++++*.+........+........+......+.....+........
    ...........+......+.....+..+..+.......+.....+.+..+.+...+..
    ....+.+........+.+...+.........+....+..+...+.+..+........+....
    .........+.....+...+......+....+.+.........+......+........
    ......+.....+..+..+..+.....+......+........+...+...+...+....
    .+.....+.......+.+.....+.....+....+...+.+.......+......
    .....+...+....+.........+.....+.+.....+.......+.+..+......+..
    .+..+........................+....+...+..+............+........
    ....+.+..+...+....+.....+......+...+.....+.......+...+..+....
    .+.........+.........+....+......+...+..............+..+.....
    ..........+.+.............+.........+....+..+......+.....+....+.
    ..+....+...+...+.....+....+.....+...+..+.+..+.......+....
    .......+...+....+.....+..+..+.....+.+..+......+.........+....
    ........+...+......+...+...+..+...+.......+..+.........
    .+.............+.........................+.+......+...........+...+
    ..+....+...+.+...............+.....+..+...+.+...+...+........
    ....+.....+......+.......+.+.+.........+......+...+...........+
    ....+.........................+...+..+.......+...+..+........+.....
    .+......+...+.+.....+...+..+..+...+.......+...+........+.....+...+.
    ...........+.............+.....+................+...+.....+++++++++++++
    +++++++++++++++++++++++++++++++++++++++++++++++++++++++++
    ```
5. `-----`
6. You are about to be asked to enter information that will be incorporated
7. into your certificate request.
8. What you are about to enter is what is called a Distinguished Name or a DN.
9. There are quite a few fields but you can leave some blank
10. For some fields there will be a default value,
11. If you enter '.', the field will be left blank.
12. `-----`
13. Common Name (eg: your user, host, or server name) [server]:vpn.server.robots.beer
14.
15. Keypair and certificate request completed. Your files are:
16. req: /etc/pki/easy-rsa/pki/reqs/server.req
17. key: /etc/pki/easy-rsa/pki/private/server.key
18.
19. root@hrb-1 /etc/pki/easy-rsa #

You will be asked for the name of the server. You can set the name of your server or a common name.
    ```

Now, when we have the cert, we need to sign that cert with the CA we created before, as shown in the following code:

```
1.  root@hrb-1 /etc/pki/easy-rsa # ./easyrsa sign-req server server
2.  Using SSL: openssl OpenSSL 3.0.2 15 Mar 2022 (Library: OpenSSL 3.0.2
    15 Mar 2022)
3.
4.  You are about to sign the following certificate.
5.  Please check over the details shown below for accuracy. Note that
    this request
6.  has not been cryptographically verified. Please be sure it came from
    a trusted
7.  source or that you have verified the request checksum with the
    sender.
8.
9.  Request subject, to be signed as a server certificate for 825 days:
10.
11. subject=
12.     commonName                  = vpn.server.robots.beer
13.
14. Type the word 'yes' to continue, or any other input to abort.
15.    Confirm request details: yes
16. Using configuration from /etc/pki/easy-rsa/pki/easy-rsa-612995.
    QMFQrV/tmp.yn0kUD
17. Enter pass phrase for /etc/pki/easy-rsa/pki/private/ca.key:
18. 40270CF7457F0000:error:0700006C:configuration file routines:NCONF_
    get_string:no value:../crypto/conf/conf_lib.c:315:group=<NULL>
    name=unique_subject
19. Check that the request matches the signature
20. Signature ok
21. The Subject's Distinguished Name is as follows
22. commonName                :ASN.1 12:'vpn.server.robots.beer'
23. Certificate is to be certified until Dec 17 10:49:55 2025 GMT (825
    days)
24.
25. Write out database with 1 new entries
26. Data Base Updated
27.
28. Certificate created at: /etc/pki/easy-rsa/pki/issued/server.crt
29.
30. root@hrb-1 /etc/pki/easy-rsa #
```

Now, we have the servers' certs we need. However, we also need a cert for our OpenVPN server as the secret. Let us create the secret as shown:

```
1.  root@hrb-1 /etc/pki/easy-rsa # openvpn --genkey --secret ta.key
2.  2023-09-14 10:51:04 WARNING: Using --genkey --secret filename is
    DEPRECATED.  Use --genkey secret filename instead.
3.  root@hrb-1 /etc/pki/easy-rsa # ls
4.  easyrsa  index.txt  openssl-easyrsa.cnf  pki  ta.key  vars  vars.
    example  x509-types
5.  root@hrb-1 /etc/pki/easy-rsa # cat ta.key
6.  #
7.  # 2048 bit OpenVPN static key
8.  #
9.  -----BEGIN OpenVPN Static key V1-----
10. d3bc43937f78508657346e57e366295b
11. 9c6ce3aaf5c779dae5aab932a39362ef
12. 2ca0db02cc7e08029be27a2e1396636c
13. 695f3cb9088b314afbda22da9dd810e6
14. 1ef434c32883684594630f2c7e0266e6
15. 070cb6809e63bf1c27fcb4bd7c0c1de3
16. 700631c84bce7b825c45535fe1a5ece8
17. b9416b1aeb934896844b5eb777e72b89
18. 517a17bfd0a0060c661c6f6f4e44cbbd
19. a0af0404fed985da2e262109abaffdbb
20. 2b1793851b611e5176d4df57edcb60dc
21. b70b1261317a2d5484f283e535bc8c76
22. fb8ce41ebf1d4fda87ce34694b06b027
23. 3facbf6bbf14d60f53442122e3915e7e
24. ddf49092223ea8dd56743130c1d1a9d7
25. 64fde38ce3e238a2caa7d6f8d4d9a71b
26. -----END OpenVPN Static key V1-----
27. root@hrb-1 /etc/pki/easy-rsa #
```

Now, we have our certs ready to start our OpenVPN server.

Let us copy the default config from **openvpn** and update the config to add the path to our certs:

```
1.  root@hrb-1 /etc/pki/easy-rsa # sudo cp /usr/share/doc/openvpn/
    examples/sample-config-files/server.conf /etc/openvpn/server/
2.  root@hrb-1 /etc/openvpn/server # vi server.conf
3.  ### Truncate to only show the parts I changed !!!!
4.
5.  ca /etc/pki/easy-rsa/pki/ca.crt
6.  cert /etc/pki/easy-rsa/pki/issued/server.crt
7.  key /etc/pki/easy-rsa/pki/private/server.key  # This file should be
    kept secret
```

8.

9. *# Diffie hellman parameters.*

10. *# Generate your own with:*

11. *#   openssl dhparam -out dh2048.pem 2048*

12. dh /etc/pki/easy-rsa/dh2048.pem

13.

14. *# on the server and '1' on the clients.*

15. tls-auth /etc/pki/easy-rsa/ta.key 0 *# This file is secret*

Start our OpenVPN server:

1. root@hrb-1 /etc/openvpn/server *# openvpn --config server.conf*

2. 2023-09-14 11:01:48 WARNING: --topology net30 support for server configs with IPv4 pools will be removed in a future release. Please migrate to --topology subnet as soon as possible.

3. 2023-09-14 11:01:48 DEPRECATED OPTION: --cipher set to 'AES-256-CBC' but missing in --data-ciphers (AES-256-GCM:AES-128-GCM). Future OpenVPN version will ignore --cipher for cipher negotiations. Add 'AES-256-CBC' to --data-ciphers or change --cipher 'AES-256-CBC' to --data-ciphers-fallback 'AES-256-CBC' to silence this warning.

4. 2023-09-14 11:01:48 OpenVPN 2.5.5 x86_64-pc-linux-gnu [SSL (OpenSSL)] [LZO] [LZ4] [EPOLL] [PKCS11] [MH/PKTINFO] [AEAD] built on Jul 14 2022

5. 2023-09-14 11:01:48 library versions: OpenSSL 3.0.2 15 Mar 2022, LZO 2.10

6. 2023-09-14 11:01:48 net_route_v4_best_gw query: dst 0.0.0.0

7. 2023-09-14 11:01:48 net_route_v4_best_gw result: via 88.99.68.65 dev enp0s31f6

8. 2023-09-14 11:01:48 Diffie-Hellman initialized with 2048 bit key

9. 2023-09-14 11:01:48 Outgoing Control Channel Authentication: Using 160 bit message hash 'SHA1' for HMAC authentication

10. 2023-09-14 11:01:48 Incoming Control Channel Authentication: Using 160 bit message hash 'SHA1' for HMAC authentication

11. 2023-09-14 11:01:48 net_route_v4_best_gw query: dst 0.0.0.0

12. 2023-09-14 11:01:48 net_route_v4_best_gw result: via 88.99.68.65 dev enp0s31f6

13. 2023-09-14 11:01:48 ROUTE_GATEWAY 88.99.68.65

14. 2023-09-14 11:01:48 TUN/TAP device tun0 opened

15. 2023-09-14 11:01:48 net_iface_mtu_set: mtu 1500 for tun0

16. 2023-09-14 11:01:48 net_iface_up: set tun0 up

17. 2023-09-14 11:01:48 net_addr_ptp_v4_add: 10.8.0.1 peer 10.8.0.2 dev tun0

18. 2023-09-14 11:01:48 net_route_v4_add: 10.8.0.0/24 via 10.8.0.2 dev [NULL] table 0 metric -1

19. 2023-09-14 11:01:48 Could not determine IPv4/IPv6 protocol. Using AF_INET
20. 2023-09-14 11:01:48 Socket Buffers: R=[212992->212992] S=[212992->212992]
21. 2023-09-14 11:01:48 UDPv4 link local (bound): [AF_INET][undef]:1194
22. 2023-09-14 11:01:48 UDPv4 link remote: [AF_UNSPEC]
23. 2023-09-14 11:01:48 MULTI: multi_init called, r=256 v=256
24. 2023-09-14 11:01:48 IFCONFIG POOL IPv4: base=10.8.0.4 size=62
25. 2023-09-14 11:01:48 IFCONFIG POOL LIST
26. 2023-09-14 11:01:48 Initialization Sequence Completed

As you see in the following line, our OpenVPN server is ready to accept connections.

Note the line, **2023-09-14 11:01:48 net_addr_ptp_v4_add: 10.8.0.1 peer 10.8.0.2 dev tun0**, here we can see the IP of our server. However, we cannot have any other IP network in the same range.

To connect our client

Go into our **easy-rsa** folder and make certs for our client. The certs will be signed by the CA on the server. The OpenVPN server will only accept connections if you have a certificate that is signed by the cert we have already created.

The following command shows how to create the client certificate:

1. root@hrb-1 /etc/pki/easy-rsa # ./easyrsa gen-req client1 nopass
2. Using SSL: openssl OpenSSL 3.0.2 15 Mar 2022 (Library: OpenSSL 3.0.2 15 Mar 2022)
3. .....+...+............+..++
   +++++++++++++++++++++*...+....+..+...+.......+.+.........+....+..
   .+...+.....+....+...+.........+...+.......+.............+++++++++++++
   ++*....+.....+....+.
   ..+.+..+......+........+.............+.....+..+.+..........+....+.+.
   ....+.....+....+...+..+.+......+.........+.........+.........+...
   ....+.+...............+...+.......+...+.......+...+..+..+..
   ..+..+...+....+............+....+.....+......+....+.......+...+..+
   .+++
4. ...+.+...............+...+...+.....+.+...+..+...+....+.......+....+..
   .+......+.......++
   +++++++++++++*........+.......+....+......+.......+.........+...+.+.+...
   ..+............+.....++
   ++++++++++++++++++++++*.......+.......+...+..+.......+...+...+..
   .+...+.+.+.....+.+...+..+.+......+..........+....+..+.+..+.......+..
   ...+..+............+.................+.........+.......+......+.
   ....+..+.+..+......+..........+........+......+++++++++
   +++

5. -----
6. You are about to be asked to enter information that will be incorporated
7. into your certificate request.
8. What you are about to enter is what is called a Distinguished Name or a DN.
9. There are quite a few fields but you can leave some blank
10. For some fields there will be a default value,
11. If you enter '.', the field will be left blank.
12. -----
13. Common Name (eg: your user, host, or server name) [client1]:
14.
15. Keypair and certificate request completed. Your files are:
16. req: /etc/pki/easy-rsa/pki/reqs/client1.req
17. key: /etc/pki/easy-rsa/pki/private/client1.key
18.
19. root@hrb-1 /etc/pki/easy-rsa # *./easyrsa sign-req client client1*
20. Using SSL: openssl OpenSSL 3.0.2 15 Mar 2022 (Library: OpenSSL 3.0.2 15 Mar 2022)
21.
22. You are about to sign the following certificate.
23. Please check over the details shown below for accuracy. Note that this request
24. has not been cryptographically verified. Please be sure it came from a trusted
25. source or that you have verified the request checksum with the sender.
26.
27. Request subject, **to be signed as a client certificate for 825 days:**
28.
29. subject=
30.   commonName   = client1
31.
32. Type the word 'yes' to continue, or any other input to abort.
33.   Confirm request details: yes
34. Using configuration from /etc/pki/easy-rsa/pki/easy-rsa-785909.afPK3a/tmp.ZwVWko
35. Enter pass phrase for /etc/pki/easy-rsa/pki/private/ca.key:
36. Check that the request matches the signature
37. Signature ok
38. The Subject's Distinguished Name is as follows

39. commonName   :ASN.1 12:'client1'
40. Certificate is to be certified until Dec 17 11:20:30 2025 GMT (825 days)
41.
42. Write out database with 1 new entries
43. Data Base Updated
44.
45. Certificate created at: /etc/pki/easy-rsa/pki/issued/client1.crt
46.
47. root@hrb-1 /etc/pki/easy-rsa #

On the Client

Now, you can log in to the client and install OpenVPN using apt-get. We can then copy the example **client.conf** to the **openvpn** folder, etc.

We need to get the certs from our OpenVPN server to the client. This is how our folder will look:

1. root@hrb:/etc/openvpn# cp /usr/share/doc/openvpn/examples/sample-config-files/client.conf /etc/openvpn/client/
2. root@hrb:/etc/openvpn/tls# pwd
3. /etc/openvpn/tls
4. root@hrb:/etc/openvpn/tls# ls
5. ca.crt client1.crt client1.key ta.key
6. root@hrb:/etc/openvpn/tls#

You will find the certs with the same name in the **easy-rsa/pki** folder on your server, where we created the certs.

Now, we can update the client config with our new settings. Our **client.conf** will appear as follows: (left some lines out that were not changed from the default config)

1. # The hostname/IP and port of the server.
2. # You can have multiple remote entries
3. # to load balance between the servers.
4. remote vpn.server.robots.beer 1194
5. ;remote my-server-2 1194
6.
7. ca /etc/openvpn/tls/ca.crt
8. cert /etc/openvpn/tls/client1.crt
9. key /etc/openvpn/tls/client1.key
10.
11. # Verify server certificate by checking that the
12. # certificate has the correct key usage set.

```
13. # This is an important precaution to protect against
14. # a potential attack discussed here:
15. #   http://openvpn.net/howto.html#mitm
16. #
17. # To use this feature, you will need to generate
18. # your server certificates with the keyUsage set to
19. #   digitalSignature, keyEncipherment
20. # and the extendedKeyUsage to
21. #   serverAuth
22. # EasyRSA can do this for you.
23. remote-cert-tls server
24.
25. # If a tls-auth key is used on the server
26. # then every client must also have the key.
27. tls-auth /etc/openvpn/tls/ta.key 1
```

You will set the remote to the address or IP of your server.

Let us start the client to verify if they are connected, as shown in the following code:

```
1.  root@hrb:/etc/openvpn/client# openvpn --config client.conf
2.
3.  {Truncated}
4.
5.  2023-09-14 13:36:58 net_route_v4_best_gw query: dst 0.0.0.0
6.  2023-09-14 13:36:58 net_route_v4_best_gw result: via 192.168.1.1 dev
    enp45s0f0np0
7.  2023-09-14 13:36:58 ROUTE_GATEWAY 192.168.1.1/255.255.255.0
    IFACE=enp45s0f0np0 HWADDR=00:0f:53:2c:ff:90
8.  2023-09-14 13:36:58 TUN/TAP device tun0 opened
9.  2023-09-14 13:36:58 net_iface_mtu_set: mtu 1500 for tun0
10. 2023-09-14 13:36:58 net_iface_up: set tun0 up
11. 2023-09-14 13:36:58 net_addr_ptp_v4_add: 10.8.0.6 peer 10.8.0.5 dev
    tun0
12. 2023-09-14 13:36:58 net_route_v4_add: 10.8.0.1/32 via 10.8.0.5 dev
    [NULL] table 0 metric -1
13. 2023-09-14 13:36:58 WARNING: this configuration may cache passwords
    in memory -- use the auth-nocache option to prevent this
14. 2023-09-14 13:36:58 Initialization Sequence Completed
```

If we run **ip a**, we can verify the new network device, as shown in the following code:

```
1.  root@hrb:/etc/openvpn/client#  ip a
2.
3.  {Truncated}
```

```
4.
5. 1166: tun0: <POINTOPOINT,MULTICAST,NOARP,UP,LOWER_UP> mtu 1500 qdisc
   fq_codel state UNKNOWN group default qlen 500
6.     link/none
7.     inet 10.8.0.6 peer 10.8.0.5/32 scope global tun0
8.        valid_lft forever preferred_lft forever
9.     inet6 fe80::f706:f62d:33bf:e66f/64 scope link stable-privacy
10.       valid_lft forever preferred_lft forever
11.
12. mattias@hrb:~$ ping 10.8.0.1
13. PING 10.8.0.1 (10.8.0.1) 56(84) bytes of data.
14. 64 bytes from 10.8.0.1: icmp_seq=1 ttl=64 time=26.4 ms
15. 64 bytes from 10.8.0.1: icmp_seq=2 ttl=64 time=26.6 ms
```

Now, we have a secure connection between our client and server. In this setup, only the traffic for 10.8.0.0/24 will go to the VPN server. So, all other traffic will use your regular network. However, you can easily change the settings for the server to force all traffic over the server. This setup is for only client-to-server setup.

WireGuard VPN

WireGuard is a more modern VPN and somewhat easier to understand, which you will grasp better in this section.

Let us start with installing WireGuard on our server, as shown in the following command:

```
1. root@hrb-1 /etc # sudo apt install wireguard
```

Now, when we have WireGuard installed, we need to create a private and a public key. To do that, WireGuard already provides some tools for us. We will first create the private key. Then, from that private key, we will generate a public key to use. This is shown in the following code:

```
1. root@hrb-1 /etc/wireguard/tls # wg genkey >> private.key
2. root@hrb-1 /etc/wireguard/tls # chmod go= private.key
3. root@hrb-1 /etc/wireguard/tls # cat private.key | wg pubkey | tee
   public.key
4. root@hrb-1 /etc/wireguard/tls # ls -l
5. total 8
6. -rw------- 1 root root 45 Sep 14 13:52 private.key
7. -rw-r--r-- 1 root root 45 Sep 14 13:53 public.key
8. root@hrb-1 /etc/wireguard/tls #
```

Now that we have our server keys, we can set our server here as shown in the following config for a server using the range 10.13.13.0:

```
1. [Interface]
2. Address = 10.13.13.1
3. ListenPort = 51820
4. PrivateKey = sMeT7YVzcjA
5. PostUp = iptables -A FORWARD -i %i -j ACCEPT; iptables -A FORWARD -o
   %i -j ACCEPT; iptables -t nat -A POSTROUTING -o eth+ -j MASQUERADE
6. PostDown = iptables -D FORWARD -i %i -j ACCEPT; iptables -D
   FORWARD -o %i -j ACCEPT; iptables -t nat -D POSTROUTING -o eth+ -j
   MASQUERADE
```

Now, add the **PrivateKey** from the files we created before. You cannot already have a network with the same range as the WireGuard here, 10.13.13.0.

Then, it is time to create clients' peers, as they are called in WireGuard. You can see the commands as follows. We will first create the private key and then the public key, just as we did on the WireGuard server.

```
1.  root@hrb:/etc/wireguard# wg genkey | tee /etc/wireguard/private.key
2.  CKgylwDb485dd21gi3PsDVy3lm+8nzF8I9eAo3b3YmM=
3.  root@hrb:/etc/wireguard# ls
4.  private.key
5.  root@hrb:/etc/wireguard# cat private.key
6.  CKgylwDb485dd21gi3PsDVy3lm+8nzF8I9eAo3b3YmM=
7.  root@hrb:/etc/wireguard# chmod go= /etc/wireguard/private.key
8.  root@hrb:/etc/wireguard# cat /etc/wireguard/private.key | wg pubkey
    | tee /etc/wireguard/public.key
9.  XEA2rYM6x4JKGFLVLWJkM2Pj4/p8ASo5ekREUV2e11M=
10. root@hrb:/etc/wireguard# ls
11. private.key  public.key
12. root@hrb:/etc/wireguard#
```

We now have a private and a public key. Now, we need to attach them to our WireGuard server config and our client. Let us start by creating a config file for our client add the following in the file **wg0.conf** in **/etc/wireguard**:

```
1.  [Interface]
2.  Address = 10.13.13.11
3.  PrivateKey =
4.  ListenPort = 51820
5.  DNS = 10.13.13.1
6.
7.  [Peer]
8.  PublicKey =
9.  PresharedKey =
10. Endpoint = IP ORE ADDRESS TO YOUR SERVER:51820
11. AllowedIPs = 10.13.13.0/24
```

PrivateKey and **PublicKey** you will get from running **cat private.key** and **cat public.key**

We also need a preshared key for our client. This can be done by running the following command:

```
1. wg genpsk > prehared.key.
```

With this, we have our clint config complete. Now, let us add the peer config to our server.

Now, we can move to our WireGuard server and add our peer config. In the **wg0.conf** file, where we added the server settings, add the following as well:

```
1. [Peer]
2. # hrb
3. PublicKey = XEA2rYM6x4JKGFLVLWJkM2Pj4/p8ASo5ekREUV2e11M=
4. PresharedKey = fM7XOI0imNNEIUE6N/FpJN4Hb+tGlfw7a25tWIkxELw=
5. AllowedIPs = 10.13.13.11/32
```

Now, verify if you have the same config for the following:

- Ip address
- PublicKey
- PresharedKey

Then, we can restart our WireGuard server and client. When our config file has the name in **/etc/wiregurad**, called **wg0.conf**, then we can run the following command:

```
1. root@hrb-1 /etc/wireguard # wg-quick down  wg0
2. [#] ip link delete dev wg0
3. [#] iptables -D FORWARD -i wg0 -j ACCEPT; iptables -D FORWARD -o wg0
   -j ACCEPT; iptables -t nat -D POSTROUTING -o eth+ -j MASQUERADE
4. root@hrb-1 /etc/wireguard # wg-quick up  wg0
5. [#] ip link add wg0 type wireguard
6. [#] wg setconf wg0 /dev/fd/63
7. [#] ip -4 address add 10.13.13.1 dev wg0
8. [#] ip link set mtu 1420 up dev wg0
9. [#] ip -4 route add 10.13.13.6/32 dev wg0
10. [#] ip -4 route add 10.13.13.5/32 dev wg0
11. [#] ip -4 route add 10.13.13.4/32 dev wg0
12. [#] ip -4 route add 10.13.13.3/32 dev wg0
13. [#] ip -4 route add 10.13.13.2/32 dev wg0
14. [#] ip -4 route add 10.13.13.11/32 dev wg0
15. [#] iptables -A FORWARD -i wg0 -j ACCEPT; iptables -A FORWARD -o wg0
    -j ACCEPT; iptables -t nat -A POSTROUTING -o eth+ -j MASQUERADE
16. root@hrb-1 /etc/wireguard #
```

Let us shut down the server and then start the VPN server again. This will add the routes for our new peer with IP 10.13.13.11. You can verify the connections of the tunnels by running the command **wg show**, which will print the status of the current connections.

VPN troubleshooting

When we set up a VPN, we connect the computer. To do that, we need to be able to send packages between them. Many things on the internet and on the local network can block our VPN. For example, the VPN can be blocked in some parts of the world.

The following are some common things to try if your VPN cannot connect:

- **Local firewall:** Verify that you do not have any firewall blocking the connections between your servers. Use tools like Telnet to verify that you can establish a connection between your server and client.

- **Package forward:** To use your VPN server and access other servers from it. You need to enable package forwarding. We did this when we used Ubuntu as a firewall.

- **Tricks:** Sometimes, your locations have blocked the ports that our VPN is using. Now, you can change the VPN port to standard ports like 80, 443, or 53 and see if that works.

Conclusion

In this chapter, we understood how we can set up a simple router to route traffic from our local network out to a public network with an Ubuntu Server. We used Iptables to set up and control what traffic can go in and out of our network.

To set up a basic IP network for desktop and server, we installed a DHCP server that will send out IP addresses to our clients in the network. We have also set up our own DNS server, allowing us to add and control DNS names within our network.

Connect two locations or connect from a client back to a server. We have looked at two different VPN solutions and how they can connect a server and a client together.

With the knowledge from this chapter, we can set up an Ubuntu Server as our primary network router and use it to control router traffic both in a workplace and in a hosting setup.

In the next chapter, we will start using virtualization and run multiple instances of Ubuntu on a single Ubuntu system.

CHAPTER 10

Running Virtualization Server Environment

Introduction

The ability to run multiple services, such as different web servers or databases, or, for example, multiple databases for various purposes, is a common use case when using Ubuntu Servers. To be able to do that and to isolate every server, we come to Virtualization for help. With Virtualization, we can take one Ubuntu metal server and turn it into several virtual servers. Then, install them separately to support our use case.

In this chapter, we will look at how you can install several **virtual machines** (**VMs**) into your Ubuntu Server. Moreover, we will also discuss how you can manage them from your desktop or over a regular webpage.

We will then look at how you can use containers and how you can achieve the same approach with containers on your Ubuntu Server.

Structure

In this chapter, we will cover the following topics:

- Installing KVM on your Ubuntu Server
- Connecting from the desktop using KVM GUI
- Installing the KVM web interface

- Creating a VM server
- Control your VM using the virsh command
- Dedicated VM Linux version
- Containers
- Podman's features
- Setup and monitoring with Grafana and Prometheus
- Reading logs with Loki
- Container-based monitoring clients

Objectives

By the end of this chapter, we will cover how to set up an Ubuntu Server as a virtual host. On that server, you spin up a new Ubuntu Server that you can install and set up services like web servers or databases.

We will understand how to manage the virtual server by cloning new servers, making backups, and setting up a network.

Once we cover virtual servers, we will move on to set up tools on our server using containers. We previously discussed Docker; here, we will use the tool Podman, which is like Docker. It is used to set up the monitoring stack we installed in a capture. We will set up everything using containers with Podman.

Moreover, we will understand how to install Podman to start containers and mount them to get access to resources from the Ubuntu Server.

Installing KVM on your Ubuntu Server

Let us install KVM, our virtualization tool, on our Ubuntu Server. For all the steps, you need SSH access to your server. We will use SSH to set up and start our VM. We will also connect our GUI tools to control the servers later.

When we run virtualization, we need support from the CPU on your server or desktop. If support is not enabled, we can still run the VM. However, its performance could be improved. In your BIOS, you can enable virtualization if your CPU supports it

First, let us install KVM. The following is the command to install KVM and to verify we can run virtualization:

```
1. root@g1:/home/mahe# sudo apt -y install bridge-utils cpu-checker
   libvirt-clients libvirt-daemon qemu qemu-kvm
2. root@g1:/home/mahe# kvm-ok
3. INFO: /dev/kvm exists
```

```
4. KVM acceleration can be used
5. root@g1:/home/mahe#
```

Let us connect some tools now that we have the core installed. The tools will run from your desktop or with a webpage to access the server and manage our VM on the Ubuntu Server. We need the tools first so we can get a screen from the server and use that to install our VM. We will also run and install an Ubuntu Server using the terminal later in this chapter.

Connecting from the desktop using KVM GUI

We have had a KVM manager installed on our desktop since we started using virtualization. Now, we can open the KVM manager to make a new connection and use SSH access.

First, add your SSH key to your server so we can access it without a password. Then, add the user you SSH into the server to the Libvirt group so it can connect to Libvirtd.

Now, open Virtual Machine Manager on your desktop and add new connections. Type in your username and host.

The following figure shows how you can set up access to a server:

Note: No password is required when running the copy SSH key command.

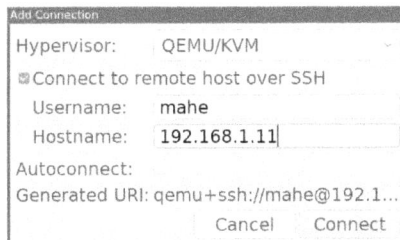

Figure 10.1: Connection to remote KVM host

Now, you can see your virtual server as shown in the following figure:

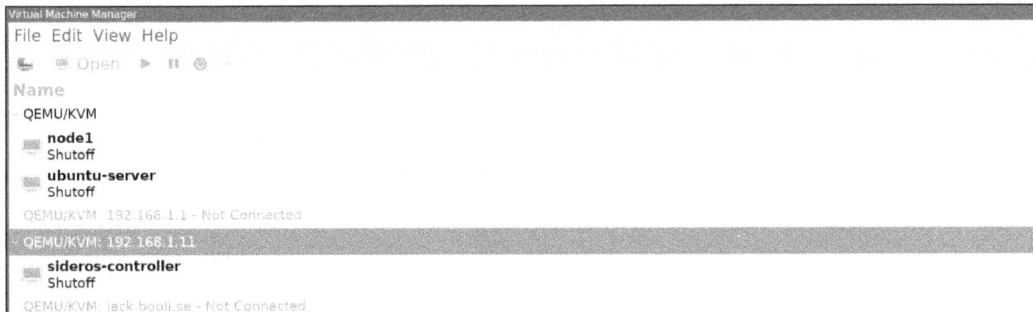

Figure 10.2: Virtual machines running

Now, you can use the GUI from your desktop to create and control your virtual server on the server in the same way as when we ran the virtual server on our desktop.

Installing the KVM web interface

We have used the tool Cockpit to set up and control our server from a web browser. The tool also has a plugin to monitor and control the KVM host.

It can be installed with the following command:

```
root@g1:/home/mahe# sudo apt install cockpit-machines
```

Now, log in to your Cockpit console, and we can see our VM running there as well, as shown in the following figure:

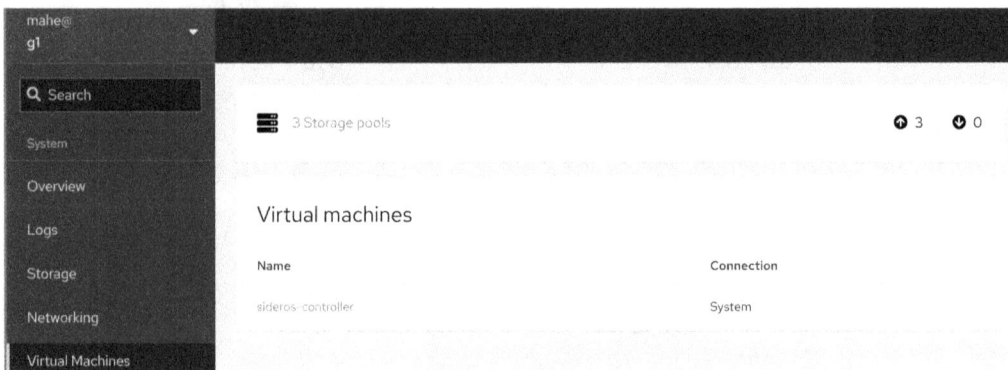

Figure 10.3: Virtual machines running are shown by Cockpit

If you are now changing any of the tools, it will also show in the other. You can run both, and if you are on your local network, use the virtual manager from your desktop. Moreover, access the virtual server from a webpage remotely.

Creating a VM server

You can use any of the tools to create a server but here we will show how you can create and connect to a server only using the terminal.

We will start the server and use our terminal to set things up. However, during the installation, we can also look at both virt manager and Cockpit to see the progress.

Create your server by running the following command:

```
1. $ sudo virt-install --name ubuntu-guest --os-variant ubuntu20.04
   --vcpus 2 --ram 2048 --location http://ftp.ubuntu.com/ubuntu/dists/
   focal/main/installer-amd64/ --network bridge=virbr0,model=virtio
   --graphics none --extra-args='console=ttyS0,115200n8 serial' --disk
   size=5
```

Now, you can follow the installation of Ubuntu, and all config is done in the terminal, as shown in the following figure:

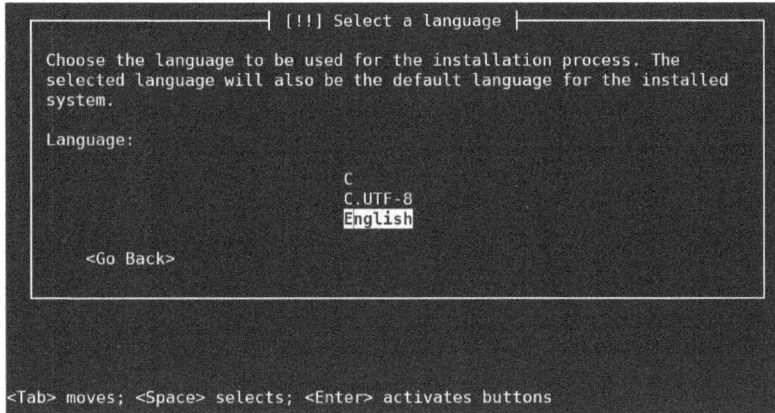

Figure 10.4: Installation of Ubuntu inside a VM from the command line

Run the installation so that you have an installed Ubuntu Server. Then, you can look at the new server from virtual manager and Cockpit and start and access the server.

Control your VM using the virsh command

Using the **virsh**, we can now clone our VM into an image and create a new one.

We can save it and send it to another server to start up there. Think of the VM image as a hard drive that, if we move it and connect it to a new computer, will boot up there as well. We can move it to a new server and start there. We can save it, so we have a backup and delete it if we do not need it anymore.

Shared storage

If you have several Ubuntu Servers, we can connect an NFS server on one of these servers and share the disk over the network with the other hosts. Now, we can save our disk image on that shared disk. Now, we can start the server from any of the Ubuntu Servers that share that disk.

Dedicated VM Linux version

Suppose you plan to run several Ubuntu Servers and have a VM running on them to create a large pool of servers. There are better tools than setting up Ubuntu Servers. Proxmox is one of those tools that is a Linux version built for running VMs. It supports multiple servers and shared storage.

With Proxmox, you can also run a pool of servers all together.

If you have even looked for a larger deployment of VMs, then OpenStack is the largest open-source tool for running large VM deployments.

Containers

In this chapter, we utilized Docker as a containerization tool. However, Docker is not the only one. Podman is a tool that is already in the Ubuntu repo. It is a drop-in replacement for Docker, so you can replace the docker with Podman, and your commands will still work. One example, you can install Podman on a server but still run Docker on the local Ubuntu Desktop.

You can choose to skip the installation part of Podman in this chapter and replace the Docker command; the output will be the same.

Podman´s features

Podman has a long list of features, and the following are some of the top ones:

- Podman supports both OCI and Docker images.
- Podman has full network integration with CNI network plugins.
- With Podman, you can combine several containers into pods, as in Kubernetes.
- It has docker support and can run both local and remote environments.
- Podman does not use a daemon. For that, it has enhanced security and will not use any resources when not running.
- Podman has a REST API that works well and can be extended like the Kubernetes API.
- Podman can also run a Pod without having full access to the host system

This also makes Podman a bit harder to run than Docker. If you plan to use containers for local dev, stick to docker over Podman. However, if you are building apps that will run in a Kubernetes cluster, it can be good to work with Podman to test if your apps are working and generate a Kubernetes manifest from your Podman setup.

Installing Podman

Installing Podman on Ubuntu is easy. It is by default in the repository and can be installed by running the following command:

```
apt-get install podman
```

This will install Podman and the tools on your Ubuntu Server. Now, we can verify if we have any containers running the following:

```
1.  root@firgate:~# podman ps
2.  CONTAINER ID   IMAGE                          COMMAND   CREATED
    STATUS         PORTS     NAMES
```

3. c4fb47f9e646 docker.io/pihole/pihole:latest   3 weeks ago
   Up 3 weeks ago   pihole
4. root@firgate:~#

The command to run to get containers is **podman ps**; however, if you use Docker, the command is **docker ps**.

Setting up Podman Repo

Before you can pull down images, you need to enable the repos that Podman can use. Docker can, as default pull from all repos, but Podman is more restricted.

Open the file **/etc/containers/registries.conf** by running the following:

1. *# # in order, and use the first one that exists.*
   [registries.search]
2. registries = ['docker.io']
3.
4. root@firgate:~# *cat /etc/containers/registries.conf*

Now, you can pull images from **docker.io**. However, if you want to pull from any other registry, you need to add those repos as well.

When we set up our tools, we make a **docker-compose** file. To use our docker compose with Podman, we need to Python package Podman compose by running the following:

1. root@firgate:/opt/monitoring# *pip3 install podman-compose*
2. Requirement already satisfied: podman-compose in /usr/local/lib/
   python3.9/dist-packages (1.0.6)
3. Requirement already satisfied: pyyaml in /usr/lib/python3/dist-
   packages (from podman-compose) (5.3.1)
4. Requirement already satisfied: python-dotenv in /usr/local/lib/
   python3.9/dist-packages (from podman-compose) (1.0.0)
5. root@firgate:/opt/monitoring#

Now we have a working setup for Podman, and we can start setting up our monitoring stack using containers and Podman/Docker compose.

Podman error with CNI plugin

When we start the Podman, we will get an error with a conflict, and the network will not start. If this happens, you must update the **cni** version in the network file.

Open the **cni** file, as follows:

1. root@pihole:/opt/monitoring# *cat /etc/cni/net.d/*87-podman-bridge.
   conflist   cni.lock
2. monitoring_default.conflist

3. root@pihole:/opt/monitoring# *cat /etc/cni/net.d/monitoring_default.*
   conflist
4. Verify the version   "cniVersion": "0.4.0",

Setup and monitoring with Grafana and Prometheus

Let us create a folder called /opt/monitoring on our server. In that folder, we are to make a **docker-compose.yaml** file. We will use this file when we set up our monitoring stack here.

During the chapter, we are to add more services to the folder and start more and more services.

You are free to follow our step-by-step guide, or you can proceed to the end to obtain the full Docker Compose file and start the full stack at once.

The following is the first version of our **docker-compose.yaml** with only **grafana**:

```
1. version: "3"
2. services:
3.   grafana:
4.     environment:
5.       - GF_PATHS_PROVISIONING=/etc/grafana/provisioning
6.       - GF_AUTH_ANONYMOUS_ENABLED=true
7.       - GF_AUTH_ANONYMOUS_ORG_ROLE=Admin
8.     image: grafana/grafana:latest
9.     volume:
10.       - ./grafana: /var/lib/grafana
11.     ports:
12.       - "3000:3000"
```

Now, we can start our stack by running the following command:

```
1. \root@pihole:/opt/monitoring# podman-compose up
2. podman-compose version: 1.0.6
3. ['podman', '--version', '']
4. using podman version: 3.4.4
5. ** excluding:  set()
6. ['podman', 'ps', '--filter', 'label=io.podman.compose.
   project=monitoring', '-a', '--format', '{{ index .Labels "io.podman.
   compose.config-hash"}}']
7. ['podman', 'network', 'exists', 'monitoring_default']
8. podman create --name=monitoring_grafana_1 --label io.podman.
   compose.config-hash=68cb8b0bb2394d0c7250f76d5c4c6c9895f1c76ad8e54
   15ba7069e9b104a03a4 --label io.podman.compose.project=monitoring
```

```
   --label io.podman.compose.version=1.0.6 --label PODMAN_SYSTEMD_
   UNIT=podman-compose@monitoring.service --label com.docker.compose.
   project=monitoring --label com.docker.compose.project.working_dir=/
   opt/monitoring --label com.docker.compose.project.config_files=docker-
   compose.yaml --label com.docker.compose.container-number=1 --label
   com.docker.compose.service=grafana -e GF_PATHS_PROVISIONING=/etc/
   grafana/provisioning -e GF_AUTH_ANONYMOUS_ENABLED=true -e GF_AUTH_
   ANONYMOUS_ORG_ROLE=Admin --net monitoring_default --network-alias
   grafana -p 3000:3000 grafana/grafana:latest
```

9. Error: error creating container storage: the container
    name "monitoring_grafana_1" is already in use by
    "a2fbe38e34f518491b749e7de84dab5aeb4368260f781d425d764eb03291392b".
    You have to remove that container to be able to reuse that name.:
    that name is already in use

10. exit code: 125

11. podman start -a monitoring_grafana_1

12. [grafana] | logger=settings t=2023-10-06T17:41:50.537470323Z
    level=info msg="Starting Grafana" version=10.1.4 commit=a676a96d91
    branch=HEAD compiled=2023-09-29T14:28:45Z

13. [grafana] | logger=settings t=2023-10-06T17:41:50.538484762Z
    level=info msg="Config loaded from" file=/usr/share/grafana/conf/
    defaults.ini

14. [grafana] | logger=settings t=2023-10-06T17:41:50.538550972Z
    level=info msg="Config loaded from" file=/etc/grafana/grafana.ini

15. [grafana] | logger=settings t=2023-10-06T17:41:50.538567889Z
    level=info msg="Config overridden from command line" arg="default.
    paths.data=/var/lib/grafana"

16. [grafana] | logger=settings t=2023-10-06T17:41:50.538582764Z
    level=info msg="Config overridden from command line" arg="default.
    paths.logs=/var/log/grafana"

17. [grafana] | logger=settings t=2023-10-06T17:41:50.538596473Z
    level=info msg="Config overridden from command line" arg="default.
    paths.plugins=/var/lib/grafana/plugins"

18. [grafana] | logger=settings t=2023-10-06T17:41:50.538610181Z
    level=info msg="Config overridden from command line" arg="default.
    paths.provisioning=/etc/grafana/provisioning"

19. [grafana] | logger=settings t=2023-10-06T17:41:50.538622431Z
    level=info msg="Config overridden from command line" arg="default.
    log.mode=console"

20. [grafana] | logger=settings t=2023-10-06T17:41:50.538636723Z
    level=info msg="Config overridden from Environment variable" var="GF_
    PATHS_DATA=/var/lib/grafana"

21. [grafana] | logger=settings t=2023-10-06T17:41:50.538649849Z
    level=info msg="Config overridden from Environment variable" var="GF_
    PATHS_LOGS=/var/log/grafana"

```
22. [grafana] | logger=settings t=2023-10-06T17:41:50.538662974Z
    level=info msg="Config overridden from Environment variable" var="GF_
    PATHS_PLUGINS=/var/lib/grafana/plugins"
23. [grafana] | logger=settings t=2023-10-06T17:41:50.538676974Z
    level=info msg="Config overridden from Environment variable" var="GF_
    PATHS_PROVISIONING=/etc/grafana/provisioning"
24. [grafana] | logger=settings t=2023-10-06T17:41:50.538693891Z
    level=info msg="Config overridden from Environment variable" var="GF_
    AUTH_ANONYMOUS_ENABLED=true"
25. [grafana] | logger=settings t=2023-10-06T17:41:50.5387076Z
    level=info msg="Config overridden from Environment variable" var="GF_
    AUTH_ANONYMOUS_ORG_ROLE=Admin"
26. [grafana] | logger=settings t=2023-10-06T17:41:50.538721892Z
    level=info msg=Target target=[all]
27. [grafana] | logger=settings t=2023-10-06T17:41:50.538754559Z
    level=info msg="Path Home" path=/usr/share/grafana
28. [grafana] | logger=settings t=2023-10-06T17:41:50.538767685Z
    level=info msg="Path Data" path=/var/lib/grafana
29. [grafana] | logger=settings t=2023-10-06T17:41:50.538782852Z
    level=info msg="Path Logs" path=/var/log/grafana
30. [grafana] | logger=settings t=2023-10-06T17:41:50.538795102Z
    level=info msg="Path Plugins" path=/var/lib/grafana/plugins
31. [grafana] | logger=settings t=2023-10-06T17:41:50.538807061Z
    level=info msg="Path Provisioning" path=/etc/grafana/provisioning
32. [grafana] | logger=settings t=2023-10-06T17:41:50.538820186Z
    level=info msg="App mode production"
33. [grafana] | logger=sqlstore t=2023-10-06T17:41:50.539735164Z
    level=info msg="Connecting to DB" dbtype=sqlite3
34. [grafana] | logger=migrator t=2023-10-06T17:41:50.708509328Z
    level=info msg="Starting DB migrations"
35. [grafana] | logger=migrator t=2023-10-06T17:41:50.74556085Z
    level=info msg="migrations completed" performed=0 skipped=493
    duration=2.093629ms
36. [grafana] | logger=secrets t=2023-10-06T17:41:50.75014303
```

In our docker-compose file, we have some settings that are extra interesting. One is the **volume**. This will make a local folder called **grafana**, and we will save our config in that file. This is how we can mount local folders from our host into our containers. The other part is the ports. This will tell us that the external post 3000 is now open into our **grafana** on port 3000. This is how we can connect from the outside to our service.

In the following file, we can see the port mapping:

```
1.      volume:
2.        - ./grafana: /var/lib/grafana
```

```
3.     ports:
4.       - "3000:3000"
```

Now, when we have Grafana running, verify you can access the Grafana GUI at **http://IP OF SERVER:3000**.

Now, we can add Prometheus to our stack. In our monitoring folder, create a new folder called **prom**, and in that folder, create our **prometheus.yaml** config file, shown as follows:

```
1.  root@pihole:/opt/monitoring# cat prom/prometheus.yml
2.  # my global config
3.  global:
4.    scrape_interval:     15s # By default, scrape targets every 15
      seconds.
5.    evaluation_interval: 15s # By default, scrape targets every 15
      seconds.
6.    # scrape_timeout is set to the global default (10s).
7.
8.    # Attach these labels to any time series or alerts when
      communicating with
9.    # external systems (federation, remote storage, Alertmanager).
10.   external_labels:
11.       monitor: 'my-project'
12.
13. # Load and evaluate rules in this file every 'evaluation_interval'
    seconds.
14. rule_files:
15.   - 'alert.rules'
16.   # - "first.rules"
17.   # - "second.rules"
18.
19. # alert
20. alerting:
21.   alertmanagers:
22.   - scheme: http
23.     static_configs:
24.     - targets:
25.       - "alertmanager:9093"
26.
27. # A scrape configuration containing exactly one endpoint to scrape:
28. # Here it's Prometheus itself.
29. scrape_configs:
30.   # The job name is added as a label `job=<job_name>` to any
    timeseries scraped from this config.
31.
```

```
32.    - job_name: 'prometheus'
33.
34.      # Override the global default and scrape targets from this job
   every 5 seconds.
35.      scrape_interval: 15s
36.
37.      static_configs:
38.          - targets: ['localhost:9090']
39.
40.    - job_name: 'cadvisor'
41.
42.      # Override the global default and scrape targets from this job
   every 5 seconds.
43.      scrape_interval: 15s
44.
45.      static_configs:
46.        - targets: ['cadvisor:8080']
47.
48.    - job_name: 'node-exporter'
49.
50.      # Override the global default and scrape targets from this job
   every 5 seconds.
51.      scrape_interval: 15s
52.
53.      static_configs:
54.        - targets: ['node-exporter:9100']
```

When the config file is in place, it is time to update our docker-compose file by running the following:

```
1.  root@pihole:/opt/monitoring# cat docker-compose.yaml
2.  version: "3"
3.  services:
4.    grafana:
5.      environment:
6.        - GF_PATHS_PROVISIONING=/etc/grafana/provisioning
7.        - GF_AUTH_ANONYMOUS_ENABLED=true
8.        - GF_AUTH_ANONYMOUS_ORG_ROLE=Admin
9.      image: grafana/grafana:latest
10.     volumes:
11.       - ./grafana: /var/lib/grafana
12.     ports:
13.       - "3000:3000"
14.   prometheus:
15.     image: prom/prometheus:latest
```

```
16.     volumes:
17.       - ./prom/:/etc/prometheus/
18.     command:
19.       - '--config.file=/etc/prometheus/prometheus.yml'
20.       - '--web.console.libraries=/usr/share/prometheus/console_
   libraries'
21.       - '--web.console.templates=/usr/share/prometheus/consoles'
22.     ports:
23.       - 9090:9090
```

As you can see, updating and adding new services go fast.

Now, start up your service using the podman-compose pre docker compose **up** command. Suppose you want them to run and not look at the other output. Replace the **up** for a **start**, and then when you want to stop, use **stop**.

Let us add our last container to get metrics from our host. It is the **Node Exporter** we used before, and now it is our **docker-compose.yaml** file should look as follows:

```
1.  root@pihole:/opt/monitoring# cat docker-compose.yaml
2.  version: "3"
3.  services:
4.    grafana:
5.      environment:
6.        - GF_PATHS_PROVISIONING=/etc/grafana/provisioning
7.        - GF_AUTH_ANONYMOUS_ENABLED=true
8.        - GF_AUTH_ANONYMOUS_ORG_ROLE=Admin
9.      image: grafana/grafana:latest
10.     volumes:
11.       - ./grafana: /var/lib/grafana
12.     ports:
13.       - "3000:3000"
14.   prometheus:
15.     image: prom/prometheus:latest
16.     volumes:
17.       - ./prom/:/etc/prometheus/
18.     command:
19.       - '--config.file=/etc/prometheus/prometheus.yml'
20.       - '--web.console.libraries=/usr/share/prometheus/console_
   libraries'
21.       - '--web.console.templates=/usr/share/prometheus/consoles'
22.     ports:
23.       - 9090:9090
24.   node-exporter:
25.     image: prom/node-exporter:v1.6.1
```

```
26.    container_name: nodeexporter
27.    volumes:
28.      - /proc:/host/proc:ro
29.      - /sys:/host/sys:ro
30.      - /:/rootfs:ro
31.    command:
32.      - '--path.procfs=/host/proc'
33.      - '--path.rootfs=/rootfs'
34.      - '--path.sysfs=/host/sys'
35.      - '--collector.filesystem.mount-points-exclude=^/
   (sys|proc|dev|host|etc)($$|/)'
36.    expose:
37.      - 9100
```

Start the stack up, and when it has started, you should be able to go to **grafana**. Set up a new data source and add our **prometheus**. Then, go to the dashboard, make a new one, and enter this number as the dashboard ID to import 1860. Now, save and open the new dashboard, and we should have some graphs in there.

We have now set up the first part of our monitoring in Podman, and we can see some metrics from our host. However, we also want to see logs from our server. Let us expand our **docker-compose.yaml** file by adding two new services.

Reading logs with Loki

Loki is a data source for storing logs and is well-integrated with Grafana. Promtail is a service that reads logfiles from your Ubuntu Server and sends them to **Loki**.

We will add these to our docker-compose and add the full stack again.

Before we can start Loki, we need to create a folder for Loki and open its permissions. Podman is enforcing hard rules on the folder inside our Docker.

The following code shows the command to create and set the permission:

```
1. root@pihole:/opt/monitoring# mkdir loki
2. root@pihole:/opt/monitoring# chmod 777 loki
```

Now, update the **docker-compose.yaml** file to look like the following:

```
1. root@pihole:/opt/monitoring# cat docker-compose.yaml
2. version: "3"
3. services:
4.   grafana:
5.     environment:
6.       - GF_PATHS_PROVISIONING=/etc/grafana/provisioning
7.       - GF_AUTH_ANONYMOUS_ENABLED=true
```

```
8.            - GF_AUTH_ANONYMOUS_ORG_ROLE=Admin
9.        image: grafana/grafana:latest
10.       volumes:
11.         - ./grafana:/var/lib/grafana
12.       ports:
13.         - "3000:3000"
14.     prometheus:
15.       image: prom/prometheus:latest
16.       volumes:
17.         - ./prom/:/etc/prometheus/
18.       command:
19.         - '--config.file=/etc/prometheus/prometheus.yml'
20.         - '--web.console.libraries=/usr/share/prometheus/console_
    libraries'
21.         - '--web.console.templates=/usr/share/prometheus/consoles'
22.       ports:
23.         - 9090:9090
24.     node-exporter:
25.       image: prom/node-exporter:v1.6.1
26.       container_name: nodeexporter
27.       volumes:
28.         - /proc:/host/proc:ro
29.         - /sys:/host/sys:ro
30.         - /:/rootfs:ro
31.       command:
32.         - '--path.procfs=/host/proc'
33.         - '--path.rootfs=/rootfs'
34.         - '--path.sysfs=/host/sys'
35.         - '--collector.filesystem.mount-points-exclude=^/
    (sys|proc|dev|host|etc)($$|/)'
36.       expose:
37.         - 9100
38.     loki:
39.       image: grafana/loki:2.9.1
40.       ports:
41.         - "3100:3100"
42.       command: -config.file=/etc/loki/local-config.yaml
43.       volumes:
44.         - ./loki:/loki:Z
45.     promtail:
46.       image: grafana/promtail:2.9.1
47.       volumes:
48.         - /var/log:/var/log
49.       command: -config.file=/etc/promtail/config.yml
```

Start up the stack by using the Podman command **podman-compose up|start** or the Docker compose command **docker compose up|start**. Navigate to data sources and add Loki as a source type at the address **http://loki:3100**. Save and test the access. Then, go to Explorer view in Grafana, show Loki as a data source, and select job filters to view any logs coming in.

This will end our base setup using Podman/Docker. We now have a monitoring stack running all in containers. We are getting logs and metrics from our host into Grafana, where we can view the Grafana and read our logs.

We have one last bit of config before we are done. That involves retrieving data from another server on our network and integrating it into our base monitoring stack. To do that, we will use a **docker-compose.yaml** file that we will start on all the servers we want to monitor, and they will start sending data to our base monitoring stack.

Before we can start our client monitoring stack, you need to have Podman or Docker running on the server we want to monitor.

Journal logs

Ubuntu uses a tool called *journal* to handle logs, and the default config in Promtail is not set up to collect logs from the journal.

To retrieve all our logs, we need to create a **Promtail** config that will collect all the logs. Then, make a new folder called prom, add a file called **config.yml**, and add the content shown as follows:

```
 1. root@pihole:/opt/monitoring# cat promtail/config.yml
 2. server:
 3.   http_listen_port: 9080
 4.   grpc_listen_port: 0
 5.
 6. positions:
 7.   filename: /tmp/positions.yaml
 8.
 9. clients:
10.   - url: http://loki:3100/loki/api/v1/push
11.
12. scrape_configs:
13. - job_name: system
14.   static_configs:
15.   - targets:
16.       - localhost
17.     labels:
18.       job: varlogs
19.       __path__: /var/log/*log
```

```
20. - job_name: journal
21.   journal:
22.     json: false
23.     max_age: 12h
24.     path: /var/log/journal
25.     matches: _TRANSPORT=kernel
26.     labels:
27.       job: systemd-journal
28.   relabel_configs:
29.     - source_labels: ['__journal__systemd_unit']
30.       target_label: 'unit'
```

Then, update our **promtail** config to use our config:

```
1.   promtail:
2.     image: grafana/promtail:2.9.1
3.     volumes:
4.       - ./promtail/:/etc/promtail/
5.       - /var/log:/var/log
6.     command: -config.file=/etc/promtail/config.yml
```

Now, restart the basic monitoring stack and verify you are getting logs from the journal.

Container based monitoring clients

Let us set up a monitoring client to return logs and metrics to our base monitoring stack. Here, we will make a **docker-compose.yaml** and save it on our client. Then, we can start a **Node Exporter** to collect metrics and a **promtail** to get logs. The logs are sent back to our Loki server. We will edit our Prometheus to collect metrics from our clients.

First, create a file for the **promtail** so you cannot set the host of the **loki** server.

The following code is what looks like from one of the nodes:

```
1.   root@g1:/opt/monitoring# cat promtail/config.yml
2.   server:
3.     http_listen_port: 9080
4.     grpc_listen_port: 0
5.
6.   positions:
7.     filename: /tmp/positions.yaml
8.
9.   clients:
10.    - url: http://192.168.1.4:3100/loki/api/v1/push
11.
12. scrape_configs:
```

```
13. - job_name: system
14.   static_configs:
15.   - targets:
16.       - localhost
17.     labels:
18.       job: varlogs
19.       __path__: /var/log/*log
20. - job_name: journal
21.   journal:
22.     json: false
23.     max_age: 12h
24.     path: /var/log/journal
25.     matches: _TRANSPORT=kernel
26.     labels:
27.       job: systemd-journal
28.   relabel_configs:
29.   - source_labels: ['__journal__systemd_unit']
30.     target_label: 'unit'
31. root@g1:/opt/monitoring#
```

Please note the following line in the aforementioned file:

```
1. clients:
2.   - url: http://192.168.1.4:3100/loki/api/v1/push
```

This is the IP of our base monitoring server where Loki is running. We also need to update our Prometheus config to pull data from the **Node Exporter**.

Open the config file on the base monitoring server and add the IP of the clients you want to monitor, as follows (The code is a snippet; the full config can be found in the GitHub repo):

```
1. root@pihole:/opt/monitoring# cat prom/prometheus.yml
2.   - job_name: 'node-exporter'
3.     # Override the global default and scrape targets from this job
   every 5 seconds.
4.     scrape_interval: 15s
5.
6.     static_configs:
7.       - targets: ['node-export
   er:9100','192.168.1.11:9100','10.0.0.17:9100']
8. root@pihole:/opt/monitoring#
```

You can see the clients on the bottom line.

Now, use **podman-compose** or **docker-compose** to start your stack.

This ends our setup by getting metrics and logs using Podman and Docker. You should now be able to see the following in your Grafana.

The following figure shows the data source to connect one to our Prometheus and one to our Loki server:

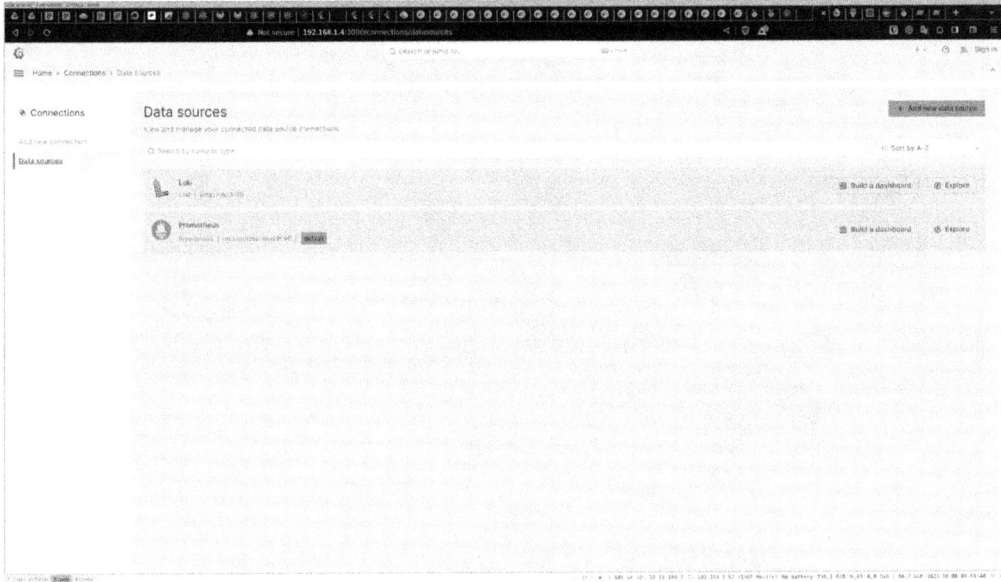

Figure 10.5: Adding Loki as a data source

If you visit the explorer view, you can see the logs from Loki by filtering on jobs as shown:

Figure 10.6: Loki logs number shown by the bars

We have the Node Exporter dashboard that you can use to view metrics from your server, as shown in the following figure:

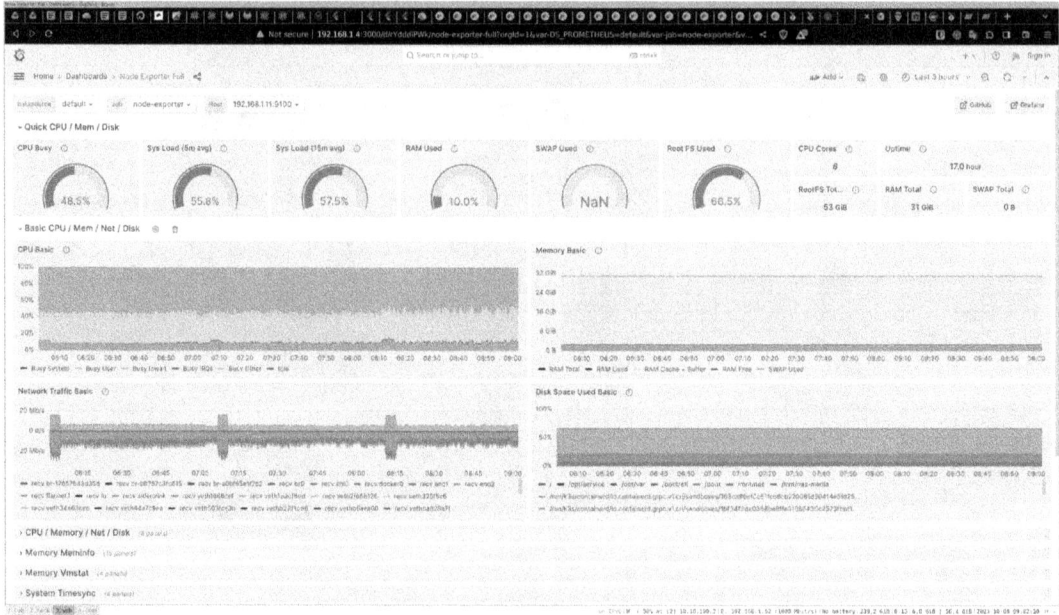

Figure 10.7: *Shows the metrics from our server in Grafana*

Conclusion

By the end of this chapter, we will have set up virtualization on an Ubuntu Server and connected and managed our VM with a GUI from our desktop and a web page. We also started and installed an Ubuntu Server VM using only the cli on our server. With this, we now know how to install and set up a VM on an Ubuntu Server in all ways possible.

We know that virtualization provides a stronger separation of services than containers, but containers are an excellent tool for starting services when they are not needed. We set up a comprehensive monitoring stack with metrics and logs, utilizing containers to optimize their use effectively. This was done using the container tools Podman and Docker.

With Podman, we slowly built up a base stack of monitoring tools until we had a full Monitoring base running. To connect clients we wanted to monitor, we set up new containers to collect and send data back to our monitoring base. With this, you can now set up services in containers and run them as a service, both as servers to collect and receive data and as clients to send data.

In the next chapter, we will discuss how to set up a Kubernetes cluster.

CHAPTER 11

Setup Webserver, Deploy and Run Webapps

Introduction

Running web applications is the standard way of running most online services today. Online applications can be from, for example, your own blog that you host, online shops, or social media platforms. So being able to host and run web applications is an important part when running and using Ubuntu Servers. Most applications on the web today have a web server that services the pages you see when you visit the page.

The database will store the data for the applications so that we can have data for the visitors of the web applications. Here, several different types of web servers display the web page to the user, and you can also use many more databases. This chapter will give a basic level of minimal knowledge of how to set up and run a simple web app using a web browser and a database.

Structure

In this chapter, we will cover the following topics:

- Web servers
- Databases
- Deploying web apps
- Webb Performance

Objectives

We will start by installing two types of web servers that are the most used today: Apache and NGINX. With our web server, we will create two domains and host simple web pages that do not require any database. We will also look into setting up some basic performance values for our web server. There are several databases for storing data for a web application, and here, we will install and set up two different types of databases. One is a document database called MongoDB, and the other is an SQL database called MariaDB. When setting up the database, we will also learn to log into our database and set some basic commands like looking at stats and taking and restoring backups.

Web servers

We will understand how to install and set up two different web servers. They both serve web pages to visitors, but they are different in some ways. For the app we will be testing, it does not really matter which one you like. But are you working with a high-performance service? Then you want to add some more time to what webserver to choose.

Apache

Let us start by installing Apache 2 as follows:

```
1. root@g1:/home/mahe# apt install apache2
```

This command will install **apache2** and create the folder where all the config files are in **/etc/apache2**:

root@g1:/etc/apache2# ls -l

```
 1. total 80
 2. -rw-r--r-- 1 root root  7224 Oct 26 13:44 apache2.conf
 3. drwxr-xr-x 2 root root  4096 Dec 20 15:25 conf-available
 4. drwxr-xr-x 2 root root  4096 Dec 20 15:25 conf-enabled
 5. -rw-r--r-- 1 root root  1782 May  3  2023 envvars
 6. -rw-r--r-- 1 root root 31063 May  3  2023 magic
 7. drwxr-xr-x 2 root root 12288 Dec 20 15:25 mods-available
 8. drwxr-xr-x 2 root root  4096 Dec 20 15:25 mods-enabled
 9. -rw-r--r-- 1 root root   320 May  3  2023 ports.conf
10. drwxr-xr-x 2 root root  4096 Dec 20 15:25 sites-available
11. drwxr-xr-x 2 root root  4096 Dec 20 15:25 sites-enabled
12. root@g1:/etc/apache2#
```

So, what does the folder structure work?

apache2.conf

This is the main config file that will be started when Apache starts. From this file, all other folders are included.

When running Apache, you can install the module. PHP is an example of one module, but it can be many more. All modules are located in mods-available. You may not need them all, so you can enable the modes you like by creating a link from mods-available to mods-enabled. Then, when Apache is started, **Apache2.conf** will include the folder mods-enabled and load the module from that folder.

Site folders are the same. For example, a site is a domain, mywapp.example.com, and you can have multiple sites in the same WordPress. For example, a web hotel may have 100 or even more sites enabled.

So, add your config (we will create the config soon) and add it to sites-available. Then, we will activate it by linking it into sites-enabled.

Webb content

We also need to have some content to run. Apache has a folder where all the files that make up the webpage are saved. The content is served from that folder. Here is why you will add your own code if you build your own app or download and copy a project.

/var/www/html is the default folder where we have our content.

First config

Let us create a folder in **/var/www/html/myapp**, and then we will create a config to display the content from that folder.

Make the folder and create a file called **index.html** in that folder. The name **index.html** is the name of the default webpage. If a web server goes to a folder and does not have a file name, it will look and load the **index.html** file.

```
1.  root@g1:/var/www/html/myapp# cat index.html
2.  <html>
3.   <title>test</title>
4.    <h2>Hello</h2>
5.  </html>
6.  root@g1:/var/www/html/myapp#
```

Now we have the content, and we need to tell our Apache server to get the files from that folder.

Here, we are updating the default file called 000-default to add our folder:

```
1.  root@g1:/etc/apache2/sites-enabled# cat 000-default.conf
2.  <VirtualHost *:80>
3.   #ServerName www.example.com
4.   ServerAdmin webmaster@localhost
5.   DocumentRoot /var/www/html/myapp
```

```
6.    ErrorLog ${APACHE_LOG_DIR}/error.log
7.    CustomLog ${APACHE_LOG_DIR}/access.log combined
8.    </VirtualHost>
9.
10. # vim: syntax=apache ts=4 sw=4 sts=4 sr noet
11. root@g1:/etc/apache2/sites-enabled#
```

Restart Apache to activate the changes, as follows:

```
1.  root@g1:/etc/apache2/sites-enabled# systemctl restart apache2
2.  root@g1:/etc/apache2/sites-enabled#
```

In the config file, we did add an access log file. Let us tail that file while we visit the page. Now go to **http:// THE IP OF YOUR SERVER.**

Tail the log file to see the access. The access or error log will give you more information if something is not working.

To read the logs, run the command as shown:

```
1.  root@g1:/etc/apache2/sites-enabled# tail -f /var/log/apache2/access.
    log
2.  192.168.1.52 - - [20/Dec/2023:16:34:49 +0000] "GET /myapp/ HTTP/1.1"
    200 336 "-" "Mozilla/5.0 (X11; Linux x86_64) AppleWebKit/537.36
    (KHTML, like Gecko) Chrome/120.0.0.0 Safari/537.36"
```

NGINX

Let us now set up NGINX, another web server, and we will set up nginx to also display our webpage. First, we must stop our Apache server; we cannot have the web server running simultaneously and listening on the same port. Run the following command to stop the Apache server:

```
1.  systemctl stop apache2
```

Then we can install NGINX as follows:

```
1.  root@g1:/etc/apache2/sites-enabled# apt install nginx
```

We will find the config files for NGINX in the **/etc/nginx** folder and then recognize the folder structure as follows:

```
1.  root@g1:/etc/nginx# ls -l
2.  total 64
3.  drwxr-xr-x 2 root root 4096 Nov 10  2022 conf.d
4.  -rw-r--r-- 1 root root 1125 Jul 27  2022 fastcgi.conf
5.  -rw-r--r-- 1 root root 1055 Jul 27  2022 fastcgi_params
6.  -rw-r--r-- 1 root root 2837 Jul 27  2022 koi-utf
7.  -rw-r--r-- 1 root root 2223 Jul 27  2022 koi-win
```

```
8.  -rw-r--r-- 1 root root 3957 Aug  2  2022 mime.types
9.  drwxr-xr-x 2 root root 4096 Nov 10  2022 modules-available
10. drwxr-xr-x 2 root root 4096 Jun 14  2023 modules-enabled
11. -rw-r--r-- 1 root root 1447 Jul 27  2022 nginx.conf
12. -rw-r--r-- 1 root root  180 Jul 27  2022 proxy_params
13. -rw-r--r-- 1 root root  636 Jul 27  2022 scgi_params
14. drwxr-xr-x 2 root root 4096 Dec 20 16:56 sites-available
15. drwxr-xr-x 2 root root 4096 Jun 14  2023 sites-enabled
16. drwxr-xr-x 2 root root 4096 Dec 20 16:56 snippets
17. -rw-r--r-- 1 root root  664 Jul 27  2022 uwsgi_params
18. -rw-r--r-- 1 root root 3071 Jul 27  2022 win-utf
```

Let us go into the folder sited-enable and edit the files default in that folder. We will update the root path to our own as follows:

```
1. # include snippets/snakeoil.conf;
2. root /var/www/html/myapp;
```

Now we can restart **nginx** and revisit our webpage over **http:// IP TO SERVER**, as follows:

```
1. root@g1:/etc/nginx/sites-enabled# systemctl restart nginx
2. root@g1:/etc/nginx/sites-enabled#
```

We can now see the same hell but now served from NGINX and not Apache.

Databases

There are many different types of databases, and they all behave differently. Here, we will test two different types, one SQL Server and one document database. They behave and work differently.

Let us start with the SQL Server.

MariaDB SQL

Let us start by installing MariaDB and setting up the SQL. For that, we will run the following command that will set up and lock down the SQL Server for us:

```
1. root@g1:/etc/nginx/sites-enabled# sudo apt install mariadb-server
   mariadb-client -y
2. root@g1:/etc/nginx/sites-enabled# mysql_secure_installation
```

During the *mysql_secure_installation*, answer all questions as questions as **y**, except the question **Switch to unix_socket authentication [Y/n] n**

... skipping

Then, set the SQL root password to a password you know.

Now, let us restart the database and log in as follows:

```
1.  root@g1:/etc/nginx/sites-enabled# systemctl restart mariadb
2.  root@g1:/etc/nginx/sites-enabled# mysql -u root -p
3.  Enter password:
4.  Welcome to the MariaDB monitor.  Commands end with ; or \g.
5.  Your MariaDB connection id is 31
6.  Server version: 10.6.12-MariaDB-0ubuntu0.22.04.1 Ubuntu 22.04
7.
8.  Copyright (c) 2000, 2018, Oracle, MariaDB Corporation Ab and others.
9.
10. Type 'help;' or '\h' for help. Type '\c' to clear the current input
    statement.
11.
12. MariaDB [(none)]> show databases;
13. +--------------------+
14. | Database           |
15. +--------------------+
16. | information_schema |
17. | mysql              |
18. | performance_schema |
19. | sys                |
20. +--------------------+
21. 4 rows in set (0.001 sec)
22.
23. MariaDB [(none)]>
```

As you aforementioned, we now also run the command **show databases;**.

This will display the databases we have in the database server. When we install new apps, we will create databases in our database server.

Run the following commands to create/list and delete a database:

MariaDB [(none)]> create database mattias;

```
1.  MariaDB [(none)]> create database mattias;
2.  Query OK, 1 row affected (0.001 sec)
3.
4.  MariaDB [(none)]> show databases;
5.  +--------------------+
6.  | Database           |
7.  +--------------------+
8.  | information_schema |
9.  | mattias            |
10. | mysql              |
```

```
11.| performance_schema |
12.| sys                |
13.+--------------------+
14.5 rows in set (0.000 sec)
15.
16.MariaDB [(none)]> drop database mattias;
17.Query OK, 0 rows affected (0.002 sec)
18.
19.MariaDB [(none)]> show databases;
20.+--------------------+
21.| Database           |
22.+--------------------+
23.| information_schema |
24.| mysql              |
25.| performance_schema |
26.| sys                |
27.+--------------------+
28.4 rows in set (0.001 sec)
29.
30.MariaDB [(none)]>
```

MongoDB

Now, we will install our other database, MongoDB, that are a document DB. For that, we need to add their repo and key, and then we can install our MongoDB database.

We are already familiar with the steps, so the following is a quick installation guide:

1. root@g1:/etc/nginx/sites-enabled# *curl -fsSL https://pgp.mongodb. com/server-7.0.asc | *

2.   sudo gpg -o /usr/share/keyrings/mongodb-server-7.0.gpg \

3.   --dearmor

4.

5.

6. root@g1:/etc/nginx/sites-enabled# *echo "deb [arch=amd64,arm64 signed-by=/usr/share/keyrings/mongodb-server-7.0.gpg] https://repo. mongodb.org/apt/ubuntu jammy/mongodb-org/7.0 multiverse" | sudo tee /etc/apt/sources.list.d/mongodb-org-7.0.list*

7. deb [arch=amd64,arm64 signed-by=/usr/share/keyrings/mongodb-server-7.0.gpg] https://repo.mongodb.org/apt/ubuntu jammy/mongodb-org/7.0 multiverse

8.

9.

10. root@g1:/etc/nginx/sites-enabled# *sudo apt-get update*

11.

12. Hit:1 http://archive.ubuntu.com/ubuntu jammy InRelease

13. Ign:2 https://repo.mongodb.org/apt/ubuntu jammy/mongodb-org/7.0 InRelease

14. Get:3 http://archive.ubuntu.com/ubuntu jammy-updates InRelease [119 kB]

15.

16. root@g1:/etc/nginx/sites-enabled# *sudo apt-get install -y mongodb-org*

17. Reading package lists... Done

18. Building dependency tree... Done

19. Reading state information... Done

20. Unpacking mongodb-org (7.0.4) ...

21. Setting up mongodb-mongosh (2.1.1) ...

22. Setting up mongodb-org-server (7.0.4) ...

23. Adding system user `mongodb' (UID 122) ...

24. Adding new user `mongodb' (UID 122) with group `nogroup' ...

25. Not creating home directory `/home/mongodb'.

26. Adding group `mongodb' (GID 126) ...

27. Done.

28. Adding user `mongodb' to group `mongodb' ...

29. Adding user mongodb to group mongodb

30. Done.

31. Setting up mongodb-org-shell (7.0.4) ...

32. Setting up mongodb-database-tools (100.9.4) ...

33. Setting up mongodb-org-mongos (7.0.4) ...

34. Setting up mongodb-org-database-tools-extra (7.0.4) ...

35. Setting up mongodb-org-database (7.0.4) ...

36. Setting up mongodb-org-tools (7.0.4) ...

37. Setting up mongodb-org (7.0.4) ...

When connecting to our MongoDB server we will use a command called **mongosh**. Here, we restart our MongoDB server and connect, as follows:

1. root@g1:/etc/nginx/sites-enabled# *systemctl restart mongod*

2. root@g1:/etc/nginx/sites-enabled# *mongosh*

3. Current Mongosh Log ID: 65833509961a4f00be52bbc0

4. Connecting to: mongodb://127.0.0.1:27017/?directConnection= true&serverSelectionTimeoutMS=2000&appName=mongosh+2.1.1

5. Using MongoDB: 7.0.4

6. Using Mongosh: 2.1.1

```
7.
8.  For mongosh info see: https://docs.mongodb.com/mongodb-shell/
9.
10.
11. To help improve our products, anonymous usage data is collected and
    sent to MongoDB periodically (https://www.mongodb.com/legal/privacy-
    policy).
12. You can opt-out by running the disableTelemetry() command.
13.
14. ------
15.    The server generated these startup warnings when booting
16.    2023-12-20T18:40:05.463+00:00: Using the XFS filesystem is
    strongly recommended with the WiredTiger storage engine. See http://
    dochub.mongodb.org/core/prodnotes-filesystem
17.    2023-12-20T18:40:06.769+00:00: Access control is not enabled for
    the database. Read and write access to data and configuration is
    unrestricted
18. ------
19.
20. test>
```

In MariaDB, we hade databases that we created, and we have similar here in the script below we create a new database called **mattias**.

In the database, we create a collection called **mattias-collections**, as follows:

```
1.  test> use mattias
2.  switched to db mattias
3.  mattias> db.createCollection("mattias-collections")
4.  { ok: 1 }
5.  mattias> show collections
6.  mattias-collections
7.  mattias>
```

Database tools

We have now installed our webserver and two different databases. But as you can see from above, managing our database is done from the command line. Let us install some tools to help us better manage our MariaDB server.

phpmyadmin

phpmyadmin is a web tool that manages MariaDB and another SQL-based server. Here, we can install it on our web server. In Ubuntu, there is a package that will install **phpmyadmin**

and setup everything for us.

So we can run it as follows:

```
1. apt install phpmyadmin php libapache2-mod-php
```

Then follow the step and set up to update the Apache2 webserver. Then, verify that our Apache2 server is running.

Go to **http:// Your IP /phpMyAdmin**, and you should see a webpage with a login. Now log in with the root and the password you set to the MYSQL SERVER.

From this webpage, you can now control your MariaDB server.

Deploying web apps

We are now ready to deploy any web app built with PHP and use a MySQL / MariaDB database. There are many different web services you can find. They all are installed in a similar setup as follows:

- We download a package with the code.

- We unpack the content to our webb folder in **/var/www/html/myapp.**

- We set the right permission for the files.

- We visit an installation page and fill in the values. The values are, for example, database name/user and password, and those we get by creating them in PHPMyAdmin.

WordPress

Let us start with the popular blog WordPress. We will download the latest WordPress and add it to our web folder. Here, we will download the **latest.zip** from WordPress, then install unzip and unzip the WordPress folder.

When we are done, we have a new folder named WordPress with the content from the ZIP we downloaded as follows:

```
1. root@g1:/var/www/html/myapp# wget https://wordpress.org/latest.zip
2. --2023-12-21 12:56:38--  https://wordpress.org/latest.zip
3. Resolving wordpress.org (wordpress.org)... 198.143.164.252
4. Connecting to wordpress.org (wordpress.org)|198.143.164.252|:443...
   connected.
5. HTTP request sent, awaiting response... 200 OK
6. Length: 25954973 (25M) [application/zip]
7. Saving to: 'latest.zip'
```

```
8.
9.  latest.zip                                         100%[=====
    ===================================================================
    =========================================================>]  24.75M
    12.6MB/s    in 2.0s
10.
11. 2023-12-21 12:56:41 (12.6 MB/s) - 'latest.zip' saved
    [25954973/25954973]
12.
13. root@g1:/var/www/html/myapp# unzip latest.zip
14. bash: unzip: command not found
15. root@g1:/var/www/html/myapp# apt install unzip
16.
17. root@g1:/var/www/html/myapp# unzip latest.zip
18. Archive:  latest.zip
19.
20.
21. root@g1:/var/www/html/myapp# ls -l
22. total 25360
23. -rwxrwxrwx 1 root root       53 Dec 20 16:34 index.html
24. -rw-r--r-- 1 root root 25954973 Dec  6 16:26 latest.zip
25. drwxr-xr-x 5 root root     4096 Dec  6 16:25 wordpress
26. root@g1:/var/www/html/myapp# rm latest.zip
27. root@g1:/var/www/html/myapp# ls -l
28. total 8
29. -rwxrwxrwx 1 root root   53 Dec 20 16:34 index.html
30. drwxr-xr-x 5 root root 4096 Dec  6 16:25 wordpress
31. root@g1:/var/www/html/myapp# https://wordpress.org/latest.zip
```

Before we can start Apache we need to set the right permission on the files. Our web server runs under the user **www-data** and group **www-data**.

```
1.  root@g1:/var/www/html/myapp# chown www-data:www-data -R wordpress/
2.  root@g1:/var/www/html/myapp#
```

We can now visit our webserver with Apache running on, and we are loading the setup page for WordPress. Follow the guide and add the following for the database. First, log in to our MariaDB from the terminal or use the PhpMyAdmin that we installed before. Then, create a new database called WordPress. Now, we can fill in our settings and add our MySQL user and password.

Using the root account, you should not do it other than for testing, as shown:

Figure 11.1: WordPress database setup

The best way is to create your account and set permissions for our WordPress.

Observium

Observium is a platform for monitoring the state of servers and switches, and it runs on PHP and MySQL. To get Observium working, we also need to add a virtual host till Apache and set and run some config commands to set our SQL and users.

Let us install it as well to test it out; notice we are now running this in the **opt** folder:

1. root@g1:/opt# *wget http://www.observium.org/observium-community-latest.tar.gz*
2. root@g1:/opt/#*tar zxvf observium-community-latest.tar.gz*
3. root@g1:/opt# *chown www-data:www-data -R observium*

Login into phpMyAdmin ore the SQL CLI and create a database for Observium. Then, we can move on to installing it by running the following commands. We copy the default config file and add our settings to our database. Then, we set up the database by installing the tables needed for Observium. After that, we create some folders and a user for us to use.

```
1.  root@g1:/opt/observium# cp config.php.default config.php
2.  root@g1:/opt/observium# vi config.php
3.  root@g1:/opt/observium# cat config.php
4.  <?php
5.
6.  ## Check https://docs.observium.org/config_options/ for documentation
    of possible settings
7.
8.  ## It's recommended that settings are edited in the web interface at
    /settings/ on your observium installation.
9.  ## Authentication and Database settings must be hardcoded here
    because they need to work before you can reach the web-based
    configuration interface
10.
11. // Database config
12. // --- This MUST be configured
13. $config['db_host']      = 'localhost';
14. $config['db_name']      = 'observium';
15. $config['db_user']      = 'root';
16. $config['db_pass']      = 'password';
17.
18. // Base directory
19. #$config['install_dir'] = "/opt/observium";
20.
21. // Default snmp version
22. #$config['snmp']['version'] = "v2c";
23. // Snmp max repetition for faster requests
24. #$config['snmp']['max-rep'] = TRUE;
25. // Default snmp community list to use when adding/discovering
26. #$config['snmp']['community'] = [ "public" ];
27.
28. // Authentication Model
29. #$config['auth_mechanism'] = "mysql";    // default, other options:
    ldap, http-auth, please see documentation for config help
30.
31. // Enable alerter
32. #$config['poller-wrapper']['alerter'] = TRUE;
33.
34. // Show or not disabled devices on major pages
35. #$config['web_show_disabled'] = FALSE;
36.
```

```
37. // Set up a default alerter (email to a single address)
38. #$config['email']['default']        = "user@your-domain";
39. #$config['email']['from']           = "Observium <observium@your-
    domain>";
40.
41. // End config.php
42. root@g1:/opt/observium#
43. root@g1:/opt/observium#
44. root@g1:/opt/observium# ./discovery.php -u
45.
46.   ___    _                                          _
47. / _ \ | |__      __      __  _ __ __  __(_) _   _ _ __ __
48. | | | | | | '_ \ / _| / _ \| '__|\ \ / /| || | | | | '_ ` _ \
49. | |_| | || |_) |\__ \|  __/| |    \ V / | || |_| || | | | | |
50. \___/ |_.__/ |___/ \___||_|     \_/  |_| \__,_||_| |_| |_|
51.                 Observium Community Edition 23.9.13005
52.                             https://www.observium.org
53.
54. Install initial database schema ... done.
55. -- Updating database/file schema
56.
57. 484 -> 485 # (db) . Done (0s).
58. -- Done.
59. -- Observium is up to date.
60. root@g1:/opt/observium# ./adduser.php matte password 1
61. Observium CE 23.9.13005
62. Add User
63.
64. User matte added successfully.
65. root@g1:/opt/observium# mkdir logs
66. root@g1:/opt/observium# mkdir rrd
67. root@g1:/opt/observium#
```

Now we have the issue that we have our WordPress running in one folder, and we have **observium** running in a different one. And we want to see both from within our web server.

To make that work, we will create a Virtual host in Apache. The setup is similar in NGINX; they both support many virtual hosts. In our Apache folder, we create a new file called **observium.conf**, and in that file, we can add the following content. Notice the **ServerAlias** value.

It tells if we go to **http://observium.lan** then this config will be activated.

```
1.  root@g1:/etc/apache2/sites-available# cat observium.conf
2.  <VirtualHost *:80>
3.      ServerAlias observium.lan
4.      ServerAdmin webmaster@localhost
5.      DocumentRoot /opt/observium/html
6.      <FilesMatch \.php$>
7.        SetHandler application/x-httpd-php
8.      </FilesMatch>
9.      <Directory />
10.           Options FollowSymLinks
11.           AllowOverride None
12.     </Directory>
13.     <Directory /opt/observium/html/>
14.           DirectoryIndex index.php
15.           Options Indexes FollowSymLinks MultiViews
16.           AllowOverride All
17.           Require all granted
18.     </Directory>
19.     ErrorLog  ${APACHE_LOG_DIR}/error.log
20.     LogLevel warn
21.     CustomLog  ${APACHE_LOG_DIR}/access.log combined
22.     ServerSignature On
23. </VirtualHost>
24. root@g1:/etc/apache2/sites-available#
```

We also need to add on our default file a server name so Apache know what config to use.

```
1.  root@g1:/etc/apache2/sites-enabled# cat 000-default.conf
2.  <VirtualHost *:80>
3.  ServerName www.lan
```

And we need to activate our config by linking the file to our **sites-enabled** folder:

```
1.  root@g1:/etc/apache2/sites-enabled# ln -s  ../sites-available/
    observium.conf .
2.  root@g1:/etc/apache2/sites-enabled# ls
3.  000-default.conf  observium.conf
4.  root@g1:/etc/apache2/sites-enabled#
```

Now restart Apache and set up the host file on your computer as well now when we do not have any DNS in our local network. From my computer:

```
1.  mattias@hrb:~$ cat /etc/hosts
2.  127.0.0.1 localhost
3.  192.168.1.11 observium.lan
```

You now have **observium** running and can visit by going to **http://observium.lan/** as shown:

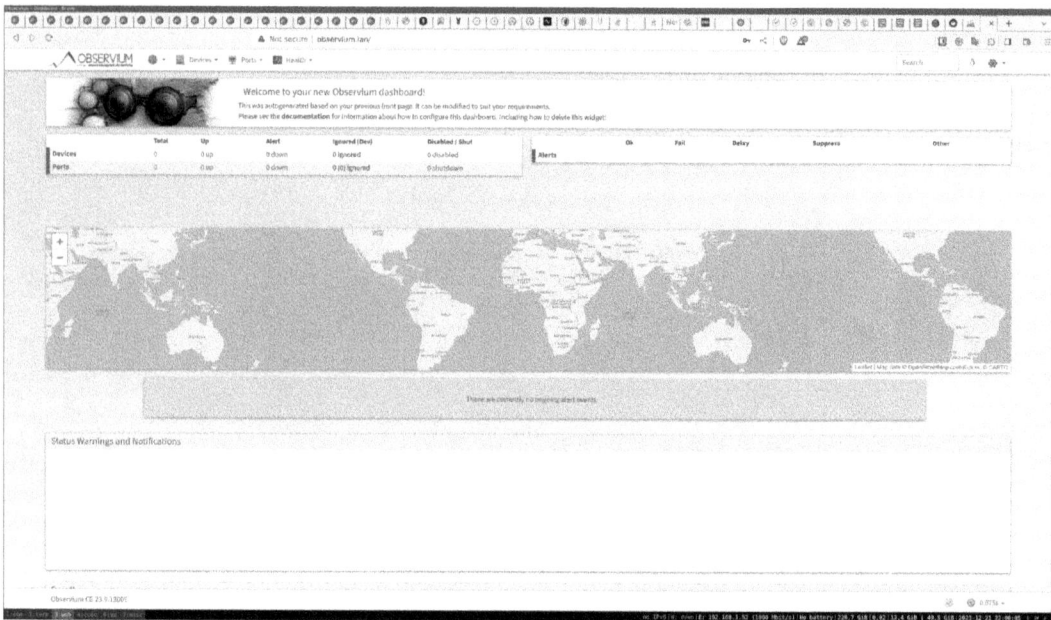

Figure 11.2: Observium main page

Rocket.Chat

Rocket.Chat is a chat application running in node. We will start here to app inside a Docker for us and then connect. Let us chat to our MongoDB server.

First, log in to our MongoDB and set up a user for our **rocket-chat**, as follows:

1. root@g1:/opt/rocket-chat*# mongosh*
2. Current Mongosh Log ID: 6584ad621f350a738e3d8239
3. Connecting to: mongodb://127.0.0.1:27017/?directConnection= true&serverSelectionTimeoutMS=2000&appName=mongosh+2.1.1
4. Using MongoDB: 7.0.4
5. Using Mongosh: 2.1.1
6.
7. For mongosh info see: https://docs.mongodb.com/mongodb-shell/
8.
9. ------
10.   The server generated these startup warnings when booting
11.   2023-12-20T18:40:05.463+00:00: Using the XFS filesystem is strongly recommended with the WiredTiger storage engine. See http://dochub.mongodb.org/core/prodnotes-filesystem

```
12.    2023-12-20T18:40:06.769+00:00: Access control is not enabled
   for the database. Read and write access to data and configuration is
   unrestricted
13. ------
14. test> use rocket
15. rocket> db.createUser(
16. ...    {
17. ...       user: "rocket",
18. ...       pwd: "rocketpass",   // or cleartext password
19. ...       roles: [ { role: "readWrite", db: "rocket" },
20. ...                { role: "read", db: "reporting" } ]
21. ...    }
22. ... )
23. { ok: 1 }
24. rocket> exit
25. root@g1:/opt/rocket-chat# mongosh -u rocket -p
   --authenticationDatabase  rocket
26. Enter password: **********
27. Current Mongosh Log ID: 6584ae48053eb4f94d7d58d6
28. Connecting to:   mongodb://<credentials>@127.0.0.1:27017/?direct
   Connection=true&serverSelectionTimeoutMS=2000&authSource=
   rocket&appName=mongosh+2.1.1
29. Using MongoDB:   7.0.4
30. Using Mongosh:   2.1.1
31.
32. For mongosh info see: https://docs.mongodb.com/mongodb-shell/
33.
34. ------
35.    The server generated these startup warnings when booting
36.    2023-12-20T18:40:05.463+00:00: Using the XFS filesystem is
   strongly recommended with the WiredTiger storage engine.
   See http://dochub.mongodb.org/core/prodnotes-filesystem
37.    2023-12-20T18:40:06.769+00:00: Access control is not enabled
   for the database. Read and write access to data and configuration
   is unrestricted
38. ------
39.
40. test> use rocket
41. switched to db rocket
42. rocket>
```

Rocket.Chat comes with a pre-setup docker-compose that we can use. We only need to update the MongoDB URL.

We also need to tell our MongoDB to listen to our network port. That is done by altering the MongoDB config, as follows:

```
1. root@g1:/opt/rocket-chat# cat /etc/mongod.conf
2. # mongod.conf
3. # network interfaces
4. net:
5.   port: 27017
6.   bindIp: 0.0.0.0
```

Update the **bindIp** from 127.0.0.1 to 0.0.0.0 and then restart the MongoDB server.

Now we can create a Docker compose file **compose.yml** and add the following content:

```
1. services:
2.   rocketchat:
3.     image: registry.rocket.chat/rocketchat/rocket.chat:${RELEASE:-latest}
4.     restart: always
5.     environment:
6.       MONGO_URL: "mongodb://rocket:rocketpass@192.168.1.11:27017/rocket"
7.       MONGO_OPLOG_URL: "mongodb://rocket:rocketpass@192.168.1.11:27017/rocket"
8.       ROOT_URL: http://192.168.1.11:3000
9.       PORT: 3000
10.      DEPLOY_METHOD: docker
11.      DEPLOY_PLATFORM: ${DEPLOY_PLATFORM:-}
12.      REG_TOKEN: ${REG_TOKEN:-}
13.    expose:
14.      - 3000
15.    ports:
16.      - 3000:3000
```

Start-up our Rocket.Chat with our **docker compose up** command. Your Rocket.Chat will be showing at **http:// IP:3000**.

Webb performance

When it comes to web performance, there are many different settings you can add to make your web server perform faster. Some are added by default, and some we need to add as well. Note that you need to test your page and settings to optimize your web server.

Some of the settings we add to our Apache server are keepalive and compress. They will keep connections open longer when you have many clients and reusing the connections and not making new ones saves time. Also, the compressed setting will compress the data when sent to the client, making it smaller and arriving faster.

The following is our Apache virtual host with **keepalive** and compress turned on:

```
1.     LoadModule deflate_module modules/mod_deflate.so
2.     KeepAlive On
3.     # MaxKeepAliveRequests: How many requests to allow during a
  persistent connection.
4.     # You can set it 0 for unlimited requests, but it is not
  recommended.
5.     MaxKeepAliveRequests 100
6.     # KeepAliveTimeout: Number of seconds to wait for the next
  request from the
7.     # same client on the same connection. Default is 5 seconds
8.     KeepAliveTimeout 15
9.     <VirtualHost *:80>
10.        ServerAdmin webmaster@localhost
11.        ErrorLog ${APACHE_LOG_DIR}/error.log
12.        CustomLog ${APACHE_LOG_DIR}/access.log combined
13.      Alias /server-status /tmp/server-stats
14.      <Directory /tmp/server-status>
15.        SetHandler server-status
16.        Order allow,deny
17.        Deny from env=go_away
18.        Allow from all
19.      </Directory>
20.    # Keep track of extended status information for each request
21.    #ExtendedStatus On
22.    # Determine if mod_status displays the first 63 characters of a
  request or
23.    # the last 63, assuming the request itself is greater than 63
  chars.
24.    # Default: Off
25.    #SeeRequestTail On
26.    <IfModule mod_proxy.c>
27.      # Show Proxy LoadBalancer status in mod_status
28.      ProxyStatus On
29.    </IfModule>
30.    <IfModule mod_deflate.c>
```

```
31.        AddOutputFilterByType DEFLATE application/javascript
32.        AddOutputFilterByType DEFLATE application/rss+xml
33.        AddOutputFilterByType DEFLATE application/vnd.ms-fontobject
34.        AddOutputFilterByType DEFLATE application/x-font
35.        AddOutputFilterByType DEFLATE application/x-font-opentype
36.        AddOutputFilterByType DEFLATE application/x-font-otf
37.        AddOutputFilterByType DEFLATE application/x-font-truetype
38.        AddOutputFilterByType DEFLATE application/x-font-ttf
39.        AddOutputFilterByType DEFLATE application/x-javascript
40.        AddOutputFilterByType DEFLATE application/xhtml+xml
41.        AddOutputFilterByType DEFLATE application/xml
42.        AddOutputFilterByType DEFLATE font/opentype
43.        AddOutputFilterByType DEFLATE font/otf
44.        AddOutputFilterByType DEFLATE font/ttf
45.        AddOutputFilterByType DEFLATE image/svg+xml
46.        AddOutputFilterByType DEFLATE image/x-icon
47.        AddOutputFilterByType DEFLATE text/css
48.        AddOutputFilterByType DEFLATE text/html
49.        AddOutputFilterByType DEFLATE text/javascript
50.        AddOutputFilterByType DEFLATE text/plain
51.        AddOutputFilterByType DEFLATE text/xml
52.    </IfModule>
53.    DocumentRoot /var/www/html
54.    </VirtualHost>
```

Here, the config for turning compress on with NGINX is as follows:

```
1. $ vim /etc/nginx/nginx.conf
2.
3. # uncomment gzip module
4. gzip on;
5. gzip_disable msie6;
6. gzip_proxied no-cache no-store private expired auth;
7. gzip_types text/plain text/css application/x-javascript application/
   javascript text/xml application/xml application/xml+rss text/
   javascript image/x-icon image/bmp image/svg+xml;
8. gzip_min_length 1024;
9. gzip_vary on;
10.gunzip on;
```

Backup

When running a database, taking backup is an important task, and for that, we have a command we can use. It is best to make a script and add it to the server to be run regularly

Here, we are exporting the databases and saving them to disk as follows:

```
1.  root@g1:/var/backups# mysqldump -u root -p wordpress > wordpress_
    backup.sql
2.  root@g1:/var/backups# mongodump mongodb://
    rocket:rocketpass@192.168.1.11:27017/rocket
3.  2023-12-21T22:00:07.579+0000 writing rocket.rocketchat_oauth_
    refresh_tokens to dump/rocket/rocketchat_oauth_refresh_tokens.bson
4.  2023-12-21T22:00:07.583+0000 done dumping rocket.rocketchat_oauth_
    refresh_tokens (0 documents)
5.  root@g1:/var/backups# ls
6.  dump  wordpress_backup.sql
7.  root@g1:/var/backups#
```

There are tools to read and restore the data back to both MariaDB and MongoDB.

Database user

When running our test, we used the root user, and it was not recommended at all. For every service you create, you want to create one user in a database to keep them separated.

We already have created a user for MongoDB. For MariaDB, you can create a user with the following command:

```
1.  CREATE USER 'dbuser'@'&' IDENTIFIED BY 'password';
2.  GRANT PRIVILEGE ON database.* TO 'dbuser'@'&';
3.  FLUSH PRIVILEGES;
```

Notice that you will update the name of the database to the database name you want to give the user access to.

Conclusions

By the end of this chapter, we looked at web servers and databases that are the base of most web applications today. Every service we use today over the internet is served by a web server and most likely has a database to store data. Apache and NGINX are two of the most used web servers, that we installed and set up in this chapter. When it comes to databases, there are many different types, but two of the most used are SQL servers, and we have installed and set up a MariaDB SQL server. The other type is a documents database, and for the document database, we have installed and set up MongoDB.

We have installed and set up two different web applications to use our Webserver and database. One is using a webform so that you, from an installation page, can set up your accounts and database settings. The other page uses config files and scripts, and here, you run and install both apps. To visit both pages on vi, configure Apache to service two virtual hosts.

Do use our MongoDB. We could install Rocket.Chat, and we could run in Docker, but it connected back to our MongoDB to store all its data.

Running a web server and database is one step, however, we also need them to be fast, and for that, we looked at simple ways of speeding up our web server. We also need backup if something happens and learned how to take a backup from both MariaDB and MongoDB. We need to make our data secure, and the first part is to make users for every service we use.

We now understand how to set up and run a web server and database in an Ubuntu Server.

In the next chapter, we will cover how to set up and run a Kubernetes cluster.

Join our book's Discord space

Join the book's Discord Workspace for Latest updates, Offers, Tech happenings around the world, New Release and Sessions with the Authors:

https://discord.bpbonline.com

CHAPTER 12

Kubernetes
Run and Setup

Introduction

In this chapter, we will look at setting up a Kubernetes cluster on an on-prem cluster of Ubuntu Servers. We will then set up some default services to ensure your cluster is operational and ready for the workload.

During the setup of the cluster, we will install services to monitor metrics and logs. Using disk and balancing traffic using ingress and load balancers.

By the end, we will deploy our WordPress deployment as a workload in the cluster.

Kubernetes clusters are available on all cloud providers today, and the content in the chapter will not just help you with Ubuntu but also help in setting up Kubernetes clusters anywhere.

Structure

In this chapter, we will cover the following topics:

- Installing Kubernetes on Ubuntu
- Installing Kubernetes
- Setting up our Kubernetes

- Deploy Kubernetes base service
- Install WordPress in Kubernetes
- Kubectl command to remember

Objectives

By the end of this chapter, we will start with installing a clean Ubuntu Server. We will then learn to set up a Kubernetes master. When the Kubernetes master is running, we will add a new Ubuntu Server as a Kubernetes worker node. And start adding workload to our Kubernetes cluster.

By the end of this chapter, you will be able to set up your own Kubernetes cluster and deploy services into the cluster. Once the cluster is set, we will continue to add cluster services to use our cluster. We will add a Load balancer to receive traffic to our cluster. We will also add tools to monitor our cluster with logs and metrics. Storage system to enable our workloads to utilize disk resources. When our core systems are installed, we can add our workload into the cluster and, like WordPress, into our cluster.

Finally, once our workload is running, we will also look at some base commands to troubleshoot our Kubernetes cluster.

Installing Kubernetes on Ubuntu

There are several tools to install Kubernetes on the Ubuntu Server. Ubuntu also has its own tool. However, here, we will examine kubeadm, a tool from Kubernetes for setting up a Kubernetes cluster.

We will start with a clean Ubuntu Server installation and install our components. Then, we will begin with setting up our master node.

Once the master node is running, we will connect our worker node to the master.

Installing Kubernetes requirements

Run the following on both the master and the worker. It will install the packages we need on our Ubuntu Server before we can start installing our Kubernetes cluster. The small bash script is a simple way to make sure our Ubuntu nodes are updated and have the correct packages and settings before we can start. This provides a good foundation for us to build upon with the Kubernetes cluster.

The following command is run on both the master and the workers:

```
1. echo "First lets update this box"
2. apt-get update
3. apt-get upgrade -y
4. echo "Lets get docker"
```

```
5. apt-get update
6.
7. apt-get install \
8.     apt-transport-https \
9.     ca-certificates \
10.    curl \
11.    gnupg \
12.    lsb-release -y
13.
14. echo "Setup cri-o"
15. export OS=xUbuntu_22.04
16. export CRIO_VERSION=1.28
    echo "deb https://download.opensuse.org/repositories/devel:/kubic:/
    libcontainers:/stable/$OS/ /"| sudo tee /etc/apt/sources.list.d/
    devel:kubic:libcontainers:stable.list
    echo "deb http://download.opensuse.org/repositories/devel:/kubic:/
    libcontainers:/stable:/cri-o:/$CRIO_VERSION/$OS/ /"|sudo tee /etc/
    apt/sources.list.d/devel:kubic:libcontainers:stable:cri-o:$CRIO_
    VERSION.list
17.
18. curl -L https://download.opensuse.org/repositories/devel:kubic:libc
    ontainers:stable:cri-o:$CRIO_VERSION/$OS/Release.key | sudo apt-key
    add -
19. curl -L https://download.opensuse.org/repositories/devel:/kubic:/
    libcontainers:/stable/$OS/Release.key | sudo apt-key add -
20. apt update
21. sudo apt install cri-o cri-o-runc -y
22.
23. echo "Setup kdeadm"
24. cat <<EOF | sudo tee /etc/modules-load.d/k8s.conf
25. br_netfilter
26. EOF
27.
28. cat <<EOF | sudo tee /etc/sysctl.d/k8s.conf
29. net.bridge.bridge-nf-call-ip6tables = 1
30. net.bridge.bridge-nf-call-iptables = 1
31. EOF
32. sudo sysctl --system
33.
34. apt-get update
35. apt-get install -y apt-transport-https ca-certificates curl
36.
37.
```

```
38. curl -fsSL https://pkgs.k8s.io/core:/stable:/v1.28/deb/Release.key |
    sudo gpg --dearmor -o /etc/apt/keyrings/kubernetes-apt-keyring.gpg
39.
40.
41. echo 'deb [signed-by=/etc/apt/keyrings/kubernetes-apt-keyring.gpg]
    https://pkgs.k8s.io/core:/stable:/v1.28/deb/ /' | sudo tee /etc/apt/
    sources.list.d/kubernetes.list
42.
43.
44. apt-get update
45. apt-get install -y kubelet kubeadm kubectl
46. apt-mark hold kubelet kubeadm kubectl
```

We also, on our master, install our kubectl cli. The **kubectl** will be the command we use to control our cluster.

Install it on the master, and if you want to connect to the cluster from your computer, run the following command:

```
apt-get install -y kubectl
```

Kubernetes cannot run with swap enabled, so we need to disable swap on our disk. Run the following command:

```
1. swapoff -a
```

This will turn the swap off. To make it over reboot, open the file **/etc/fstab** and comment out the swap line shown as follows:

```
1. root@k8sworker1:/etc# cat /etc/fstab
2. # /etc/fstab: static file system information.
3. #
4. # Use 'blkid' to print the universally unique identifier for a
5. # device; this may be used with UUID= as a more robust way to name
   devices
6. # that works even if disks are added and removed. See fstab(5).
7. #
8. # <file system> <mount point>   <type>  <options>       <dump>
   <pass>
9. # / was on /dev/ubuntu-vg/ubuntu-lv during curtin installation
10. /dev/disk/by-id/dm-uuid-LVM-cfGHvajJTd3kAImwQnpYjlKIdlibPnigLy3eug4t
    ETdyLQoEMklbvgGFdKNKwsMx / ext4 defaults 0 1
11. # /boot was on /dev/vda2 during curtin installation
12. /dev/disk/by-uuid/a05358b5-b729-4962-ab39-53f6bcf016d9 /boot ext4
    defaults 0 1
13. /swap.img none swap sw 0 0
14.
15. #/swap.img none swap sw 0 0
```

Your file should have the line with *swap* commented out, as aforementioned.

We also need to update/hack so that **containerd** starts running the following command to verify our **containerd**:

1. rm /etc/containerd/config.toml
2. systemctl restart containerd

Setting up our Kubernetes cluster

We are now ready to install Kubernetes, and we will do that by running an **init** command on the master node. We will also set an IP range for our pod in the **init** command.

The **init** script will run and make all the config. When the **init** is done, we will add our worker node. Then, we must add a network plugin that creates the network for the pods in the cluster. There are several network plugins, and they all give different values, shown as follows:

1. root@k8smaster:/etc# kubeadm init --cri-socket /var/run/crio/crio.sock --pod-network-cidr=10.244.0.0/16
2. W1106 21:05:51.319644   20918 initconfiguration.go:120] Usage of CRI endpoints without URL scheme is deprecated and can cause kubelet errors in the future. Automatically prepending scheme "unix" to the "criSocket" with value "/var/run/crio/crio.sock". Please update your configuration!
3. W1106 21:05:51.323164   20918 version.go:104] could not fetch a Kubernetes version from the internet: unable to get URL "https://dl.k8s.io/release/stable-1.txt": Get "https://dl.k8s.io/release/stable-1.txt": dial tcp: lookup dl.k8s.io on 127.0.0.53:53: server misbehaving
4. W1106 21:05:51.323178   20918 version.go:105] falling back to the local client version: v1.28.3
5. [init] Using Kubernetes version: v1.28.3
6. [preflight] Running pre-flight checks
7. [preflight] Pulling images required for setting up a Kubernetes cluster
8. [preflight] This might take a minute or two, depending on the speed of your internet connection
9. [preflight] You can also perform this action in beforehand using 'kubeadm config images pull'
10. [certs] Using certificateDir folder "/etc/kubernetes/pki"
11. Logs between has remove for visibilty
12. [[bootstrap-token] Configured RBAC rules to allow certificate rotation for all node client certificates in the cluster
13. [bootstrap-token] Creating the "cluster-info" ConfigMap in the "kube-public" namespace

14. [kubelet-finalize] Updating "/etc/kubernetes/kubelet.conf" to point to a rotatable kubelet client certificate and key
15. [addons] Applied essential addon: CoreDNS
16. [addons] Applied essential addon: kube-proxy
17.
18. Your Kubernetes control-plane has initialized successfully!
19.
20. To start using your cluster, you need to run the following as a regular user:
21.
22.   mkdir -p $HOME/.kube
23.   sudo cp -i /etc/kubernetes/admin.conf $HOME/.kube/config
24.   sudo chown $(id -u):$(id -g) $HOME/.kube/config
25.
26. Alternatively, if you are the root user, you can run:
27.
28.   export KUBECONFIG=/etc/kubernetes/admin.conf
29.
30. You should now deploy a pod network to the cluster.
31. Run "kubectl apply -f [podnetwork].yaml" with one of the options listed at:
32.   https://kubernetes.io/docs/concepts/cluster-administration/addons/
33.
34. Then you can join any number of worker nodes by running the following on each as root:
35.
36. kubeadm join 192.168.122.162:6443 --token s139j1.2zdnneea0v6d8e7u \
37.   --discovery-token-ca-cert-hash sha256:29d849da533a16d55ee4da7b02534135eee998d674e8f73a8bd989cd82cdb2cf
38.

Now, our Kubernetes master has been set up and ready. We can now run the **join** command on our worker to add it to the cluster. This can be done by running the following code:

1. root@k8sworker1:/etc# kubeadm join 192.168.122.162:6443 --token 8ojxkg.nc73dumshya6616t --cri-socket /var/run/crio/crio.sock --discovery-token-ca-cert-hash sha256:6a0866192f3c308cd78cf336ce22afeeb7e969262e09dbb06b1888d49e8ffeb2

2. W1106 20:52:36.423681   9268 initconfiguration.go:120] Usage of CRI endpoints without URL scheme is deprecated and can cause kubelet errors in the future. Automatically prepending scheme "unix" to the "criSocket" with value "/var/run/crio/crio.sock". Please update your configuration!

3. [preflight] Running pre-flight checks

4. [preflight] Reading configuration from the cluster...

5. [preflight] FYI: You can look at this config file with `'kubectl -n kube-system get cm kubeadm-config -o yaml'`

6. [kubelet-start] Writing kubelet configuration to file `"/var/lib/kubelet/config.yaml"`

7. [kubelet-start] Writing kubelet environment file with flags to file `"/var/lib/kubelet/kubeadm-flags.env"`

8. [kubelet-start] Starting the kubelet

9. [kubelet-start] Waiting for the kubelet to perform the TLS Bootstrap...

10.

11. This node has joined the cluster:

12. * Certificate signing request was sent to apiserver and a response was received.

13. * The Kubelet was informed of the new secure connection details.

14.

15. Run `'kubectl get nodes'` on the control-plane to see this node join the cluster.

16. root@k8sworker1:/etc#

The join token is valid for a while, but you can easily create a new token later if you want to add more nodes.

To access your cluster, we need a config with the URL and certs to grant access. Kubeadmin has generated it for us, and we can use it with the following command:

1. export KUBECONFIG=/etc/kubernetes/admin.conf

You can copy this to your computer and then run the **kubectl** command from it. This token is the admin token that you should keep secure. There are many ways you can make users and roles in Kubernetes, but we will only use the admin token. As shown in the following code, we add our config and request our Kubernetes API to determine what nodes are connected. The following code shows how to set up the access to our Kubernetes cluster:

1. root@k8smaster:/etc# *export KUBECONFIG=/etc/kubernetes/admin.conf*

2. root@k8smaster:/etc# *kubectl get nodes*

```
3. NAME           STATUS    ROLES           AGE      VERSION
4. k8smaster      Ready     control-plane   3m41s    v1.28.3
5. k8sworker1     Ready     <none>          46s      v1.28.3
6. root@k8smaster:/etc#
```

We have our cluster up and connected. Let us do our last step before we start using our cluster, which is adding a network plugin. This can be done by running the following:

1. root@k8smaster:/etc# *kubectl apply -f https://github.com/flannel-io/flannel/releases/latest/download/kube-flannel.yml*
2. namespace/kube-flannel created
3. serviceaccount/flannel created
4. clusterrole.rbac.authorization.k8s.io/flannel created
5. clusterrolebinding.rbac.authorization.k8s.io/flannel created
6. configmap/kube-flannel-cfg created
7. daemonset.apps/kube-flannel-ds created
8. root@k8smaster:/etc#

Here, we use our **kubectl** command and apply the flannel network plugin to our cluster. We have now added our first workload into the cluster and made it ready for our next step.

Let us verify that all our pods are running as they should:

1. root@k8smaster:/opt/cni/bin# kubectl get pods -A

	NAMESPACE	NAME	READY	STATUS	RESTARTS
2.					
	RESTARTS	AGE			
3.	kube-flannel	kube-flannel-ds-16d9j	1/1	Running	0
	18m				
4.	kube-flannel	kube-flannel-ds-tqlg5	1/1	Running	0
	18m				
5.	kube-system	coredns-5dd5756b68-1mmfl	1/1	Running	0
		13s			
6.	kube-system	coredns-5dd5756b68-zn5w4	1/1	Running	0
		19m			
7.	kube-system	etcd-k8smaster	1/1	Running	8
		20m			
8.	kube-system	kube-apiserver-k8smaster	1/1	Running	9 (21m ago)
		20m			
9.	kube-system	kube-controller-manager-k8smaster	1/1	Running	0
		20m			
10.	kube-system	kube-proxy-87szh	1/1	Running	0
		19m			
11.	kube-system	kube-proxy-fmn7q	1/1	Running	0
		18m			
12.	kube-system	kube-scheduler-k8smaster	1/1	Running	9
		20m			

Deploy Kubernetes base service

We will now start adding workload to our cluster. To do that, we will use kubectl as we did before and a tool called **Helm**. Helm is like a package manager for Kubernetes, and with it, we can add workloads as packages.

You will learn to make your manifest and deploy it to the cluster later in this chapter, but for now, we will be using already-built tools.

We will move fast now and install a lot of services into the cluster. Then, when we are done with the core service, we will deploy our service.

So, for now, hold on, and it will be clear later what all the different services will do.

Installing Helm

Helm, the package manager for Kubernetes, is installed by running the following commands:

```
1. root@k8smaster:~# curl https://raw.githubusercontent.com/helm/helm/
   main/scripts/get-helm-3 | bash
2.   % Total    % Received % Xferd  Average Speed   Time     Time
     Time  Current
3.                                  Dload  Upload   Total    Spent
     Left  Speed
4. 100 11664  100 11664    0     0  76712        0 --:--:-- --:--:-- --:-
   -:-- 76736
5. Downloading https://get.helm.sh/helm-v3.13.1-linux-amd64.tar.gz
6. Verifying checksum... Done.
7. Preparing to install helm into /usr/local/bin
8. helm installed int
```

Storage

Let us start by adding storage. There are many different storage solutions, and we will use one called **OpenEBS**. OpenEBS can be used with lvm and many different types of storage, but here, for simplicity, we will be using a simple **hostpath**. This works well in base clusters, but another way of storage is needed if you are to make larger clusters.

If you are a cloud provider, they already have storage ready for you. The following code shows how to install **openebs** storage into our Kubernetes cluster:

```
1. root@k8smaster:/opt/cni/bin# kubectl apply -f https://openebs.
   github.io/charts/openebs-operator.yaml
2. namespace/openebs created
3. serviceaccount/openebs-maya-operator created
4. clusterrole.rbac.authorization.k8s.io/openebs-maya-operator created
5. clusterrolebinding.rbac.authorization.k8s.io/openebs-maya-operator
   created
6. customresourcedefinition.apiextensions.k8s.io/blockdevices.openebs.io
   created
```

7. customresourcedefinition.apiextensions.k8s.io/blockdeviceclaims.
   openebs.io created
8. configmap/openebs-ndm-config created
9. daemonset.apps/openebs-ndm created
10. deployment.apps/openebs-ndm-operator created
11. deployment.apps/openebs-ndm-cluster-exporter created
12. service/openebs-ndm-cluster-exporter-service created
13. daemonset.apps/openebs-ndm-node-exporter created
14. service/openebs-ndm-node-exporter-service created
15. deployment.apps/openebs-localpv-provisioner created
16. storageclass.storage.k8s.io/openebs-hostpath created
17. storageclass.storage.k8s.io/openebs-device created
18. root@k8smaster:/opt/cni/bin#

We have added some base storage that will use the node files as a base. We need to run one more command in Kubernetes to use this storage as default.

If we do not run this command, we will have some problems when we deploy into our cluster:

1. kubectl patch storageclass openebs-hostpath -p '{"metadata":
   {"annotations":{"storageclass.kubernetes.io/is-default-
   class":"true"}}}'

Monitoring

Let us add monitoring to our stack to know what is going on with our pods. To do that, we will be using helm.

We start by adding the repo and adding the Prometheus-community repo. To load the repo, we run the command "**helm repo update**". We now have the repo and can install it.

It follows the same way as our Ubuntu package manager; we can install Prometheus using **helm** into our cluster as follows:

1. root@k8smaster:~# helm repo add prometheus-community https://
   prometheus-community.github.io/helm-charts
2. "prometheus-community" has been added to your repositories
3. root@k8smaster:~# helm repo update
4. Hang tight while we grab the latest from your chart repositories...
5. ...Successfully got an update from the "prometheus-community" chart
   repository
6. Update Complete. ⏉Happy Helming!⏉
7. root@k8smaster:~# helm install monitoring prometheus-community/kube-
   prometheus-stack

```
8.  NAME: monitoring
9.  LAST DEPLOYED: Tue Nov  7 17:28:04 2023
10. NAMESPACE: default
11. STATUS: deployed
12. REVISION: 1
13. NOTES:
14. kube-prometheus-stack has been installed. Check its status by
    running:
15.    kubectl --namespace default get pods -l "release=monitoring"
16.
17. Visit https://github.com/prometheus-operator/kube-prometheus for
    instructions on how to create & configure Alertmanager and Prometheus
    instances using the Operator.
18. root@k8smaster:~#
```

We now will have some more Pods, and we can see what we have running now:

```
1.  root@k8smaster:~# kubectl get pods -A
2.  NAMESPACE        NAME
    READY    STATUS    RESTARTS       AGE
3.  default          alertmanager-monitoring-kube-prometheus-
    alertmanager-0   2/2      Running    0              3m56s
4.  default          monitoring-grafana-67656d977b-k5qdz
    3/3      Running   0            4m7s
5.  default          monitoring-kube-prometheus-operator-557564d7f4-v74t5
    1/1      Running   0            4m7s
6.  default          monitoring-kube-state-metrics-66f77d9d-sf2kn
    1/1      Running   0            4m7s
7.  default          monitoring-prometheus-node-exporter-bw2fd
    1/1      Running   0            4m7s
8.  default          monitoring-prometheus-node-exporter-pz6s5
    1/1      Running   0            4m7s
9.  default          prometheus-monitoring-kube-prometheus-prometheus-0
    2/2      Running   0            3m56s
```

You should already be familiar with these Pods as we have used them before. The Node Exporter will get all the metrics from our node and display them to Prometheus. Then, we have Grafana, which will display the data for us.

Ingress

The ingress controller in Kubernetes is the one that will receive all traffic to the cluster. It will then route the traffic to the exemplary service behind. We need an ingress controller in the cluster to share the same entry service for them. There are several different ingress controllers, and here we have chosen to use one called **traefik**.

You will use the same approach as before with Helm, as follows:

1. root@k8smaster:~*# helm repo add traefik https://traefik.github.io/ charts*
2. "traefik" has been added to your repositories
3. root@k8smaster:~*# helm repo update*
4. Hang tight while we grab the latest from your chart repositories...
5. ...Successfully got an update from the "traefik" chart repository
6. ...Successfully got an update from the "prometheus-community" chart repository
7. Update Complete. ⏾Happy Helming!⏾
8. root@k8smaster:~*# helm install traefik traefik/traefik*
9. NAME: traefik
10. LAST DEPLOYED: Tue Nov 7 17:36:49 2023
11. NAMESPACE: default
12. STATUS: deployed
13. REVISION: 1
14. TEST SUITE: None
15. NOTES:
16. Traefik Proxy v2.10.5 has been deployed successfully on default namespace !
17. root@k8smaster:~*#*

Then, we can check what Pods are running:

1. default   traefik-784fbdd7dc-dlbbv
   1/1   Running   0   87s

Load balancer

Traefik, which we installed before, will take care of routing the traffic right inside our cluster. However, we also need traffic to hit our cluster. For that, we need an external load balancer. In the cloud, you will get one from the cloud providers, but here, we will use MetalLB. MetalLB will take IP from our local network. Then, that IP will be used by our clusters and for you to access.

We can install MetalLB with the following command:

1. root@k8smaster:~# kubectl apply -f https://raw.githubusercontent. com/metallb/metallb/v0.13.12/config/manifests/metallb-native.yaml
2.
3. namespace/metallb-system created
4. customresourcedefinition.apiextensions.k8s.io/addresspools.metallb.io

```
    created
5.  customresourcedefinition.apiextensions.k8s.io/bfdprofiles.metallb.io
    created
6.  customresourcedefinition.apiextensions.k8s.io/bgpadvertisements.
    metallb.io created
7.  customresourcedefinition.apiextensions.k8s.io/bgppeers.metallb.io
    created
8.  customresourcedefinition.apiextensions.k8s.io/communities.metallb.io
    created
9.  customresourcedefinition.apiextensions.k8s.io/ipaddresspools.metallb.
    io created
10. customresourcedefinition.apiextensions.k8s.io/l2advertisements.
    metallb.io created
11. serviceaccount/controller created
12. serviceaccount/speaker created
13. role.rbac.authorization.k8s.io/controller created
14. role.rbac.authorization.k8s.io/pod-lister created
15. clusterrole.rbac.authorization.k8s.io/metallb-system:controller
    created
16. clusterrole.rbac.authorization.k8s.io/metallb-system:speaker created
17. rolebinding.rbac.authorization.k8s.io/controller created
18. rolebinding.rbac.authorization.k8s.io/pod-lister created
19. clusterrolebinding.rbac.authorization.k8s.io/metallb-
    system:controller created
20. clusterrolebinding.rbac.authorization.k8s.io/metallb-system:speaker
    created
21. configmap/metallb-excludel2 created
22. secret/webhook-server-cert created
23. service/webhook-service created
24. deployment.apps/controller created
25. daemonset.apps/speaker created
26. validatingwebhookconfiguration.admissionregistration.k8s.io/metallb-
    webhook-configuration created
27. root@k8smaster:~#
```

Let us take a look if we have some new Pods that have started

```
1.  root@k8smaster:~# kubectl get pods -A
2.  NAMESPACE          NAME
    READY    STATUS    RESTARTS       AGE
3.  metallb-system     controller-786f9df989-m8mgn
    1/1      Running   0              59s
4.  metallb-system     speaker-grqkl
```

```
       1/1      Running    0              59s
5.  metallb-system    speaker-whfcx
       1/1      Running    0              59s
6.  root@k8smaster:~#
```

Logs

Now, it is time to set up our last tool. For that, we need to add more values to our Helm chart. We will create a file with the extra values and then pass the file into our **helm** command. This is standard practice when installing Helm charts.

Create a new file on the master node named **values.yaml** and add the following content:

```
1.  loki:
2.    commonConfig:
3.      replication_factor: 1
4.    storage:
5.      type: 'filesystem'
6.  singleBinary:
7.    replicas: 1
```

Now, we will add the **grafana** Helm repo and install **loki**:

```
1.  root@k8smaster:~/loki# cat values.yaml
2.  loki:
3.    commonConfig:
4.      replication_factor: 1
5.    storage:
6.      type: 'filesystem'
7.  singleBinary:
8.    replicas: 1
9.  root@k8smaster:~/loki# helm repo add grafana https://grafana.github.
    io/helm-charts
10. "grafana" has been added to your repositories
11. root@k8smaster:~/loki# helm repo update
12. Hang tight while we grab the latest from your chart repositories...
13. ...Successfully got an update from the "traefik" chart repository
14. ...Successfully got an update from the "grafana" chart repository
15. ...Successfully got an update from the "prometheus-community" chart
    repository
16. Update Complete. ⎈Happy Helming!⎈
17. root@k8smaster:~/loki# helm install --values values.yaml loki
    grafana/loki-stack
18. NAME: loki
```

```
19. LAST DEPLOYED: Tue Nov  7 19:10:40 2023
20. NAMESPACE: default
21. STATUS: deployed
22. REVISION: 1
23. NOTES:
24. ********************************************************************
    ***
25.  Welcome to Grafana Loki
26.  Chart version: 5.36.3
27.  Loki version: 2.9.2
28. ********************************************************************
    ***
29.
30. Installed components:
31. * grafana-agent-operator
32. * loki
33. root@k8smaster:~/loki#
```

Let us see if our Pods are running:

```
1. root@k8smaster:~/loki# kubectl get pods -A
2. NAMESPACE          NAME
   READY     STATUS     RESTARTS        AGE
3. default            alertmanager-monitoring-kube-prometheus-
   alertmanager-0    2/2      Running    0              143m
4. default            loki-0
   1/1       Running    0              5m32s
5. default            loki-promtail-fjm47
   1/1       Running    0              5m32s
6. default            loki-promtail-vcbjf
   1/1       Running    0              5m32s
7. default            monitoring-grafana-67656d977b-k5qdz
   3/3       Running    0              143m
8.
```

We can see we now have some Loki Pods running.

Install WordPress in Kubernets

Now, we have added our core service, and we can start adding our service.

We will start by adding a WordPress installation. It will be a MySQL server and a WordPress Pod. We will then set up and use the core service we install to view and monitor our service.

When we deploy WordPress, we will be making manifest files. These files are the config that we send to our Kubernetes cluster to make it start running our service.

There are many values we are not covering here, and if you are to build a deployment for a production server, you need to add more value to the deployment.

MySQL

Let us start by adding our MySQL server. Create a file called **mysql.yaml** on the k8s master or on a computer that has access to Kubernetes.

Then, add the following content:

```
1.  apiVersion: apps/v1
2.  kind: Deployment
3.  metadata:
4.    name: mysql
5.  spec:
6.    selector:
7.      matchLabels:
8.        app: mysql-pod
9.    replicas: 1
10.   template:
11.     metadata:
12.       labels:
13.         app: mysql-pod
14.     spec:
15.       containers:
16.         - image: mysql:5.6
17.           imagePullPolicy: Always
18.           name: mysql-pod
19.           args: ["--default-authentication-plugin=mysql_native_
      password"]
20.           env:
21.             - name: MYSQL_USER
22.               value: mysql
23.             - name: MYSQL_PASSWORD
24.               value: 'password'
25.             - name: MYSQL_ROOT_PASSWORD
26.               value: rootpassword
27.             - name: MYSQL_DATABASE
28.               value: wordpress
29.           ports:
30.             - containerPort: 3306
```

```
31.                name: sql
32.            resources:
33.              requests:
34.                cpu: 100m
35.            volumeMounts:
36.              - name: mysql-persistent-storage
37.                mountPath: /var/lib/mysql
38.        volumes:
39.          - name: mysql-persistent-storage
40.            persistentVolumeClaim:
41.              claimName: mysql-disk
42. ---
43. apiVersion: v1
44. kind: Service
45. metadata:
46.   name: mysql
47.   labels:
48.     app: mysql-pod
49. spec:
50.   type: ClusterIP
51.   ports:
52.     - port: 3306
53.       targetPort: 3306
54.       protocol: TCP
55.   selector:
56.     app: mysql-pod
57. ---
58. kind: PersistentVolumeClaim
59. apiVersion: v1
60. metadata:
61.   name: mysql-disk
62. spec:
63.   accessModes:
64.     - ReadWriteOnce
65.   resources:
66.     requests:
67.       storage: 1Gi
```

When we look at this file, we see three things. First is the deployment. This is the manifest for starting a MySQL container inside Kubernetes. We have the container name, and we set how much CPU it will use. And we set where our disk for storage will go.

The env section is where we set our configs. We tell the container to create a new database named mysql and a user named mysql, and we give the user the passwords.

We will use this info later when we deploy our WordPress.

The second part in our file is the service. It will be like opening a port in the firewall and setting port 3306 on and the name of the service mysql. This is where you will find this MySQL server.

The last bit is us adding the disk we need for our MySQL server.

Let us apply our manifest with the command:

kubectl apply -f mysql.yaml

When you have deployed, verify that the Pods are running as before.

WordPress

Let us make a new YAML file called **wordpress.yaml** and add the following content:

```
1.  kind: PersistentVolumeClaim
2.  apiVersion: v1
3.  metadata:
4.    name: wordpress-storage
5.  spec:
6.    accessModes:
7.      - ReadWriteOnce
8.    resources:
9.      requests:
10.       storage: 2Gi
11.
12. ---
13. apiVersion: v1
14. kind: Service
15. metadata:
16.   name: wordpress
17.   labels:
18.     app: wordpress-pod
19. spec:
20.   type: ClusterIP
21.   ports:
22.     - port: 80
23.       targetPort: 80
24.       protocol: TCP
25.       name: http
26.   selector:
```

```
27.     app: wordpress-pod
28. ---
29. apiVersion: apps/v1
30. kind: Deployment
31. metadata:
32.   name: wordpress
33. spec:
34.   replicas: 1
35.   selector:
36.     matchLabels:
37.       app: wordpress-pod
38.   template:
39.     metadata:
40.       labels:
41.         app: wordpress-pod
42.     spec:
43.       containers:
44.       - image: wordpress
45.         imagePullPolicy: Always
46.         name: wordpress-pod
47.         env:
48.         - name: WORDPRESS_DB_HOST
49.           value: mysql
50.         - name: WORDPRESS_DB_PASSWORD
51.           value: password
52.         - name: WORDPRESS_DB_USER
53.           value: mysql
54.         - name: WORDPRESS_DB_NAME
55.           value: wordpress
56.         ports:
57.         - containerPort: 80
58.           name: www
59.         resources:
60.           requests:
61.             memory: "64Mi"
62.             cpu: "250m"
63.           limits:
64.             memory: "256Mi"
65.             cpu: "500m"
66.         volumeMounts:
67.         - name: wordpress-storage
68.           mountPath: /var/www/html
```

```
69.        securityContext:
70.          fsGroup: 200
71.        volumes:
72.          - name: wordpress-storage
73.            persistentVolumeClaim:
74.              claimName: wordpress-storage
```

This file looks like our MySQL. You can see that in the env section, we are setting the values for our MySQL. However, they do not look the same.

That is because every image has its own way of setting values, and MySQL and WordPress do not use the same values.

Suppose you go to the docker hub and look at the image of, for example, WordPress or MySQL. The readme for that image will tell you what values you can use.

Let us apply WordPress to our cluster using **kubectl** and the apply command.

Then, verify that the Pod is running.

Access our WordPress

Now, when our WordPress is running, we want to access it with a web browser. To do that, we will be using two different methods. First, we will open a port directly to the WordPress service we append.

The second uses an ingress controller and a local IP. We have already installed the tools needed for this.

Let us start with the **NodePort**.

In the WordPress file, go to the service and alter the service so it looks like the following:

```
1.  apiVersion: v1
2.  kind: Service
3.  metadata:
4.    name: wordpress
5.    labels:
6.      app: wordpress-pod
7.  spec:
8.    type: NodePort
9.    ports:
10.     - port: 80
11.       targetPort: 80
12.       protocol: TCP
13.       name: http
14.   selector:
```

```
15.     app: wordpress-pod
16.
```

Then, apply for your WordPress again. We have now changed the service to open a port in our Kubernetes server and route that to our WordPress. Let us find our port by typing the following command:

```
1.  root@k8smaster:~/deploy# kubectl get service wordpress
2.  NAME          TYPE        CLUSTER-IP      EXTERNAL-IP     PORT(S)
    AGE
3.  wordpress     NodePort    10.96.52.119    <none>          80:31360/TCP
    5m18s
4.  root@k8smaster:~/deploy#
```

Under port, we can see a port number 31360. Now, you can open a browser and go to:

http:// IP OF ONE OF THE WORKERS : 31360

http://192.168.122.26:31360/

You should now see the WordPress install page there.

However, we want this to work with a DNS name so we can go to **wordpress.home.lan** and see our WordPress.

For that, we need to add an ingress and an LB.

Setup MetalLB

Make a YAML file called **metallb.yaml** and add the following content:

```
1.  apiVersion: metallb.io/v1beta1
2.  kind: IPAddressPool
3.  metadata:
4.    name: pool
5.    namespace: metallb-system
6.  spec:
7.    addresses:
8.    - 192.168.122.133/32
9.  ---
10. apiVersion: metallb.io/v1beta1
11. kind: L2Advertisement
12. metadata:
13.   name: pool
14.   namespace: metallb-system
15. spec:
16.   ipAddressPools:
```

```
17.    - pool
18.
```

Look at the address 192.168.122.133, the IP we want to use in our network. You need to update that IP to match your own network.

Apply the config using **kubectl apply -f** command. Now, for us to start using the IP, we need to add it to our **traefik** (ingress) service:

```
1.  root@k8smaster:~/deploy# kubectl annotate service traefik  metallb.
    universe.tf/address-pool=pool
2.  service/traefik annotated
3.  root@k8smaster:~/deploy# kubectl get svc traefik
4.  NAME       TYPE           CLUSTER-IP      EXTERNAL-IP       PORT(S)
    AGE
5.  traefik   LoadBalancer   10.105.142.83   192.168.122.133   80:31731/
    TCP,443:32717/TCP    2d3h
6.  root@k8smaster:~/deploy#
```

Here, we are now adding an annotation to our service and then checking our service. As you can see, the IP is now set to our **traefik** service.

If you open a browser and go to that IP, you will see a 404 page as expected.

Time to make an ingress. Now we can make ingress and point our WordPress.home.local to our WordPress. For that, we need a new file, and we will call it **wordpress-ingress. yaml** and add the following content:

```
1.  apiVersion: networking.k8s.io/v1
2.  kind: Ingress
3.  metadata:
4.    annotations:
5.       kubernetes.io/ingress.class: traefik
6.    name: wordpress
7.  spec:
8.    rules:
9.    - host: "wordpress.home.lan"
10.     http:
11.       paths:
12.       - backend:
13.           service:
14.             name: wordpress
15.             port:
16.               number: 80
17.         path: /
18.         pathType: Prefix
```

Then, we also need to tell our computer where to find WordPress. You can set up the DNS record there if you have a DNS server installed or, you can open your **/etc/hosts** and add the following:

```
192.168.122.133 wordpress.home.lan
```

You need to update the IP to the same IP you use in our **metallb config**.

Now open your browser, visit **WordPress.home.lan**, and install WordPress.

Monitoring Kubernetes cluster with Grafana

Let us make another ingress. Make a new file called **grafan-ingress.yaml** and add the following content:

```
1.  apiVersion: networking.k8s.io/v1
2.  kind: Ingress
3.  metadata:
4.    annotations:
5.      kubernetes.io/ingress.class: traefik
6.    name: grafana
7.  spec:
8.    rules:
9.    - host: "grafana.home.lan"
10.     http:
11.       paths:
12.       - backend:
13.           service:
14.             name: monitoring-grafana
15.             port:
16.               number: 80
17.         path: /
18.         pathType: Prefix
19.
```

Then, update your DNS server ore your local host file to point to the correct IP of your cluster.

```
192.168.122.133 wordpress.home.lan
192.168.122.133 grafana.home.lan
```

Now you can visit Grafana on *grafana.home.lan*.

Now you can add more and more services and set them up, so they have their own ingress.

During our cluster setup, we added metrics and logs, and with Grafana, you can now look at the data. Log into your Grafana, and we can add the data sources for you. We did this in the monitoring chapter.

To find the URLs to the sources, use the command:

kubectl get svc

It will give the name and the port as follows:

```
monitoring-kube-prometheus-prometheus       ClusterIP       10.111.200.89
<none> 9090/TCP,8080/TCP                     2d14h
```

When connecting to Prometheus, use the URL **http://monitoring-kube-prometheus-prometheus:9090.**

Kubernetes stores passwords in something called secrets. The secrets are not encrypted but encoded in base64. To obtain the secret, we need to edit the secret and then decode it from base64. This is a good practice to use.

First, open the secret with an edit, such as:

kubectl edit secret monitoring-grafana

```
1.  apiVersion: v1
2.  data:
3.    admin-password: cHJvbS1vcGVyYXRvcg==
4.    admin-user: YWRtaW4=
5.    ldap-toml: ""
6.  kind: Secret
7.  metadata:
8.    annotations:
9.      meta.helm.sh/release-name: monitoring
10.     meta.helm.sh/release-namespace: default
11.   creationTimestamp: "2023-11-07T17:28:14Z"
12.   labels:
13.     app.kubernetes.io/instance: monitoring
14.     app.kubernetes.io/managed-by: Helm
15.     app.kubernetes.io/name: grafana
16.     app.kubernetes.io/version: 10.1.5
17.     helm.sh/chart: grafana-6.60.6
18.   name: monitoring-grafana
19.   namespace: default
20.   resourceVersion: "139101"
21.   uid: e739a7e6-0ca7-4bfc-9fb5-29966dfd5178
22. type: Opaque
```

Let us copy the base64 encoded string and decode it:

```
1.  root@k8smaster:~/deploy# echo cHJvbS1vcGVyYXRvcg== | base64 -d
2.  prom-operator
3.
4.  root@k8smaster:~/deploy#
```

The password for the admin user in Grafana is prom-operator.

Kubectl command to remember

When working with the Kubernetes cluster, there are several commands that are particularly useful.

There are many more, but this will work with the Kubernetes cluster we have set up now and will give us some base knowledge on finding and troubleshooting a Kubernetes cluster.

Pods

Pods are running in a different namespace. Run the following command to find and locate Pods in your cluster. If we want to look more into our Pod, use the get pods to find a Pod:

```
kubectl get pods -A
kubectl get pods
kubectl get ns
kubectl get pods -n openebs
```

Then, we can get more info from those Pods by running the following command and adding the name of the pod as follows:

```
kubectl describe pod traefik-NAME_FROM_YOUR_CLUSTER
kubectl logs -f traefik-NAME_FROM_YOUR_CLUSTER
kubectl edit pod traefik-NAME_FROM_YOUR_CLUSTER
```

As you see, we are using the command **get**/describe/edit, and you can run the same command on all resources in Kubernetes.

Now try to find and run the commands on the resources here, as follows:

```
kubectl get deployments -A
kubectl get service -A
kubectl get ingress -A
```

Conclusions

By the end of this chapter, we have completed the setup of a Kubernetes cluster from the base and metal server using Ubuntu. We also installed the tools needed to run Kubernetes and provisioned the Kubernetes cluster based on one master and a worker node cluster. To use the ore cluster, we installed tools to use storage so that our service in the cluster can store data. Moreover, we set up a load balancer so we can access our service. Then, to monitor our cluster, we added tools to view metrics and logs from our cluster and services. When our base tool was ready, we made our own deployments of a MySQL server and a WordPress and installed them into our cluster. With this, we gained basic knowledge of how to set up the Kubernetes cluster and install and add services to the cluster. We can also make and deploy our own apps into a Kubernetes cluster.

In the next chapter, we will start automating our task, making bash scripts, and using Ansible and Terraform.

Join our book's Discord space

Join the book's Discord Workspace for Latest updates, Offers, Tech happenings around the world, New Release and Sessions with the Authors:

https://discord.bpbonline.com

CHAPTER 13

Task Automations, CI/CD Pipeline, and Service Deployment

Introduction

In this chapter, we will look at the automation of tasks we do by moving the script and commands into code. Instead of running the commands one by one, we execute the commands with a script or a tool like Terraform or Ansible. We can see the state of the script. We will permanently control and verify that we run the script the same way every time.

This way, we can move away from mistakes and misses in the process of installing or setting up a server and service. It is the same approach we used when we installed the server using MAAS. We know the outcome will always be the same.

Moreover, we will examine some tools and scripts that can help automate certain tasks covered in this book.

Structure

In this chapter, we will cover the following topics:

- Basic Bash
- Automate tasks with Ansible
- Run host command from Docker

- Build and push Docker images
- Deploy with terraform against Kubernetes

Objectives

In this chapter, we will begin by setting up a simple Bash script that will serve as our document when installing a service and run some basic commands for us.

From the basic Bash script that we can run simply, we will move over to the tool called Ansible. Ansible will help us run our commands in a more controlled way and verify the output. We can now also run our commands on multiple computers simultaneously.

From Ansible, we will use a docker to run tasks inside the Docker. This will help us verify that we always have the same set of tools. We will start by running Ansible inside Docker and then transition to using Ansible to execute Docker commands on the host.

Basic Bash

Bash scripts are commands that you can run in order. You can do a lot more in Bash, but for this section, we will use Bash to set up scripts and run them in order. We have done some Bash scripting before, for example, when installing docker.

We will now create a script to run for Docker installation. We can then save this script in a folder. When we have a new server, we can copy over the script and execute it to install Docker. Now, we can easily restore a server to a point and have the Bash scripts as a document for us later.

Let us create a simple Bash script to install Docker. Copy the following code into a file and name the file **install_docker.sh**, as follows:

```
 1. root@server:~# cat install_docker.sh
 2. #!/bin/bash
 3.
 4.
 5. echo "Lets get docker"
 6. apt-get update
 7.
 8. echo "Installing req packages"
 9. apt-get install \
10.     apt-transport-https \
11.     ca-certificates \
12.     curl \
13.     gnupg \
14.     lsb-release -y
15.
```

```
16. echo "Getting repo keys"
17. curl -fsSL https://download.docker.com/linux/ubuntu/gpg | sudo gpg
    --dearmor -o /usr/share/keyrings/docker-archive-keyring.gpg
18.
19. echo "Settings up repo"
20. echo \
21.   "deb [arch=amd64 signed-by=/usr/share/keyrings/docker-archive-
    keyring.gpg] https://download.docker.com/linux/ubuntu \
22.   $(lsb_release -cs) stable" | sudo tee /etc/apt/sources.list.d/
    docker.list > /dev/null
23.
24. echo "Install Docker"
25. apt-get update
26. apt-get install docker-ce docker-ce-cli containerd.io -y
27.
```

Before we can run the command, we need to make the file executable. Then, we can run the script as follows:

```
1. root@server:~# chmod +x install_docker.sh
2. root@server:~# ./install_docker.sh
3.
```

As you can see, it will run the command and install Docker. It is good practice to add the commands you run in a file, so you have them saved.

You can also use Bash script to detect the state of your server. By running some commands that will print output, we can quickly get the state of our server. It would be great if there were some issues with the server, and troubleshooting was needed. Jump in and run a script to get some basic data on the problem. It will save you a lot of time if an incident happens. Here is a script that prints data to help resolve Ubuntu issues. You can also add more scripts to expand it.

The following example code is a good start:

```
1. #!/bin/bash
2. echo "Disk"
3. df -h
4. du -h --max-depth=0 /
5. du -h --max-depth=0 /var
6. echo "iniode"
7. for i in `find . -type d `; do echo `ls -a $i | wc -l` $i; done |
    sort -n
8.
9. echo "Network"
10. ip a
```

```
11. ip r
12. cat /etc/resolv.conf
13.
14.
15. echo "Memory"
16. free
```

Automate tasks with Ansible

So, a Bash script is easy; however, if I have more servers and want to run a command to install Docker on all of them. For that, there are several commands that you can use. In this chapter, we will look at one of the tools called Ansible.

With Ansible, you can run a script, and it will run the commands on the selected server. You can also group them so that they only run a set of tools on one type of server. For example, only install MySQL on your MySQL server.

We will now install and set up Ansible to run on our server. We will run Ansible in a Docker image. That way, we can always guarantee our ansible will work and that the version of ansible will always be the same as the docker image. Let us set up a docker-compose to run our ansible.

Create a docker-compose file and add the following content:

```
1.  services:
2.    ansible:
3.      build: .
4.      volumes:
5.        - ./playbooks:/opt/playbooks
6.        - ./files:/opt/files
7.        - ./hosts:/etc/ansible/
8.        - ./ssh:/root/.ssh
9.
10.     command: tail -f /etc/fstab
```

Here, we are making an Ansible folder and mounting it in 4 folders. Playbooks will be the command we run; hosts are the machines on which we will run the command, and the files are the files we want to copy over to our server. The last folder is to keep our hostkey over Docker restart.

We also need to build a Docker image to use and, for that, make a Dockerfile with the following content:

```
1.  FROM ubuntu:latest
2.  RUN apt update
3.  RUN apt install software-properties-common -y
```

```
4. RUN add-apt-repository --yes --update ppa:ansible/ansible
5. RUN apt install ansible -y
```

Now that we have the base parts ready, we can add our host. In the host folder, create files only named host and add the following:

```
1. root@72f9e0eecd79# cat hosts
2. all:
3.   vars:
4.     ansible_connection: ssh
5.     ansible_user: matte
6.     #ansible_ssh_pass: vagrant
7.   hosts:
8.     192.168.122.133:
9. docker:
10.   hosts:
11.     192.168.122.133:
12. apache:
13.   hosts:
14.     192.168.122.133:
```

Here, you will need to update so that the username and IP match what you are using.

Now, we are ready to create our first playbook. For that, in the playbook folder, create a file called **install_docker.yaml** and add the following content:

```
1. root@72f9e0eecd79# cat install-docker.yaml
2. - name: Install Docker
3.   hosts: all
4.
5.   tasks:
6.   - name: Creates directory
7.     file:
8.       path: /opt/files/
9.       state: directory
10.     become: yes
11.   - name: Copy file hosts with permissions
12.     ansible.builtin.copy:
13.       src: /opt/files/install_docker.sh
14.       dest: /opt/files/install_docker.sh
15.       mode: '0644'
16.     become: yes
17.
18.   - name: Upgrade all apt packages
19.     apt:
```

```
20.      force_apt_get: yes
21.      upgrade: dist
22.   become: yes
```

We are now ready to start Ansible and run the playbook against our host. start by building the image and then start a shell inside our Docker as follows:

1. **mattias@hrb:~/projects/hrb/ansible$ docker compose build**

2. [+] Building 0.0s (9/9) FINISHED
   docker:default

3. => [ansible internal] load build definition from Dockerfile
   0.0s

4. => => transferring dockerfile: 265B
   0.0s

5. => [ansible internal] load .dockerignore
   0.0s

6. => => transferring context: 2B
   0.0s

7. => [ansible internal] load metadata
   for docker.io/library/ubuntu:latest
   0.0s

8. => [ansible 1/5] FROM docker.io/library/ubuntu:latest
   0.0s

9. => CACHED [ansible 2/5] RUN apt update
   0.0s

10. => CACHED [ansible 3/5] RUN apt
   install software-properties-common -y
   0.0s

11. => CACHED [ansible 4/5] RUN add-apt-
   repository --yes --update ppa:ansible/ansible
   0.0s

12. => CACHED [ansible 5/5] RUN apt install ansible -y
   0.0s

13. => [ansible] exporting to image
   0.0s

14. => => exporting layers
   0.0s

15. => => writing image
   0.0s

16. => => naming to docker.io/hrb/api
   0.0s

17. **mattias@hrb:~/projects/hrb/ansible$ docker compose run ansible /bin/bash**

18. root@a0e829791762:/#

We are now in our docker, and we can run our command. Ansible has a strict host check, so before we can SSH into a server, we need to add it to our **ssh** host key. It is done by simply running the ssh IP of the server. This is required only one time, the host keys are stored outside the docker.

When are we then ready to run our Ansible command as follows:

```
 1. root@d848399327c7:/# ansible-playbook --ask-pass --ask-become-pass /
    opt/playbooks/install-docker.yaml
 2. SSH password:
 3. BECOME password[defaults to SSH password]:
 4.
 5. PLAY [Install Docker] ********************************************
    ******************************************************************
    *******************************************
 6.
 7. TASK [Gathering Facts] *******************************************
    ******************************************************************
    *******************************************
 8. ok: [192.168.122.133]
 9.
10. TASK [Creates directory] *****************************************
    ******************************************************************
    *********************************************
11. ok: [192.168.122.133]
12.
13. TASK [Copy file hosts with permissions] **************************
    ******************************************************************
    ***********************************************
14. ok: [192.168.122.133]
15.
16. TASK [Upgrade all apt packages] **********************************
    ******************************************************************
    ********************************************
17. ok: [192.168.122.133]
18.
19. PLAY RECAP *******************************************************
    ******************************************************************
    **********************************************
20. 192.168.122.133            : ok=4    changed=0    unreachable=0
    failed=0    skipped=0    rescued=0    ignored=0
21.
22. root@d848399327c7:/#
```

The command will ask you for the password and **sudo** password and then what playbook to run. You can make more playbooks and do other tasks.

```
1. ansible-playbook --ask-pass --ask-become-pass /opt/playbooks/
   install-docker.yaml
```

Go to the Ansible homepage and look at all the modules there. And you can rewrite the tools. So, instead of copying over the file, it can run the task for you.

Run host command from Docker

When running our server, sometimes we may need to install a small package that is only needed for one thing. Then, we want to remove it directly after. Ore, we want to troubleshoot, and for that, we need some tools. But we do not want to install them on the server before. Ore, we do not want to have a tool installed on our server, but we want to update a file. Then, we can start a Docker container, grant it access to the host file system, and let it add and update the file on the host. This is a common way to update server configurations when using a Kubernetes cluster. We can create a pod and add it to Kubernetes to run on all hosts. The Pod will update the host's settings.

Let us build a simple Pod that will update our DNS server on our server. Here, we will use an Ubuntu Docker image and a docker-compose that mounts the host folder **/etc** into the container as **/mnt/etc**. We do not want to mount it as **/etc**, inside the container. It will be bad. Now, if we have the tool installed in the container, we can run commands on the host files.

The following is our Docker file:

```
#Docker file
1. from ubuntu:latest
```

A simple docker-compose is as follows:

```
1. services:
2.   host-update:
3.     build: .
4.     volumes:
5.       - /etc:/mnt/etc
```

Now, we can run it as follows:

```
1. mattias@hrb:~/projects/hrb/book/docker/host-update$ docker compose
   run host-update cat /mnt/etc/passwd
2. root:x:0:0:root:/root:/bin/bash
3. daemon:x:1:1:daemon:/usr/sbin:/usr/sbin/nologin
4. bin:x:2:2:bin:/bin:/usr/sbin/nologin
5. sys:x:3:3:sys:/dev:/usr/sbin/nologin
```

You can now update and modify anything on a host system using container images. By moving this into Kubernetes, you can scale your setup.

Build and push Docker images

One of the tasks we run on the Ubuntu Server is to run some servers. We will now make a NGINX webserver and add a static HTML page into a docker. We will then run an Ansible script to copy, download our Docker, and run it on our server.

Docker hub

Before we begin, we need a docker registry. This is where we can upload the Docker images that we build.

We will use the docker hub for our images in this example. But you need to add your image to push images, too. In the Docker chapter, we looked at setting up a Docker hub account.

Build local

Create a Docker compose project by making a **docker-cmpose.yaml** file and add the following content. Now, make a folder called html and add a file called **index.html**.

In that file **index.html**, add the following content:

```
1.  <htm>
2.      <head>
3.          <title>Home</title>
4.      </head>
5.      <body>
6.          <h1>Home</h1>
7.          <p>Home page</p>
8.      </body>
9.  </htm>
```

Here, we use a simple HTML page, but you can have anything inside the Docker, such as a Java application ore some other code project. The process of building and deploying is the same setup here. When you have the tools to build and deploy, you can update to run anything here.

Build and push

Now, we can make a small Bash script to build our Docker and push it to the Docker hub. We also pass on the argument for the version of the image.

Create a Bash file and add the following content:

```
1.  #!/bin/bash
2.  VERSION=$1
3.  docker build -t mattiashem/ubuntu-static:$VERSION .
4.  docker push mattiashem/ubuntu-static:$VERSION
```

You must replace the Docker image path to match your Docker hub settings. Now, we can build and push our image by running the command. Our next part is using Terraform and deploying our container. Terraform is the most common tool when using IoC, and we will only use it against a Kubernetes cluster here. But it is mainly used by agent cloud providers, and you can change to deploy our app to anything.

Deploy with terraform against Kubernetes

To get started, we will need two files, one to **init** our terraform and one to run the command. To make it easy, we installed Terraform in the same Docker as Ansible, and our Dockerfile will look as follows:

```
FROM ubuntu
1. RUN apt update &&  apt install wget unzip software-properties-
   common gnupg  -y
2. RUN add-apt-repository --yes --update ppa:ansible/ansible
3. RUN apt update && apt install ansible -y
4. WORKDIR /opt
5. RUN wget https://releases.hashicorp.com/terraform/1.6.5/
   terraform_1.6.5_linux_amd64.zip && \
6.     unzip terraform_1.6.5_linux_amd64.zip && \
7.     mv terraform /usr/local/bin/terraform && \
8.     rm terraform_1.6.5_linux_amd64.zip
9. RUN terraform --version
```

We also updated our **docker-compose.yaml** file as follows:

```
1. services:
2.   terrableansible:
3.     build: .
4.     image: hrb/api
5.     volumes:
6.       - ./playbooks:/opt/playbooks
7.       - ./files:/opt/files
8.       - ./hosts:/etc/ansible/
9.       - ./terraform:/opt/terraform
10.      - ./ssh:/root/.ssh
11.      - ./kube:/root/.kube
12.    command: tail -f /etc/fstab
```

Init Terraform

Jumo into our Docker with all the tools by running the following command:

```
1. docker compose run terrableansible /bin/bash
```

To make this work, we need the kubeconfig file that grants us access to the cluster and a config file with our app. In the folder Terraform, create the file **tarraform.ft** and add the following content:

```
1.  root@b2218a9105ac:/opt/terraform# cat terraform.tf
2.  terraform {
3.    backend "local" {
4.      workspace_dir = "/opt/terraform/state/terraform.tfstate.d"
5.    }
6.  }root@b2218a9105ac:/opt/terraform#
```

Then we need a file to run the command **deploy.tf** with the following content:

```
1.  root@b2218a9105ac:/opt/terraform# cat deployments.tf
2.  resource "kubernetes_deployment" "static" {
3.    metadata {
4.      name = "static-data"
5.      labels = {
6.        test = "static"
7.      }
8.    }
9.
10.   spec {
11.     replicas = 3
12.
13.     selector {
14.       match_labels = {
15.         app = "static"
16.       }
17.     }
18.
19.     template {
20.       metadata {
21.         labels = {
22.           app = "static"
23.         }
24.       }
25.
26.       spec {
27.         container {
28.           image = "mattiashem/ubuntu-static:$VERSION"
29.           name  = "static"
30.
31.           resources {
32.             limits = {
```

```
33.                 cpu     = "0.5"
34.                 memory  = "512Mi"
35.             }
36.           requests = {
37.                 cpu     = "250m"
38.                 memory  = "50Mi"
39.             }
40.         }
41.
42.         liveness_probe {
43.           http_get {
44.             path = "/"
45.             port = 80
46.
47.             http_header {
48.                 name  = "X-Custom-Header"
49.                 value = "Awesome"
50.             }
51.           }
52.
53.           initial_delay_seconds = 3
54.           period_seconds        = 3
55.         }
56.       }
57.     }
58.   }
59. }
60. }root@b2218a9105ac:/opt/terraform#
```

To access the cluster, copy a kubeconfig file into the Kube folder named config.

Here, we have the kubeconfig of one of my clusters in Hertzner. The kubeconfig file should always be secure, and you need to update the scripts when running against production workloads.

```
1.  root@924332efbdd9:/opt/terraform# cat /root/.kube/config
2.  apiVersion: v1
3.  kind: Config
4.  clusters:
```

Terraform commands

This is the first command you will run to **init** our **terraform**. It will set up the state and download the modules you need.

```
terraform init
```

Terraform plan

The plan command will verify that we can connect and show what changes Terraform would like to make. This is a good command, and if you run Terraform against a cloud env, you would like to run a plan to verify that your server is always in sync with the code.

Terraform apply

This is the command that will make the change.

```
Plan: 1 to add, 0 to change, 1 to destroy.
1.
2.  Do you want to perform these actions?
3.    Terraform will perform the actions described above.
4.    Only 'yes' will be accepted to approve.
5.
6.    Enter a value: yes
7.
8.  kubernetes_deployment.static: Destroying... [id=default/static-data]
9.  kubernetes_deployment.static: Destruction complete after 0s
10. kubernetes_deployment.static: Creating...
11. kubernetes_deployment.static: Creation complete after 8s
    [id=default/static-data]
12.
13. Apply complete! Resources: 1 added, 0 changed, 1 destroyed.
14. root@924332efbdd9:/opt/terraform#
```

Also, if we log in to the cluster, we can see the Pods running as follows:

```
1.  [core@ubuntu]$ kubectl get pods
2.  NAME                            READY   STATUS    RESTARTS   AGE
3.  static-data-555757f6d4-4zpvr    1/1     Running   0          12s
4.  static-data-555757f6d4-cw7kj    1/1     Running   0          12s
5.  static-data-555757f6d4-gcz4z    1/1     Running   0          12s
```

CI/CD

We now have our building block for making CI/CD pipelines. Most pipelines are a set of scripts put together to perform the actions you want. Here, we can now run Ansible to install packages. We can run our batch scripts that will build and push images, and we can, with our terraform, deploy our image into a Kubernetes cluster. This block set up the base for us to build CI/CD pipelines.

Conclusion

By the end of this chapter, we will have worked with tools to help us document our work more effectively by incorporating commands into the code. We also started to move from SSH into the server and running commands to the more modern approach of having a script and using the tool to set up our server. This will help us when we start working with servers professionally. Additionally, we examined the Ansible tool, which aligns well with Linux and Ubuntu Servers. We then moved to test and run Terraform to deploy our docker image to a Kubernetes cluster. We now have the tools to set up the server as we want it using Ansible. Build and push docker images with Bash ore docker-compose, then deploy what we have built into a cluster, bringing us to a full pipeline. Running all these tools inside docker also makes them super easy to run in CI/CD tools like GitLab or GitHub.

This is the last chapter; once you have gone through all the chapters, you will know how to work with Ubuntu, from installing the desktop and server to configuring, deploying the Kubernetes cluster, securing the network, and deploying applications. With this, we are ready to start our journey in Ubuntu and Linux.

Join our book's Discord space

Join the book's Discord Workspace for Latest updates, Offers, Tech happenings around the world, New Release and Sessions with the Authors:

https://discord.bpbonline.com

Index

www.ingramcontent.com/pod-product-compliance
Lightning Source LLC
Chambersburg PA
CBHW061808210326
41599CB00034B/6922